Technologies of Suspicion and the Ethics of Obligation in Political Asylum

SERIES IN HUMAN SECURITY

Series editors: Geoffrey Dabelko, Brandon Kendhammer, and Nukhet Sandal

---

The Series in Human Security is published in association with Ohio University's War and Peace Studies and African Studies programs at the Center for International Studies and the Environmental Studies Program at the Voinovich School of Leadership and Public Affairs.

Technologies of Suspicion and the Ethics of Obligation in Political Asylum, edited by Bridget M. Haas and Amy Shuman

Technologies of Suspicion and the Ethics of Obligation in Political Asylum

Edited by

BRIDGET M. HAAS AND AMY SHUMAN

OHIO UNIVERSITY PRESS | ATHENS

Ohio University Press, Athens, Ohio 45701
ohioswallow.com

Printed in the United States of America
Ohio University Press books are printed on acid-free paper ∞ ™

29 28 27 26 25 24 23 22 21 20 19 5 4 3 2 1

Library of Congress Cataloging-in-Publication Data

Names: Haas, Bridget M., editor. | Shuman, Amy, date, editor.
Title: Technologies of suspicion and the ethics of obligation in political asylum / edited by Bridget M. Haas and Amy Shuman.
Description: Athens, Ohio : Ohio University Press, 2019. | Series: Series in human security | Includes bibliographical references and index.
Identifiers: LCCN 2018056335| ISBN 9780821423783 (hardback : alk. paper) | ISBN 9780821446676 (pdf)
Subjects: LCSH: Political refugees--Government policy--Case studies. | Political refugees--Legal status, laws, etc.--Case studies. | Asylum, Right of--Case studies. | National security--Technological innovations--Case studies. | Immigration enforcement--Technological innovations--Case studies. | BISAC: POLITICAL SCIENCE / Political Freedom & Security / Human Rights. | SOCIAL SCIENCE / Anthropology / General.
Classification: LCC JV6346 .T43 2019 | DDC 323.6/31--dc23
LC record available at https://lccn.loc.gov/2018056335

Contents

Acknowledgments

The idea for this volume started to take shape when we, the editors of this volume, organized a panel, "Asylum and Politics of Suspicion," for the 2014 American Anthropological Association (AAA) conference in Washington, DC. Several of the contributors to this volume presented papers at the panel or served as discussants. Thanks to Heath Cabot for chairing that panel and for her insights and important contributions to that discussion. Following the AAA panel, we received funding from the Wenner-Gren Foundation and the Mershon Center for International Security Studies at the Ohio State University (OSU) to hold a day-and-a-half workshop on Asylum and the Politics of Suspicion in March 2015 at OSU. We thank the Wenner-Gren Foundation and Richard Herrmann, director of the Mershon Center, for their generous support, without which the workshop would not have been possible. We would like to also thank Nick Spitulski, program coordinator at OSU, for his outstanding job handling the logistics of the workshop, arranging transportation, lodging, and meals for the group. The OSU workshop brought together participants of the earlier AAA panel as well as additional scholars doing important work on political asylum. The papers presented at that workshop were revised and crafted into the essays you see in this volume.

We would like to thank the contributors who participated in the original workshop and contributed their essays to this volume. The depth and breadth of intellectual work represented in these pages is impressive, and we are very fortunate to be able to include their work together in this book.

We would like to thank the editors and staff at Ohio University Press / Swallow Press, including the editors of the Series in Human Security: Geoffrey Dabelko, Brandon Kendhammer, and Nukhet Sandal; and managing editor Nancy Basmajian. Thank you to copyeditor Don McKeon for his excellent work. We would particularly like to thank Rick Huard at Ohio University Press, who has guided this project toward completion. The editors and authors of the volume would like to thank two anonymous reviewers, whose thoughtful and valuable feedback strengthened the individual chapters and the book as a whole.

Introduction

Negotiating Suspicion, Obligation, and Security in Contemporary Political Asylum Regimes

BRIDGET M. HAAS AND AMY SHUMAN

Asylum seekers are increasingly the focus of global debates surrounding humanitarian obligations on the one hand and concerns surrounding security and border control on the other. Asylum seekers are at turns portrayed as innocent victims in need of humanitarian protection and as "queue jumpers" or threats to the body of the host nation. Recent coverage of the European migration crisis illustrates these competing representations of asylum seekers.

On September 2, 2015, newspapers across the globe carried the sobering image of the lifeless body of Alan Kurdi, a three-year-old Syrian boy who had washed up on a beach in Turkey. He, along with his mother and two siblings, had died fleeing their homeland in search of safety in the European Union (EU). This incident served to reframe the narrative of the migrant crisis that had started earlier that year and had reached immense proportions by this time. The view of migrants, and Syrian ones in particular, began to shift from suspicious Other or potential terrorist to humanitarian victim.

If coverage of Kurdi's death represented a shift in the narrative of the migrant crisis, it was short-lived. On November 13, 2015, a series of coordinated terrorist attacks in Paris transfixed the world. It was soon revealed that one of the terrorists held a fake Syrian passport and had entered France through the migrant trail that flowed from the Middle East, passing through Greece, Macedonia, and Serbia and into Western Europe. The global response to the Paris terrorist attacks was swift: borders closed and the processing of refugees was slowed or temporarily ceased at EU countries' borders.

The shifting public narratives and policy responses concerning the EU migrant crisis represent a new iteration of tensions between humanitarian ethics and security concerns that are generated by international migration. This tension between humanitarian obligations and the security of the state have been evident since the inception of international refugee policy, though events such as the 2001 terrorist attacks on the World Trade Center and the November 13, 2015, attacks in Paris bring these tensions to the fore, as they are acutely experienced and debated. Indeed, in a post-9/11 landscape (and now reinvigorated after 11/13), volatile debates have taken place pitting humanitarian ethics against notions of security and border control.[1] To be sure, at the time of completing this introductory chapter, US president Donald Trump issued an executive order barring refugees and immigrants from seven predominantly Muslim countries from entering the United States. The travel ban, quickly dubbed a "Muslim ban" by media and opponents of the measure, was soon met with widespread protests and legal challenges across the country. Months later, in October 2017, Trump laid out a new immigration strategy that focused on overhauling the US asylum system, including narrowing the standards required to gain asylum and imposing penalties on asylum seekers who file claims deemed to be "fraudulent." The strong divisiveness of the debate surrounding these measures speaks to the enduring and entrenched nature of the tensions between humanitarian obligations and concerns over national security.

The "paradoxical preoccupation with globalization and domestic security" manifests in an increase in the circulation of goods and technologies with the simultaneous attempt to constrain human mobility (Fassin 2011; Muller 2004, 52). The asylum seeker emerges as a central figure in this debate, exposing the fragility of modern sovereignty (Muller 2004) and challenging "both the norms and the exceptions of the state" (Squire 2009, 3).

As Giorgio Agamben (2000) asserts, "If the refugee represents such a disquieting influence in the order of the nation-state, this is primarily because, by breaking the identity between the human and the citizen and that between nativity and nationality, it brings the originary fiction of sovereignty into crisis" (20–21). Yet, as Nyers (2003, 2006) reminds us, the state is still a powerful entity, and it is through the construction of "the refugee" that "the citizen" is simultaneously created and maintained.

Indeed, it is the liminality of the asylum seeker, as a figure "betwixt and between" (Turner 1967)—neither fully included in nor fully excluded from a host country—that offers a critical lens into the workings of the state. Close attention to contexts of liminality and marginalization can provide important observations into larger political and cultural forces (Das and Poole 2004; Fassin 2015, 3). In providing fine-tuned analyses of political asylum systems and the adjudication of asylum claims across a range of sociocultural and geopolitical contexts, this volume offers critical insights into the processes by which tensions between humanitarianism and security/border control are negotiated and enacted at the local level.

Although asylum seekers have vastly different situations, political asylum is a global policy, requiring the collaboration of nations with different resources and different attitudes toward both refugees and economic migrants. Research on political asylum has always relied on in-depth understanding of the complex situations people are fleeing, including the particular forms of persecution and corruption. In this book, we integrate the particulars with the larger issues of policy. We are writing at an important moment in time in terms of forced migration and increasing numbers of asylum seekers. This particular cultural historical moment is defined by a global war on terrorism, in which suspicion has supplanted compassion and trust in many cases. The rise of an ethos or culture of suspicion as a defining characteristic of asylum regimes is evidenced, for example, by an increase in the rates of denial of asylum claims in the United States (TRAC 2016), the closing of borders to asylum seekers in the EU, and the rise of anti-immigration—particularly anti–asylum seeker—sentiments and rhetoric across the globe.

While we opened up this introduction with a discussion about the perceived threat of terrorism that underlined global fears of the asylum seeker, the contributions to this volume do not focus on asylum seekers as terrorist threats. Rather, we use this description of the contemporary political landscape to highlight two key themes, or aims, of this volume. First, recounting the shifting narratives surrounding asylum seekers in the EU and United States illustrate both the constructed nature of suspicious subjects and the fluidity and malleability of these constructed categories. This volume provides detailed ethnographic analyses of how categories of suspicious asylum subjects are produced in disparate locally and culturally specific ways. This framing turns our attention to how migrants are often produced as suspicious subjects by the very asylum regimes to which they appeal for protection. Second, a focus on the widespread tensions between protection and control, between humanitarian obligations and national security, brings to the fore the dominance of a lens of suspicion regarding asylum at this particular moment in time and place. Our contention in this volume is that this broader ethos or lens of suspicion comes to bear in powerful ways on the everyday adjudication of asylum claims, albeit in uneven and locally contingent ways and very often with deleterious consequences for those who claim a need for protection.

ASYLUM SEEKER: VICTIM VERSUS THREAT

Part of the recent fear of refugees fleeing the Syrian, Iraqi, and Afghan conflicts is attributed to the possibility that terrorists are mingling with refugees and crossing into Europe with them. Many of our discussions in this book address the consequences resulting from the more general suspicion of refugees for people seeking asylum. These issues are not new, and as many political asylum scholars have observed, what we are calling a lens of suspicion has been part of the assessment of disparities in the asylum system since its inception (Macklin 2009), often described in terms of questions of credibility determinations (Daniel and Knudsen 1995; Einhorn 2009). In her discussion of lesbian political asylum applicants, Claire Bennett (2014) describes a "culture of disbelief" by decision-makers. She writes, "Questioning a person's credibility is a legitimate line of enquiry as stipulated under Section 8 of the Asylum and Immigration (Treatment of Claimants) Act of 2004. This clearly states that suspicion should be raised if individuals fail to answer specific questions, hide or provide misleading information, produce false documentation, or file an asylum application later than is reasonably expected" (Bennett 2014, 151).

Asylum seekers are refugees who are fleeing their homelands and whose cases have not yet been assessed by national systems designed to consider whether or not they qualify for protected status. At the end of 2016, there were 2.8 million asylum seekers worldwide (UNCHR 2017).[2] To qualify for asylum, one must prove he or she meets the definition of a refugee under international law, as outlined in the 1951 Convention Relating to the Status of Refugees and its 1967 Protocol Relating to the Status of Refugees. Article 1A of the convention, as amended by the 1967 protocol, defines a refugee as

> a person who owing to a well-founded fear of being persecuted for reasons of race, religion, nationality, membership of a particular social group or political opinion, is outside the country of his nationality and is unable, or owing to such fear, is unwilling to avail himself of the protection of that country; or who, not having a nationality and being outside the country of his former habitual residence as a result of such events, is unable or, owing to such fear, is unwilling to return to it. (UN General Assembly 1967)

In addition to meeting the definition of refugee as specified in international law, one must also meet the requirements of the particular domestic asylum laws of the country within which one is seeking asylum. While the refugee convention undergirds domestic asylum laws, the postconvention development of asylum bureaucracies took different forms, and there is a lack of uniformity in asylum adjudication across national boundaries.

When focusing specifically on asylum claims and asylum systems, scholarly attention has been primarily on the adjudication of asylum cases that occur in countries where national asylum systems are in place, namely within the forty-four "industrialized countries" of first asylum identified by the United Nations High Commissioner for Refugees (UNCHR 2015). These are the nations of Europe, the United States, Canada, Australia, New Zealand, Japan, and the Republic of Korea (with Western European countries, the United States, and Canada receiving the highest proportion of asylum claims and also much scholarly attention). There is sometimes a theoretical and empirical distinction made between refugee status determination (RSD) hearings conducted by the UNCHR in settings where asylum systems are not in place and the adjudication of asylum claims that are lodged within and processed by individual nation-states.

In this volume, the majority of contributors analyze the adjudication of asylum claims by various individual nation-states, though some address RSD processes in contexts where a national system of asylum is nonexistent. We consider these under the same analytical lens because both sets of processes engage in the assessment of legitimacy of migrants and rely, in theory, on similar criteria. Moreover, we see the tensions between humanitarian imperatives and security concerns as central to all asylum-adjudication contexts. We are interested in the situated practices and logics that are variously deployed in the assessment of these claims, as these tensions are negotiated in locally contingent ways.

The ways in which asylum seekers have been understood and acted upon, in both academic and policy arenas, has shifted over time. Scholars and activists who have held an interest in human rights have focused on asylum seekers as rights-bearing individuals within the context of international law (Edwards 2005; Hathaway 1991). Yet this human rights framework has been increasingly supplanted by the discourse of humanitarianism, whereby participating actors increasingly appeal to compassion and moral sentiments (Fassin and Rechtman 2009; Feldman 2007; Ticktin 2006, 2011). In this framework, the asylum seeker is reconfigured, moving from a strictly rights-bearing individual to that of humanitarian victim.

This deployment of humanitarianism has been complicated, however, by a rise in the criminalization and securitization of asylum and asylum seekers, particularly in the Global North (Adamson 2006; Anderson 2013; Bigo 2002; Coutin 2011; Gibney 2004; Kerwin 2005; Squire 2009). Indeed, migration, and asylum in particular, is increasingly seen as foremost an issue of security. Victoria Squire (2009) has examined the exclusionary politics of asylum in Europe and the United Kingdom, arguing that the state, in constructing the asylum seeker as a threat to be managed, "effectively generates the 'problem' or 'threat' to which it is opposed," thereby engaging in an endless cycle of restriction and control (3). The increasing dominance of the securitization paradigm of asylum has produced "the 'criminal/terrorist'" as "another figure along the refugee-migrant spectrum" (Holmes and Castañeda 2016, 18).

The criminalization and securitization of migration has also meant the emergence and implementation of an array of restrictive border-control measures, ranging from the collection of biometric data to detention, interdiction, and deportation (Bigo 2007; Broeders 2007; De Genova and Peutz

2010; Fassin 2011; Huysmans 2006; Mountz 2010, Schuster 2003). The discourse of national security has been mobilized by states to repress the rights of migrants or to justify the infliction of violence upon them (Carens 2003; Fassin 2011; Mountz 2010; Schuster 2003; Squire 2009).

If the asylum seeker as potential terrorist represents one kind of threat that needs to be addressed through the adjudication of asylum claims, then the asylum seeker as economic siphon or threat to cultural identity represents another iteration of security threat (Innes 2010; Mountz 2010; Schuster 2003). To be sure, media representations of transnational migrants as "queue jumpers" or otherwise "bogus" asylum seekers abound, so much so that the dominant public perception of asylum seekers is that the majority of them are not truly humanitarian victims but rather those (illegitimately) seeking economic opportunity (Anderson 2013; Kmak 2015). The "bogus" asylum seeker has become a central figure in the debates surrounding security, migration, and humanitarian ethics (Zimmerman 2011). The putative distinction between the economic migrant and the humanitarian/political refugee lies at the heart of asylum adjudication. While the distinction between these two categories of migrants has been shown to be untenable, it remains a cornerstone of policies and discourses surrounding asylum seekers (Bohmer and Shuman 2010; Dauvergne 2004; Essed and Wesenbeek 2004). The presumptive distinction between proper (humanitarian/political) and improper (economic) reasons for mobility becomes a way of "morally delineating the deserving refugee from the undeserving migrant" (Holmes and Castañeda 2016, 13).

The fear that political asylum seekers might actually be economic migrants, that they might overtax fragile economic systems, or that they might be terrorists is not new (Gibney 2002). Some asylum and refugee scholars have argued that the system has always been vulnerable, that it was designed initially to offer safe haven to people fleeing Soviet countries rather than to refugees from the Global South and the Middle East (Pirouet 2001, 124–26). The association between asylum seekers and terrorists, however unfounded, was intensified after 2001, and these concerns have been applied not only to people seeking asylum in Europe, Australia, the United Kingdom, Canada, and the United States but also in East Africa, where, Monica Kathina Juma and Peter Mwangi Kagwanja (2008) write, "Refugees, generally perceived as a liability, are likely to become pawns in a wider geopolitical game in which they are redefined as agents of insecurity and terrorism" (225). Whether seen as a threat to the nation-state, the welfare state, and/or liberal democracies (Schuster 2003), asylum seekers often bear the brunt of public and political anxieties.

ASYLUM ADJUDICATION AS CRITICAL LENS

If asylum systems produce migrants as legitimate (humanitarian refugees) or illegitimate (unqualified or fraudulent) applicants, then we must understand the mechanisms by which this production happens. As this volume underscores, it is of vital importance to more fully understand *who* becomes understood as a threat, *how* they emerge as suspicious (or not), and how these categories of inclusion and exclusion shift, temporally and spatially.

In this volume, we emphasize an understanding of asylum systems as not solely political-legal institutions but also ones that comprise systems and practices that are inherently sociomoral. That is, in declaring—and thus producing—an asylum seeker as either an illegitimate/"bogus" asylum seeker or a legitimate "true refugee," asylum systems confer a moral standing for these particular individuals. Asylum seekers, like other precarious subjects managed by state institutions, can "easily slip from one side of this moral line to the other, from the role of suspect to the status of victim and vice versa" (Fassin 2015, 2). Is an asylum seeker a suspect and dangerous Other—a terrorist posing as a vulnerable figure or a fraudulent malingerer trying to siphon the economic and social resources of the host country? Or is the asylum seeker a "true refugee," a victim of political persecution who deserves protection and care?

This volume posits in-depth anthropological attention to multiple sites of asylum adjudication as a critical lens in which to interrogate the broader sociocultural, historical, and political-economic forces shaping refugee and asylum policies and practices. It is in these microlevel contexts—courtrooms, offices of nongovernmental organizations (NGOs), United Nations High Commissioner for Refugees (UNHCR) interviews—that asylum seekers are produced as either legitimate or illegitimate subjects and their fates are decided. By providing an array of accounts of how global and national discourses and policies regarding asylum are "locally reckoned" (Willen 2012), the contributors to this volume add to our understanding about the disparate and uneven nature of asylum adjudication. That is, while it is not new to recognize the inequitable and uneven outcomes of asylum and RSD systems both across and within borders (Einolf 2001; Hamlin 2014; Legomsky 2009; Ramji-Nogales et al. 2007; Schoenholtz 2005), the mechanisms, technologies, and everyday interactions that produce such uneven outcomes warrant more attention (Jubany 2011, 2017).

Below we discuss three overarching themes that inform contemporary political asylum systems and the analyses of the contributors to this volume: obligation, suspicion, and security. These thematic domains are not discrete and should not be taken to be clearly delineated areas of inquiry but rather constructs with which to think, as applied to various ethnographic and textual material. Indeed, these domains are intersecting and interdependent, and most contributions to this volume speak to more than one of these themes.

Obligation

We posit obligation as a central concept to our analyses of political asylum. More specifically, we borrow from Nadia El-Shaarawi (this volume) the idea of an "ethics of obligation," by which we mean to underscore the moral character and implications of claims to protection and obligations to protect. While El-Shaarawi explicitly offers the ethics of obligation as her primary intervention, many other contributors to this volume—Ilil Benjamin, Bridget M. Haas, John B. Haviland, and Charles Watters—highlight the ethical relationships involved in the struggle over the meaning of the "obligation to protect."

It is not sufficient on either a theoretical or a policy level to merely claim that states are obligated to protect refugees and asylum seekers. Rather, this claim is our point of departure—it is the assertion of the obligation to protect asylum seekers that the contributors to this volume interrogate. For example, while the decisions of states and other institutions to adjudicate and admit asylum seekers are legally based upon the Geneva Convention, the issue of whom to admit and the processes for assessing this are issues that are locally and subjectively negotiated and informed by moral assumptions. "In order to substantiate obligation," Claudia Tazreiter (2004) asserts, "the moral standing of a person or people must be articulated" (29). In asylum adjudication, institutional actions have direct implications for human suffering. Asylum seekers, as opposed to refugees, pose a different kind of ethical challenge: "What gives asylum seekers a vital moral claim, however, is the fact that their arrival involves the state directly and immediately in their fate" (Carens 2003, 101).

Ultimately, asylum is about states' obligations to protect certain categories of persons deemed vulnerable. But *to whom* states are obligated emerges as a contentious, shifting, and muddy question. The question of to whom states and other institutions are obligated is also a matter of geopolitical interests and ideologies, which shape which groups are seen as deserving of protection at a particular place and moment in time (Coutin 2011; Holmes and Castañeda 2016). Attention to circulating discourses and authoritative claims concerning asylum politics can offer critical insight "about how the responsibility for suffering is shifted; how fears of cultural, ethnic, and religious difference are mobilized; and how boundaries of social categories are made and unmade," thereby creating a "hierarchy of deservingness" (Holmes and Castañeda 2016, 13, 19).

Yet, as the contributions to this volume elucidate, the question of who deserves protection is just as much a matter of locally specific factors as it is larger geopolitical factors. Asylum is a socially and culturally shaped process and set of institutions, and conceptions of legitimate subjects (those deserving asylum status) are always historically and socioculturally contingent. Asylum adjudication, while informed by broader discourses and ideologies, is also a thoroughly intersubjective and interpersonal process, and the collision of logic systems—between the culture of asylum adjudicators and the culture of asylum seekers—has been well documented (Blommaert 2001; Bohmer and Shuman 2007, 2008, 2018; Jacquemet 2009, 2011; Rousseau et al. 2002). The local, as much as the global, is key here. For example, categories of deservingness are often highly contingent on affective and narrative performance within adjudication arenas (Bohmer and Shuman 2008; McKinnon 2009), what El-Shaarawi (this volume), drawing on Jarret Zigon, deems "local moralities."

States' obligations to its own citizens must simultaneously be privileged in asylum politics and practices. As the opening discussion of responses to the current EU migrant crisis illustrated, the very question of who is under threat is far from clear and often lacks consensus. Asylum seekers are at turns constructed as the threat and the threatened (Innes 2010).

It is important to acknowledge the multiple stakeholders and myriad actors involved in political asylum systems. While asylum adjudication sometimes involves simply a claimant and an adjudicator (asylum officer, UNCHR official, immigration judge), it is more often the case that asylum claims involve the participation of many mediating actors. Thus, legal aid advocates, immigration attorneys, and human rights or other NGO members often play an integral part in asylum systems and processes. Given these different stakeholders, it is essential to consider the competing conceptions of asylum seekers that may be at play at any given time during the adjudication of asylum claims. The role of NGOs in the asylum process is framed as one of asylum claimant advocacy, though on the ground their effects appear more complex (Cabot 2013, 2014; Ticktin 2011). Naomi Millner (2011), for example, challenges the view that NGO refugee advocates can subvert dominant, pejorative representations of asylum seekers by enacting an ethos of hospitality precisely because these humanitarian actors are drawing on the same discursive and conceptual logic of the state, thereby reproducing the same categories of belonging and exclusion as the state. She describes these moments of categorization as "ethical framings which invest such governmental orders with legitimacy" (Millner 2011, 321). Ilil Benjamin's essay in this volume vividly illustrates the complexity of the relationships between aid workers and asylum claimants—a context in which obligation to protect is by no means straightforward.

The contributors to this volume examine the ways in which the concept of obligation is engaged both directly and indirectly, bringing to the fore the complex ways in which a dominant ethos of suspicion works on both a global and local level to reshape questions of *to whom* we are obligated and how that obligation is determined and legitimated. The chapters by Haviland and Watters, drawing on very different ethnographic material, shed light on how the construction of particular categories of migrants mobilize a sense of obligation over other categories of migrants.

Security

Political asylum and national and international security have always been intertwined, but the connection has intensified in recent years. In essence, asylum adjudication is the negotiation of two sets of anxieties about security: the asylum seeker's quest for physical or existential security and anxieties about the economic, physical, and/or cultural threat that asylum seekers pose to national security. We have emphasized throughout this introduction the tensions between humanitarian obligation and national security / border control. As Daniel M. Goldstein (2007) has pointed out, rights can be revoked in the name of security.

Yet security and obligation are inextricably linked, in that fulfilling an obligation—be it to asylum seekers or the state—is a prerequisite for security. On the one hand, meeting humanitarian obligations to protect deserving refugees is necessary to ensure asylum seekers' personal and existential security. Indeed, the life-or-death stakes of asylum decisions are recognized not only by asylum claimants and their advocates but also by asylum adjudicators who wrestle with making these decisions, as the ethnographic data presented in Haas's chapter reveals. On the other hand, recognizing the obligation to protect citizens from outside threat is seen as essential for national security. Put differently, getting obligation "right"—protecting those who need protection and denying those who do not—is framed as necessary to security on a broad level.

Security always incorporates and references its inverse: insecurity. Matthew Gibney (2002) underlines the irony in viewing asylum seekers as a threat since by definition they are victims of insecurity. Jef Huysmans (2006) highlights the inequities regarding security that arise in political asylum processes. Framing asylum seekers' claims as "alternative security claims," Huysmans notes that the asylum seekers' requests for protection "often remain subordinated to the security of the State and its citizenry" (6). Thus, a central question in asylum adjudication is, *whose* security matters? The shifting and contextual definitions of who is deemed morally deserving expose the fact that security (and insecurity) itself is socioculturally and historically constructed. As Claudia Aradau, Jef Huysmans, Andrew Neal, and Nadine Voelkner (2014) note, "For something to become a security concern, institutional, political, technological, and various other work is performed that makes it a matter of insecurity" (3; see also Huysmans 2006). Security and insecurity, therefore, must be understood as situated practices that require the anticipation and subsequent control of perceived risks (Amoore 2013; Goldstein 2007). These threats and perceived risks are themselves social constructions, often reflecting broader ideological and political agendas, as several of the essays in this volume make clear (Rachel Lewis, Sara McKinnon, Watters).

This volume examines the struggle over claims for security and protection as they are deployed in contexts of political asylum. We consider how the idea of security or insecurity comes into play on many levels in political asylum. We ask: Whose security is at stake, and how is the security of asylum seekers measured against the security of the state? Who needs protection? Who gets to decide this? Further, we ask how insecurity is configured, especially in the expectation that asylum seekers will articulate their vulnerability as a central part of their claims. In fact, the articulation of vulnerability could be considered the primary "currency" in asylum adjudication (James 2004, 2011). Many of the contributions to this volume attend to the struggle over claims for protection—between adjudicators and claimants (El-Shaarawi, Lewis, McKinnon, Amy Shuman, and Carol Bohmer), between aid workers and asylum seekers (Benjamin), and between "objective" sources of evidence and "subjective" narratives of asylum seekers (Haas, Marco Jacquemet, Benjamin N. Lawrance). The contribution from Haviland is particularly noteworthy in this regard in that he turns the problematic of "a politics of protection" on its head and asks what happens when those who do not understand themselves in need of protection get defined as such by the state.

Suspicion

Though we are framing suspicion as its own conceptual domain here, this is, as the volume's title indicates, an overarching theme of the book as a whole. Indeed, suspicion is the primary point of organization for this volume. The ethical quandaries and challenges that underlie the control of borders have long been recognized by scholars (Carens 1992; Gibney 1988). However, in this volume, we argue that the rise of suspicion as the dominant ethos of asylum adjudication—the stance that asylum seekers are "always already untrustworthy"—is reconfiguring notions of who can claim protection and who is obligated to protect (Holmes and Castañeda 2016, 19; see also Bohmer and Shuman 2007; Griffiths 2013; Jacquemet 2011; Maryns 2006).

Didier Fassin and Richard Rechtman (2009) describe refugees as "objects of suspicion," tracing their emergence as perceived competitors in the labor market. Asylum policy, then, was subordinated to the economics of migration (256). Following this, they argue that the "hunt for bogus refugees became a leitmotif in public discourse, used to justify the increasing harshness of adjudications" (256). Our discussion of suspicion examines both the larger conceptual framework of suspicion and particular, localized discourses of suspicion in the political asylum process. Though the adjudication of asylum is an individualized process, its effects are much greater:

"the discredit of asylum seekers as individuals signifies the delegitimation of asylum as an institution" (Fassin 2011, 220).

Suspicion generates technologies to measure and assess deservingness and, more specifically, credibility, and several essays in this book discuss these various "technologies of suspicion" (Campbell, 2004), including chapters by Haas, Jacquemet, Lawrance, and Lewis. This volume's contributors ask: What are these technologies of suspicion? How and when are they deployed and by whom? What are the effects, both intended and unintended, of these technologies? While recognizing suspicion as a dominant ethos of asylum systems, contributors also attend to its slippages, ambivalences, and indeterminacies.

While asylum adjudication and RSD processes are putatively concerned with "getting *at* the 'truth,'" the contributions to this volume underscore the ways in which asylum systems actually engage in the production of truth (Fassin 2013). Thus, technologies of suspicion are simultaneously "technologies of truth" (Merry and Coutin 2014). For example, in many cases, as Lawrance's chapter demonstrates, outside expert witnesses or state-produced country condition reports are granted ultimate authority over the testimony of the asylum seeker herself (see also Good 2007; Lawrance and Ruffer 2015). Our contention in this book is that asylum systems are not just contexts in which certain categories and performances are rewarded and legitimated but also contexts in which these very categories of personhood are themselves produced.

A key effect of these technologies of suspicion is a narrowing of the lens of who can be considered morally deserving. That is, if states are obligated to protect "true refugees" who are worthy of protection, then by narrowing the criteria by which this deservingness is met also serves to limit the number to whom the state is obligated. This allows for states to restrict migration while keeping their claim to humanitarian obligation intact. This is reflected in the assertion by asylum institutions that a rise in asylum denials reflects a rise in "bogus" asylum seekers. We agree with Fassin (2015), who suggests that this instead reflects a rise in the *production* of suspicious subjects rather than a rise in their presence (see also Kmak 2105, 396). Indeed, numerous essays provide fine-grained analyses of the production of suspicious subjects across a variety of settings (Haviland, Lewis, McKinnon, Shuman and Bohmer, Watters).

OUTLINE OF THE BOOK

All of the contributors to the book engage with concepts of obligation, security, and suspicion, albeit from different theoretical, geopolitical, and methodological perspectives. As we have been elaborating in this introduction, these concepts shift across time and space, and the essays in this book investigate their localization and their impact on the security and well-being of asylum seekers.

The essays that constitute part I, "Asylum and Protection as Contested Categories," lay important groundwork for the volume and the subsequent chapters. These three chapters address different cultural and geographical contexts but cohere around an engagement with the ways in which asylum as a category can be murky and contested. Each of these chapters richly illuminates disparate examples of disconnection between asylum bureaucracies' claims to protect and migrants' experiences of these bureaucratic procedures. They show that asylum regimes and their associated notions of obligation and protection are often at odds with migrants' experiences of the asylum process and of migrants' conceptions of themselves, including their desires, goals, sense of agency, and understandings of dignity. The contributors to the chapters in part I focus on how politics of suspicion mediate culturally complicated—and often conflicting—notions surrounding asylum on the ground. Moreover, these chapters reveal important insights surrounding the sociocultural, political, and experiential consequences of these contestations.

Part I opens with Nadia El-Shaarawi's chapter focusing on the politics of obligation as it relates to US refugee policy toward Iraqi refugees in the wake of the Iraq War. As she notes, the RSD of Iraqi refugees was informed by an explicitly moral framework whereby preferential access was given to those whose persecution could be traced directly to their association with the American forces or other allied organizations in Iraq. El-Shaarawi urges us to think about how questions of moral responsibility intervene in tensions between humanitarianism impulses and security concerns and further trouble the category of asylum. Though notions of moral responsibility, as other essays illustrate, are not usually as explicitly outlined in asylum policies, El-Shaarawi's emphasis on obligation as a necessary category of analysis is highly instructive. Her data reveal the multiple and conflicting ways in which obligation is imagined and experienced within a broader politics of suspicion—a theme that resonates across essays in this book.

Charles Watters's essay examines the moral economy of deservingness that is at play in the management of asylum seekers broadly, as well as within the specific research site of Zeebrugge, a port city in Belgium through which migrants seek to pass en route to the United Kingdom. Watters importantly attends to how refugees themselves interpret and respond to institutional and/or governmental tensions between protection and control as they creatively navigate "problem spaces." The disconnect between migrants' understandings of themselves and their institutional categorization can result in the effacement of particular aspects of refugees' narratives and experiences. For instance, articulations of aspiration or agency are viewed as suspect and delegitimated, as such characteristics fail to conform to the role of the passive refugee, deemed most deserving of protection within asylum regimes.

John B. Haviland's essay, which concludes part I, likewise considers the tensions that arise when subjects are recognized in ways that are at odds with their own self-understandings. It is unique to this volume in two ways. First, Haviland richly draws on his complex role as both ethnographer and interpreter in immigration cases involving Tzotzil speakers. This dual role allows Haviland a rare opportunity to observe the multiple actors and "different orders of engagement" involved in the construction of suspicious subjects, which he presents via deep analyses of transcripts between multiple actors (himself, a migrant in US custody, a US Immigration and Customs Enforcement agent, a social worker). Second, as noted earlier, Haviland sets out "to stand the notion of 'suspicion' upside down," focusing on migrants who did not identify as refugees or asylum seekers but instead found themselves as objects of what he terms "coerced asylum." He examines the consequences for migrant minors from Central America and Mexico as they become the subjects of American "ideologically driven legal resolutions" whereby the US government positions itself as morally obligated to protect vulnerable and victimized (Other) children.

Having established asylum as a contested and cumbersome category, part II, "Technologies of Suspicion," looks more specifically at forms of knowledge production within asylum systems. The contributions in this section provide critical analyses of new and dominant technologies of putatively getting at the truth of asylum claims. Whether conceived of as "technologies of suspicion" (Campbell 2004), "technologies of truth" (Merry and

Coutin 2014), or "technologies of morality" (Kmak 2015), these new forms of assessing truth, legitimacy, and deservingness—and their flip sides of disbelief and illegitimacy—are reconfiguring not only *how* one becomes seen as worthy of protection but also *who* becomes worthy of protection. While many other contributors in this volume address various technologies of suspicion deployed within asylum adjudication, the three essays of this section take specific and/or emergent technologies of suspicion as their primary focus.

Bridget M. Haas's chapter ethnographically explores asylum officers in the United States and the ways in which these adjudicators wrestle with the dual imperative to protect both the state and legitimate, deserving asylum seekers. Asylum officers, who conceive of themselves as "moral gatekeepers," are acutely aware of the humanitarian imperative facing them and of the life-or-death stakes of their decisions. Yet concerns over and commitments to national security are also seen as moral issues. Thus, asylum officers must weigh their obligation to the state against their obligation to a foreign, unknown Other. To do this, asylum officers engage various technologies of truth in their adjudication of claims, including credibility assessments, the use of corroborating material or other "objective" evidence, and the evaluation of psychological affidavits. Haas traces the unevenness of the implementation of these technologies and the ambivalence with which asylum officers approach them. Such ambivalence, along with the fact that asylum officers rely on their own emotions to make asylum decisions, reveals the fissures in these technologies of truth. Haas also underscores the adjudication process as one that constructs particular categories of personhood and deservingness, challenging the putative notion that categories such as "humanitarian victim," "security threat," or "bogus" asylum seeker are self-evident or exist prior to one's involvement with the asylum process.

Benjamin Lawrance, in his chapter on magical African asylum claims, argues that the politics of suspicion that characterize political asylum results in the increasing emphasis on the importance of empirical research in establishing asylum claimant credibility. In particular, Lawrance examines the use of country of origin information (COI), such as State Department reports and reports crafted by other national and international organizations. Adjudicators view COI as authoritative, thus offering legitimacy to cases that can effectively use these data sources to support their claims. Lawrance uses case examples from West African women refugees who invoked various forms of witchcraft in their persecution narratives to illustrate that that claims of magic and witchcraft were unable to find support in COI. Consequently, lawyers recrafted these women's testimonies, reformulating witchcraft asylum claims into claims of gender violence, which could be more suitably supported by expert evidence and COI. While Lawrance acknowledges that this legal strategy may serve to increase the chances of a successful outcome, he pushes us to consider the human and social costs of this legal move, framing it as an example of bureaucratic violence. Lawrance's chapter urges consideration of which technologies and information get understood as authoritative and why, as well as how this production of knowledge shapes who gets recognized (or not) as deserving of protection.

The final chapter in this part addresses emergent digital and Web-based technologies that are transforming asylum systems. In his examination of the affordances and limitations of asylum going digital, Marco Jacquemet describes the technologies used in asylum hearings, including on-site immediate examinations of Google Earth websites, search engines, and machine translation to corroborate or dispute applicants' assertions. While on the surface these new techniques may seem benign, even beneficial, to asylum adjudication, Jacquemet suggests that they are in fact power technologies that serve to implement the ideology of suspicion in the asylum process. Although these new technologies may help "speed things up," they also carry the "risk of communicative breakdown and bias against asylum seekers." Along with the other contributions to this volume, Jacquemet's essay allows for an understanding of asylum systems and their associated technologies as both producing suspicion and governing suspicious subjects. Thus, asylum systems work to bring into existence the very suspicions that they then presumptively need to control and manage.

The chapters in the third and final part of the volume, "Enacting and Navigating Suspicion," offer analyses of the micropolitics of asylum adjudication, with particular attention to how these technologies mediate interactions between adjudicators or advocates and asylum claimants. These chapters shed light on how asylum seekers navigate the technologies of suspicion introduced in the previous section and how broader global and national discourses, ideologies, and policies come to be locally enacted in varied and complex ways. Contributors highlight how notions of deservingness are both performed and assessed within arenas increasingly characterized by an ethos of suspicion.

Ilil Benjamin's chapter addresses the complex yet highly influential roles that NGO advocates play within asylum regimes. Using data collected at a refugee legal aid organization in Israel, Benjamin explores the difficulties that confront NGO workers as they try to help refugees reframe their asylum testimonies to fit the requirements of the asylum system. Benjamin's analysis reveals multiple iterations of the tension between suspicion and responsibility. Within the Israeli asylum regime, there are particular categories—economic migrant, for example—as well as certain national affiliations or kinds of narrative performances that are deemed more suspicious than others. Benjamin argues that while asylum advocates try to mediate these factors, over time they often "parted with many illusions of honesty and good faith in the asylum system." And as Benjamin shows, they too are sometimes confronted with their own suspicions about particular asylum seekers, posing personal moral dilemmas for these NGO workers.

The essay by Sara McKinnon keenly illustrates an analytic tacking between macro- and microlevel politics of asylum. Important to her project is her assertion that a close examination of local-level responses to new forms of incorporation—here, transgender asylum claimants—reveals much about US anxieties and aspirations. In particular, McKinnon considers shifts in the framing and language of asylum claims for transgendered women, noting a rhetorical separation of gender and gender identity. As McKinnon explicates, this microlevel shift produced significant (negative) changes in outcomes of these claims and served "to create boundaries around a suspicious and fearful figure in US law and politics—the figure of the reproductive brown woman." McKinnon's chapter reveals not only the geopolitical shaping of who can be considered "incorporable as an immigrant subject" but the highly gendered and racialized aspects of this process as well.

The final two chapters shed important light on how the complexities and contradictions of asylum systems are navigated by asylum seekers themselves. Rachel Lewis's chapter deftly examines how particular groups of subjects—in her case lesbian asylum claimants—are configured as suspect. Her analysis critically connects local practices of credibility assessment to larger discourses surrounding gender, sexuality, race, and class. Lewis demonstrates the mechanisms by which these larger cultural and discursive forces are locally enacted to construct queer asylum seekers as deportable subjects, echoing McKinnon's observations of the gendered and racialized nature of the construction of suspicious subjects. The issue of credibility and its local negotiation on which Lewis reflects is a key theme in other essays as well. For Lewis, accounting for the intersections of race, class, gender, and sexuality as they shape credibility assessments for gay and lesbian asylum claimants is a necessary step in conceptualizing effective forms of queer antideportation activism.

The final essay of part III, by Amy Shuman and Carol Bohmer, continues the investigation into credibility assessments and the enactment of suspicion in their examination of the tensions between asylum seekers' trauma narratives and asylum officials' cultural expectations of narrative performance. Beginning with an analysis of the case of Rwandan Paul Rusesabagina, Shuman and Bohmer highlight the highly contested nature of claims to protection, obligation, and security. Continuing with the observation that political asylum hearings are both interrogations and narrative performances, Shuman and Bohmer investigate three dimensions of narrative that are used as tools in asylum claimant credibility assessments: orientation, positioning, and narrative logic. Through a detailed narrative analysis of an asylum case, they demonstrate the incompatibility of interrogation and trauma narratives. Shuman and Bohmer pay particular attention to the fact that asylum seekers' experiences are saturated with contradictions. Of necessity, asylum seekers often occupy multiple and contradictory subject positions in order to survive, and they must create a coherent narrative to persuade asylum officials of their credibility. These "narrative failures" can have devastating results, ranging from the delegitimation of personal and collective suffering to the forcible removal of migrants back to situations of existential insecurity.

We close with a conclusion in which we reflect on the contributions of the volume, especially as they relate to ongoing and emergent discourses and practices surrounding asylum. In particular, we examine the insights gleaned from the volume's essays on the relationship between credibility and legibility. Further, we reflect on the role of ethnography, cultural analysis, and the positionality of scholars in the study of asylum regimes.

Ultimately our intent in this volume is to emphasize the very human stakes involved in the adjudication of refugee and asylum claims. That the contemporary landscape of humanitarian crises and forced migration described in the opening pages of this introduction is increasingly dominated by an ethos of suspicion does not just provide a case for theoretical inquiry.

The tensions and slippages between humanitarianism and border control surrounding political asylum, whereby suspicion often supplants protection, has profound human and social consequences. A more robust understanding of how these broader forces and tensions come to be locally enacted in ways that differentially shape the lived experiences of those fleeing persecution and claiming the need for protection is essential if we are to compassionately respond to the scope of suffering and mobility in the contemporary moment.

NOTES

1. According to Marisa Cianciarulo (2006), political asylum has become "a lightning rod for the national immigration debate, forcing the country to balance the traditional humanitarian interests against weighty security concerns" (110). See also Hamlin (2014, 5).

2. The United Nations High Commissioner for Refugees estimates that at the end of 2016, there were 65.6 million forcibly displaced persons worldwide. Of this total, 22.5 million were refugees, 40.3 million were internally displaced people, and 2.8 million were asylum seekers (UNCHR, 2016).

REFERENCES

Adamson, Fiona B. 2006. "Crossing Borders: International Migration and National Security." *International Security* 31 (1): 165–99.

Agamben, Giorgio. 2000. "Beyond Human Rights." In *Means without End: Notes on Politics*. Translated by V. Bienitti and C. Casarino, 15–28. Minneapolis: University of Minnesota Press.

Amoore, Louise. 2013. *The Politics of Possibility: Risk and Security beyond Probability*. Durham, NC: Duke University Press.

Anderson, Bridget. 2013. *Us and Them? The Dangerous Politics of Immigration Control*. Oxford: Oxford University Press.

Aradau, Claudia, Jef Huysmans, Andrew Neal, and Nadine Voelkner. 2014. *Critical Security Methods: New Frameworks for Analysis*. New York: Routledge.

Bennett, Claire. 2014. "Lesbians and United Kingdom Asylum Law: Evidence and Existence." In *Gender in Refugee Law: From the Margins to the Centre*, edited by Efrat Arbel, Catherine Dauvergne, and Jenni Milbank, 138–56. New York: Routledge.

Bigo, Didier. 2002. "Security and Immigration: Toward a Critique of the Governmentality of Unease." *Alternatives* 27:63–92.

———. 2007. *Policing Insecurity Today: Defense and Internal Security*. Houndmills, UK: Palgrave Macmillan.

Blommaert, Jan. 2001. "Investigating Narrative Inequality: African Asylum Seekers' Stories in Belgium." *Discourse and Society* 12 (4): 413–49.

Bohmer, Carol, and Amy Shuman. 2007. "Producing Epistemologies of Ignorance in the Political Asylum Application Process." *Identities: Global Studies in Culture and Power* 14:603–29.

———. 2008. *Rejecting Refugees: Political Asylum in the 21st Century*. London: Routledge.

———. 2010. "Contradictory Discourses of Protection and Control in Transnational Asylum Law." *Journal of Legal Anthropology* 1 (2): 212–29.

———. 2018. *Political Asylum Deceptions: The Culture of Suspicion*. Cham, Switzerland: Palgrave Macmillan.

Broeders, Dennis. 2007. "The New Digital Borders of Europe EU Databases and the Surveillance of Irregular Migrants." *International Sociology* 22 (1): 71–92.

Cabot, Heath. 2013. "The Social Aesthetics of Eligibility: NGO Aid and Indeterminacy in the Greek Asylum Process." *American Ethnologist* 40 (3): 452–66.

———. 2014. *On the Doorstep of Europe: Asylum and Citizenship in Greece*. Philadelphia: University of Pennsylvania Press.

Campbell, Nancy. 2004. "Technologies of Suspicion: Coercion and Compassion in Post-Disciplinary Surveillance Regimes." *Surveillance and Society* 2 (1): 78–92.

Carens, Joseph H. 1992. "Refugees and the Limits of Obligation." *Public Affairs Quarterly* 6 (1): 31–44.

———. 2003. "Who Should Get In? The Ethics of Immigration Admissions." *Ethics and International Affairs* 17 (1): 95–110.

Cianciarulo, Marisa Silenzi. 2006. "Terrorism and Asylum Seekers: Why the Real ID Act Is a False Promise." *Harvard Journal on Legislation* 43 (1): 101–43.

Coutin, Susan Bibler. 2011. "The Rights of Noncitizens in the United States." *Annual Review of Law and Social Science* 7:289–308.

Daniel, E. Valentine, and John Chr. Knudsen, eds. 1995. *Mistrusting Refugees*. Berkeley: University of California Press.

Das, Veena, and Deborah Poole, eds. 2004. *Anthropology at the Margins of the State*. Santa Fe, NM: School of American Research Press.

Dauvergne, Catherine. 2004. "Making People Illegal." In *Critical Beings: Law, Nation and the Global Subject*, edited by Peter Fitzpatrick, 83–100. Hampshire, UK: Ashgate.

De Genova, Nicholas P., and Nathalie Peutz, eds. 2010. *The Deportation Regime: Sovereignty, Space, and the Freedom of Movement*. Durham, NC: Duke University Press.

Edwards, Alice. 2005. "Human Rights, Refugees, and the Right 'to Enjoy' Asylum." *International Journal of Refugee Law* 17 (2): 293–330.

Einhorn, Bruce J. 2009. "Consistency, Credibility, and Culture." In Ramji-Nogales, Schoenholtz, and Schrag, *Refugee Roulette*, 187–201.

Einolf, Christopher J. 2001. *The Mercy Factor: Refugees and the American Asylum System*. Chicago: Ivan Dee.

Essed, Philomena, and Rianne Wesenbeek. 2004. "Contested Refugee Status: Human Rights, Ethics, and Social Responsibilities." In *Refugees and the Transformation of Societies: Agency, Policies, Ethics and Politics*, edited by Philomena Essed, 53–66. New York: Berghahn Books.

Fassin, Didier. 2011. "Policing Borders, Producing Boundaries: The Governmentality of Immigration in Dark Times." *Annual Review of Anthropology* 40:213–26.

———. 2013. The Precarious Truth of Asylum. *Public Culture* 25 (1): 39–63.
———. 2015. Introduction: Governing Precarity. In *At the Heart of the State: The Moral Worlds of Institutions*, edited by Didier Fassin, 1–12. London: Pluto Press.
Fassin, Didier, and Estelle d'Halluin. 2007. "Critical Evidence: The Politics of Trauma in French Asylum Policies." *Ethos* 35 (3): 300–329.
Fassin, Didier, and Richard Rechtman. 2009. *Empire of Trauma: An Inquiry into the Condition of Victimhood.* Princeton, NJ: Princeton University Press.
Feldman, Ilana. 2007. "Difficult Distinctions: Refugee Law, Humanitarian Practice, and Political Identification in Gaza." *Cultural Anthropology* 22:129–69.
Gibney, Mark. 1988. *Open Borders? Closed Societies? The Ethical and Political Issues.* New York: Greenwood.
Gibney, Matthew. 2002. "Security and the Ethics of Asylum after 11 September." *Forced Migration Review* 13:40–42.
———. 2004. *The Ethics and Politics of Asylum: Liberal Democracy and the Response to Refugees.* Cambridge: Cambridge University Press.
Goldstein, Daniel M. 2007. "Human Rights as Culprit, Human Rights as Victim: Rights and Security in the State of Exception." In *The Practice of Human Rights: Tracking Law between the Global and the Local,* edited by Mark Goodale, 49–77. Cambridge: Cambridge University Press.
Good, Anthony. 2007. *Anthropology and Expertise in the Asylum Courts.* London: Routledge.
Griffiths, Melanie. 2012. "'Vile Liars and Truth Distorters': Truth, Trust and the Asylum System." *Anthropology Today* 28 (5): 8–12.
Hamlin, Rebecca. 2014. *Let Me Be a Refugee: Administrative Justice and the Politics of Asylum in the United States, Canada and Australia.* Oxford: Oxford University Press.
Hathaway, James C. 1991. "Reconceiving Refugee Law as Human Rights Protection." *Journal of Refugee Studies* 4 (2): 113–31.
Holmes, Seth M., and Heide Castañeda. 2016. "Representing the "European Refugee Crisis" in Germany and Beyond." *American Ethnologist* 43 (1): 12–24.
Huysmans, Jef. 2006. *The Politics of Insecurity: Fear, Migration and Asylum in the EU.* New York: Routledge.
Innes, Alexandria J. 2010. "When the Threatened Become the Threat: The Construction of Asylum Seekers in British Media Narratives." *International Relations* 24 (4): 456–77.
Jacquemet, Marco. 2009. "Transcribing Refugees: The Entextualization of Asylum-Seekers' Hearings in a Transidiomatic Environment." *Text and Talk* 29 (5): 525–46.
———. 2011. "Crosstalk 2.0: Asylum and Communicative Breakdowns." *Text and Talk* 31 (4): 475–97.
James, Erica C. 2004. "The Political Economy of 'Trauma' in Haiti in the Democratic Era of Insecurity." *Culture, Medicine and Psychiatry* 28 (2): 127–49.
———. 2011. Haiti, Insecurity and the Politics of Asylum. *Medical Anthropology Quarterly* 25 (2): 357–76.
Jubany, Olga. 2011. "Constructing Truths in a Culture of Disbelief: Understanding Asylum Screening from Within." *International Sociology* 26 (1): 74–94.
———. 2017. *Screening Asylum in a Culture of Disbelief: Truths, Denials, and Skeptical Borders.* Cham, Switzerland: Palgrave Macmillan.

Juma, Monica Kathina, and Peter Mwangi Kagwanja. 2003. "Securing Refuge from Terror: Refugee Protection in East Africa after September 11." In *Problems of Protection: The UNHCR, Refugees, and Human Rights*, edited by N. Steiner, M. Gibney, and G. Loescher, 225–36. New York: Routledge.

Kerwin, Donald. 2005. "The Use and Misuse of 'National Security' Rationale in Crafting US Refugee and Immigration Policies." *International Journal of Refugee Law* 17 (4): 749–63.

Kmak, Magdalena. 2015. "Between Citizen and Bogus Asylum Seeker: Management of Migration in the EU through the Technology of Morality." *Social Identities* 21 (4): 395–409.

Lawrance, Benjamin N., and Galya Ruffer, eds. 2015. *Adjudicating Refugee and Asylum Status: The Role of Witness, Expertise, and Testimony*. Cambridge: Cambridge University Press.

Legomsky, Stephen H. 2009. "Learning to Live with Unequal Justice: Asylum and the Limits to Consistency." In Ramji-Nogales, Schoenholtz, and Schrag, *Refugee Roulette*, 250–87.

Macklin, Audrey. 2009. "Asylum and the Rule of Law in Canada: Hearing the Other (Side)." In *Refugees, Asylum Seekers and the Rule of Law*, edited by S. Kneebone, 78–121. Cambridge: Cambridge University Press.

Maryns, Katrijn. 2006. *The Asylum Speaker: Language in the Belgian Asylum Procedure*. New York: Routledge.

McKinnon, Sara L. 2009. "Citizenship and the Performance of Credibility: Audiencing Gender-Based Asylum Seekers in US Immigration Courts." *Text and Performance Quarterly* 29 (3): 205–21.

Merry, Sally Engle, and Susan Bibler Coutin. 2014. "Technologies of Truth in the Anthropology of Conflict: AES/APLA Presidential Address, 2013." *American Ethnologist* 41 (1): 1–16.

Millner, Naomi. 2011. "From 'Refugee' to 'Migrant' in Calais Solidarity Activism: Re-Staging Undocumented Migration for a Future Politics of Asylum." *Political Geography* 30 (6): 320–28.

Mountz, Alison. 2010. *Seeking Asylum: Human Smuggling and Bureaucracy at the Border*. Minneapolis: University of Minnesota Press.

Muller, Benjamin. 2004. Globalization, Security, Paradox: Towards a Refugee Biopolitics. *Refuge: Canada's Journal on Refugees* 22 (1): 49–57.

Nyers, Peter. 2003. "Abject Cosmopolitanism: The Politics of Protection in the Anti-Deportation Movement." *Third World Quarterly* 24 (6): 1069–93.

———. 2006. *Rethinking Refugees: Beyond States of Emergency*. New York: Routledge.

Pirouet, Louise. 2001. *Whatever Happened to Asylum in Britain? A Tale of Two Walls*. New York: Berghahn Books.

Ramji-Nogales, Jaya, Alexander Schoenholtz, and Peter G. Schrag. 2007. "Refugee Roulette: Disparities in Asylum Adjudication." *Stanford Law Review* 60 (2): 295–411.

———. 2009. *Refugee Roulette: Disparities in Asylum Adjudication and Proposals for Reform*. New York: New York University Press.

Rousseau, Cécile, François Crépeau, Patricia Foxen, and France Houle. 2002. "The Complexity of Determining Refugeehood: A Multidisciplinary Analysis of the

Decision-Making Process of the Canadian Immigration and Refugee Board." *Journal of Refugee Studies* 15 (1): 43–70.

Schoenholtz, Andrew. 2005. "Refugee Protection in the United States Post-September 11th. *Columbia Human Rights Law Review* 36 (2): 323–64.

Schuster, Liza. 2003. *The Use and Abuse of Political Asylum in Britain and Germany*. London: Frank Cass.

Shuman, Amy, and Carol Bohmer. 2004. "Representing Trauma: Political Asylum Narratives." *Journal of American Folklore* 117:394–414.

Squire, Victoria. 2009. *The Exclusionary Politics of Asylum*. Hampshire, UK: Palgrave Macmillan.

Steiner, Niklaus, Mark Gibney, and Gil Loescher, eds. 2003. *Problems of Protection: The UNHCR, Refugees, and Human Rights*. New York: Routledge

Tazreiter, Claudia. 2004. *Asylum Seekers and the State: The Politics of Protection in a Security-Conscious World*. Burlington, VT: Ashgate.

Ticktin, Miriam. 2006. "Where Ethics and Politics Meet: The Violence of Humanitarianism in France." *American Ethnologist* 33 (1): 33–49.

———. 2011. *Casualties of Care: Immigration and the Politics of Humanitarianism in France*. Berkeley: University of California Press.

Transactional Records Access Clearinghouse (TRAC). 2016. *Continued Rise in Asylum Denial Rates: Impact of Representation and Nationality*. Syracuse University. www.trac.syr.edu/immigration/reports/448.

Turner, Victor. 1967. "Betwixt and Between: The Liminal Period in Rites de Passage." In *The Forest of Symbols: Aspects of Ndembu Ritual*. Ithaca, NY: Cornell University Press.

UN General Assembly. 1967. Protocol Relating to the Status of Refugees, 31 January 1967, United Nations, Treaty Series, vol. 606. http://www.refworld.org/docid/3ae6b3ae4.html.

UN High Commissioner for Refugees (UNHCR). 2015. *Asylum Trends 2014: Levels and Trends in Industrialized Countries*. http://www.refworld.org/docid/5513bd3b4.html.

———. 2017. *Global Trends: Forced Displacement in 2016*. http://www.unhcr.org/5943e8a34.pdf.

Willen, Sarah. 2012. "How Is Health-Related "Deservingness" Reckoned? Perspectives from Unauthorized Im/migrants in Tel Aviv." *Social Science and Medicine* 74 (6): 812–21.

Zagor, Matthew. 2015. "The Struggle of Autonomy and Authenticity: Framing the Savage Refugee." *Social Identities* 21 (4): 373–94.

Zimmermann, Susan E. 2011. "Reconsidering the Problem of 'Bogus' Refugees with 'Socio-economic Motivations' for Seeking Asylum." *Mobilities* 6 (3): 335–52.

Part I

Asylum and Protection as Contested Categories

Chapter 1

Troubling the Ethics of Durable Solutions in the Age of Suspicion

Iraq War Refugees and the Politics of Obligation

NADIA EL-SHAARAWI

"In front of Iraqi people I am now a traitor, having cheated my country, and in front of Americans I don't have a case." As Mustafa and I sat in the waiting room of a Cairo refugee legal aid organization, his angry condemnation filled me with shame. That afternoon, I had noticed him come into the clinic carrying a thin folder of paper and drop onto a seat in the waiting room, visibly upset. Around him, the hustle and bustle of work went on as usual: clients waited to be seen as legal advocates interviewed refugees, filled out forms, and entered data. I, the ethnographer, had been encouraged to speak with Mustafa by the director, who noted in hushed tones that Mustafa had just been rejected for resettlement to the United States and "needed to talk." While Mustafa could appeal the decision, we knew how difficult it would be and how unlikely it was to be successful.

Resettlement rejections often came with almost no explanation for why a case had been refused in the first place, making appeals challenging. And while the legal aid clinic provided its clients with assistance before and after the resettlement interviews, refugees were almost never allowed to bring a legal advocate to the interviews that would decide their fate. A conversation with an anthropologist in a moment like this felt inadequate, empty of comfort. I knew that the director had asked me to speak with Mustafa because there was nothing substantive to offer him in that moment. Mustafa, who had been forced to flee Iraq because of his association with the Americans, had, in his estimation, risked reidentifying himself as a "traitor" in exile by applying to be resettled to the United States. Yet because his affiliation with the United States in Iraq had not been judged to fit the specific criteria of the US resettlement program, his application was rejected. Mustafa, like many Iraqis I met in Cairo, was caught in between: he didn't quite fit the bureaucratic specificities of the programs designed to provide protection to Iraqi refugees, despite believing himself to be in need of such protection.

According to the United Nations High Commissioner for Refugees (UNHCR), there are 25.4 million refugees in the world today. Refugee status is, by definition, intended to be temporary. Yet displacement is increasingly protracted, with a global average length of displacement of twenty years. Nonetheless, the framing of displacement as a "temporary crisis" demands a solution, and the conventional framework employed by international organizations and states includes three discrete, so-called durable solutions: repatriation to the country of origin, local integration, and third-country resettlement. The framework of durable solutions may be less familiar and pressing in contexts where national asylum systems lead to permanent residence or citizenship for people granted asylum, but in states where national asylum systems are absent and where refugees are allowed to reside on a temporary basis only, like in Egypt, the question of a durable solution to displacement takes on urgency for refugees and humanitarians alike.

This volume focuses on the ways that discourses of humanitarianism and securitization play out in a wide range of asylum adjudication contexts. In this chapter, I focus on Iraqi refugees' experiences of adjudication—not of asylum but of third-country resettlement, one of the durable solutions. Resettlement involves the selection and transfer of refugees from the country where they have sought refuge to a new country that has agreed to provide them with residence and, usually, a pathway to citizenship. Once the preferred solution to the "refugee problem" (Loescher and Scanlan 1998), resettlement has become the least-used durable solution. Only approximately 1 percent of refugees are resettled. Resettlement is typically only a possibility for people who have already been granted refugee status. It is often intended as an additional form of protection when asylum is insufficient. Yet, as in asylum, resettlement adjudication decides who is included and who is excluded. Both processes are complex arenas of contestation in which questions of obligation, security, humanitarianism, and protection are played out.

While resettlement and asylum processes share some similarities, there are key differences. First, while theoretically people who meet the definition of a refugee under the 1951 Convention Relating to the Status of Refugees and its 1967 protocol have the right to claim asylum, no such right to resettlement exists. Resettlement is entirely at the discretion of the resettlement state, which decides which refugees to admit and the manner in which they will be admitted. The United States has for a long time resettled the most refugees of any of the twenty-eight resettlement countries and has the most nationally independent program of any resettlement state (Van Selm 2014). Second, persons can claim asylum when they reach the territory of the state to which they have fled. Resettlement, on the other hand, allows states to select the refugees they would like to admit before they travel to the resettlement country. It is therefore not surprising that states often hold up resettlement programs as "orderly" against the uncontrolled, and therefore suspicious, mobility of asylum seekers (Van Selm 2014), who are often stigmatized as dangerous or illegitimate "queue jumpers." But this is not always the case. For example, populist politicians in the United States have recently used versions of both of these discourses as justification for restrictions or moratoriums on refugee resettlement.

Scholars, as well as politicians, have deliberated at length about what responsibilities states have to admit refugees (Gibney 2004). In this chapter, I move away from an approach grounded in the ethical underpinnings or policy implications of inclusion and exclusion that, while important, tend to center the state in their analysis (Aleinikoff 1995). Instead I argue for an anthropological approach that focuses on Iraqi refugees' lived experiences of the resettlement process and the ways in which the logics that underpinned resettlement were negotiated locally in Cairo. This method pays attention to the ways in which these larger geopolitical questions are made and remade in everyday encounters during the resettlement process. How do refugees like Mustafa experience, understand, and engage with questions of obligation in the context of the resettlement process?

Although resettlement has become an exceptional solution, its impact reaches far beyond the few refugees who are resettled each year. Yet research on resettlement often does not include a focus on refugees' own hopes, plans, and experiences related to resettlement. Much scholarship on resettlement instead focuses on the integration of resettled populations, especially in the United States and Canada, and not on the process of resettlement itself, with important exceptions (e.g., Thomson 2012; Jansen 2008; Horst 2006). In addition, as Katy Long (2013) notes, the durable-solutions framework itself has rarely been subject to scholarly critique.

This chapter draws on several periods of ethnographic fieldwork with Iraqi refugees in Egypt from 2007 to 2012. During this time, I conducted interviews with refugees and humanitarians and engaged in participant observation in a refugee legal aid clinic and other key sites for the Iraqi community in Egypt. When I began my research, the resettlement process was not a primary focus of my project. However, over time I came to realize how centrally resettlement figured in the daily lives of my interlocutors, many of whom were seeking to be resettled to a third country, such as the United States. The lived experience of urban exile could not be understood without attention to the bureaucratic process that characterized much of their lives during this period.

DISPLACEMENT AND THE IRAQ WAR

In order to make sense of Iraqis' experiences with the resettlement process, it is essential to consider why they became refugees and how they experienced life in exile. In 2007, when I began my fieldwork, the flight of Iraqis from their country was at its apex. The 2003 Iraq War and the violence and unrest that followed led to the displacement of 4.7 million Iraqis. Some 2.7 million were internally displaced, while 2 million lived as refugees, mostly in countries in the region such as Jordan, Syria, Lebanon, and Egypt. Although it would soon be eclipsed by the forced migration caused by the Syrian Civil War, at the time the Iraqis represented the largest mass migration in the Middle East after 1948 (Fagan 2007).

The March 2003 invasion of Iraq, dubbed Operation Iraqi Freedom, was justified by the premise that Saddam Hussein possessed weapons of mass destruction, a rationale that was later demonstrated to be false. In April of that year, Baghdad fell, ending the twenty-four-year rule of Saddam and the Ba'ath Party. US troops would remain in Iraq until their official withdrawal in 2011. There was significant protest and public criticism of the war, which many likened to that of the Vietnam War. Criticism focused on a number of different issues, including the legality of the invasion, the human costs and financial costs, which have been estimated at more than $823 billion (Crawford 2014), abuses by the armed forces and private contractors, and failure to plan for the transition of power.

Immediately following the toppling of Saddam's regime, policymakers expected large-scale population movement both into and out of the country. However, the initial refugee movements did not materialize. Instead, beginning in 2005 and reaching its apex in 2006–7, escalating sectarian violence led to the mass displacement of millions of Iraqis, catching policymakers and practitioners unaware. After the fall of Saddam's regime, the absence of a strong state and a climate of insecurity further encouraged Iraqis to turn to other groupings, including tribal, sectarian, ethnic, and regional allegiances, in order to provide security and protection (Al-Mohammad 2010; Boyle 2009). This built on patterns of allegiance under the previous regime in which the stifling of political opposition was such that Iraqis identified with religious, tribal, and ethnic leaders for authority separate from that of the state. However, in a climate of fear and uncertainty, this plurality of groups led to great insecurity. In 2005, the number of militias, insurgent groups, tribal groups, and criminal gangs carrying out attacks exceeded one hundred (Filkins 2008). At the same time as the military, police, and other organs of the state were disbanded, weapons and ammunition became widely available in the marketplace, leading to well-armed civilians and militias and the absence of governmental authority (Sahlins 2011).

Many people fled Iraq after experiencing death threats, kidnappings, or other forms of violence in the climate of escalating sectarian violence and unrest. A smaller number of Iraqis were forced to leave the country when they were targeted as a result of their work (or their perceived affiliation) with the US war effort. Iraqis who had worked for the Americans were identified as collaborators by militias and subject to threats, kidnapping, or murder. At the same time, some Americans who had worked in Iraq and later received pleas from their terrorized interpreters and other Iraqi associates were actively pressing the US government to assist Iraqis who were in danger because of their association with the American war effort (Johnson 2013).

IRAQI REFUGEES IN EGYPT AND THE HOPE FOR DURABLE SOLUTIONS

At the height of their displacement, a population of approximately 150,000 Iraqis sought exile in Egypt (Yoshikawa 2007), primarily in urban Cairo. Although Egypt is a signatory to the 1951 refugee convention, it is difficult if not impossible for refugees to realize their rights in practice due to reservations Egypt has entered to the convention and a lack of implementing domestic legislation. These reservations limit the state's legal obligations to refugees, passing most of the administration and management of refugee populations onto the UNHCR and nongovernmental organizations (NGOs), in an example of what Aihwa Ong (2000) has referred to as graduated sovereignty.

Because of the state's "benign neglect" (Sadek 2010), Iraqi refugees could not work or access public education in Egypt, and they lived with precarious residency status, granted on the basis of their refugee claim but requiring renewal every six months. Citizenship is conferred on the basis of descent in Egypt and thus is not available to refugees. As a result, I found that Iraqis did not conceive of Egypt as a home but often spoke of their time there as "a station," "a temporary place," or "a problem to be solved," and conditions in Egypt contributed to Iraqi refugees' inability to settle more permanently in the country. In visits to my interlocutors' homes, I often saw the material evidence of this existential limbo (Haas 2017): the temporariness of life in Egypt combined with the uncertainty of the resettlement process often meant that people lived with their bags packed and ready to go, just in case. As my work has illustrated and as has been documented in a number of other asylum and migration contexts (El-Shaarawi 2015; Griffiths 2013, 2014; Haas 2017; Horst and Grabska 2015), living in protracted waiting can have deleterious effects on refugees' well-being.

If any type of meaningful integration into Egyptian society was not possible, return was also not an option. By 2010, the UNHCR had assisted some three thousand Iraqis to return to their country from countries of asylum, although they simultaneously did not formally encourage return to Iraq (UN News Service 2010). In 2010, a UNHCR survey found that the majority of Iraqi refugees who had returned to Baghdad regretted their decision to go back. Among the main reasons cited for this regret were insecurity, economic hardship, and a lack of basic services (UN News Service 2010). Many who had returned reported being forced to do so because they could no longer afford to live in the countries where they had sought asylum, not because they felt that the situation in Iraq had improved.

As a result, many Iraqi refugees were "stuck" in host countries such as Egypt—unable to return to Iraq, integrate in their host societies, or establish residence elsewhere. These circumstances, combined with policies that facilitated the resettlement of Iraqis, led to the importance of resettlement. Resettlement promised an escape from a difficult present and an uncertain future. It also provided opportunities to imagine an escape to the "Western world" (Horst 2006; Jansen 2008) in a context where other possibilities for such travel were foreclosed or dangerous. In Cairo, where residency, education, health care, and employment were unstable for refugees, the hope for resettlement was for more than protection but included the ability to rebuild lives following displacement.

RESETTLEMENT AND OBLIGATION

When I first met Mustafa in 2009, he and other Iraqi refugees were in the strange position of seeking protection, in the form of resettlement, in the country that arguably was responsible for their displacement in the first place. At that time, there were two main ways that Iraqi refugees could be resettled to the United States. The first, the US Department of State's so-called Direct Access Program, provided priority processing to Iraqis who had aided the US war effort and had been persecuted as a result. This was the program from which Mustafa had just been rejected when we met. The second was through UNHCR referral, which prioritized refugees who had exceptional protection needs in their country of asylum: victims of violence and torture, refugees with medical needs that could not be treated in Egypt, unaccompanied children, and others who for various reasons could not live safely in Egypt. If we think of morality as relational, the first mode of resettlement found its moral logic in allegiance and recompense for sacrifice, while the second is based on a more traditionally impartial humanitarian logic that privileges need and vulnerability. Both resettlement programs combine, in various ways, the securitized and humanitarian logics that increasingly characterize the refugee system. Although in many cases these logics represent a shift from a rights-based, legalistic approach to a humanitarian, moral one (Fassin 2005), this shift does not fully account for the dynamics of contemporary or historical refugee resettlement. With resettlement, we see a third logic in operation as well, one more clearly associated with a sense that the resettlement state is responsible for causing harm and displacement. In this chapter, I am interested in considering how the logic of obligation plays out in the resettlement process for Iraqi refugees in Egypt.

Resettlement primarily serves the humanitarian function of "protection"—it is often intended to be the solution of last resort for refugees whose human rights cannot be protected in their current location in exile. Yet resettlement policy and practice is not just humanitarian. It often serves specific political goals at the same time that it espouses humanitarian aims. For the United States, which resettles the largest number of refugees worldwide, a sense of moral obligation frequently plays into decisions about which refugees will be offered the possibility of resettling to the United States and, eventually, becoming American.

From a theoretical perspective, I introduce the question of obligation partly to trouble our ideas of the ethics of humanitarianism and human rights. Both ethics make universalist claims that are sometimes in conflict with one another and are often invoked in tandem, especially in discussion about asylum seekers or refugees. As Ilana Feldman and Miriam Ticktin (2010) have noted, anthropologists have contributed to our understanding of these universalist claims by offering evidence of the particular and, more recently, by turning to the effects of universalist claims making. In this chapter, I consider questions of obligation as a bridge between gift and entitlement, between humanitarianism and human rights. Questions of obligation, in a sense, introduce particularism into universals by creating categories of people who might make certain moral claims to humanitarian goods—that is, who might be entitled to the gift. Yet the claims of Iraqis who worked with the US forces and other organizations in Iraq trouble easy distinctions between "us" and "them" based on seemingly clear-cut notions of citizenship and inclusion.

Anthropologists have recently considered how universalist claims, transmuted into action, often have particularist effects. Humanitarian organizations, with limited mandates and means, face what Peter Redfield (2013) has termed "the troubling logic of choice." In some contexts, medical and psychological suffering, often developed into evidence through expert knowledge and documentation, serves as a proxy to identify "true" refugees or asylum seekers (Ticktin 2011; Fassin and d'Halluin 2007). While other analyses have focused on the political or antipolitical (Ticktin 2011) effects of these shifts in the context of asylum, I am interested here in thinking through the effects of moral claims of obligations on the subjective experience of refugees seeking resettlement as a lens to considering the connections between gifts, entitlements, and obligations. To do so, I consider the local moralities, to borrow Jarrett Zigon's (2008) term, surrounding Iraqi refugees' subjective experiences of the Direct Access Program.

An investigation of the local moralities associated with refugee resettlement reveals the important but contested role that questions of obligation play in people's lives. Michael M. J. Fischer's (2003) approach to understanding the interaction of people and larger moral systems of societies is a useful starting point for considering how the ethics of obligation are experienced, negotiated, and constituted through social relations. In order to consider these questions in more detail, I turn first to a brief historiography of the US resettlement program, with a focus on obligation, and then to some insights from fieldwork with Iraqi refugees as they navigated the resettlement program in Cairo.

RESETTLEMENT TO THE UNITED STATES

In US law, the term "refugee" refers specifically to people who have been brought to the country through the official government resettlement program. Any person who arrives in the United States of his or her own volition is categorized as an asylum seeker and, if their claim is granted, they become an asylee. While asylees and refugees may have identical claims and may undergo similar status-determination procedures, resettled refugees must prove their case before they ever reach US territory. They also typically must meet additional resettlement-specific criteria in addition to being determined to fit the definition of a refugee. When asylum seekers enter the United States, their presence and their request for asylum triggers certain legal obligations on the part of the state. Resettlement is not governed by any such entitlements. Refugee resettlement policy in the United States has been characterized by a tension between self-interest and humanitarianism since its inception. While the 1951 UN refugee convention, the 1967 protocol, and the United States Refugee Act of 1980 all require that the decision to provide refugee protection should not be governed by foreign policy objectives (Waibsnaider 2006), a brief survey of US refugee resettlement indicates that geopolitics play an important role in policy decisions.

The Displaced Persons Act of 1948, the first US refugee policy, allowed for the admission of people who had entered Allied zones in Germany, Austria, or Italy prior to 1945—essentially limiting the number of Jewish refugees who could claim protection following World War II (Waibsnaider 2006). The act was described by President Harry S. Truman as "flagrantly discriminatory. It mocks the American tradition of fair play" and met with sharp public criticism (Bockley 1995). It was subsequently revised twice, once in 1950 to include refugees from communist China, and once in 1951 to allow for the admission of European refugees who had been displaced after 1945 (Waibsnaider 2006). By the second half of the twentieth century, the United States was focused on admitting refugees from communist countries as a way of showing that the citizens of those countries were fleeing, while also propping up its image in the world (Waibsnaider 2006). Refugees from countries that the United States supported, meanwhile, were rarely granted refugee status, instead being cast as "economic migrants" (Bockley 1995). Before the 1980s, more than 90 percent of refugees admitted to the United States were from communist countries.

The 1980 Refugee Act adopted the United Nations definition of a refugee. The act was designed to develop a more uniform resettlement process and move US refugee policy away from an emphasis on communism and Europeans. However, in 1980 and afterward, the United States continued to "prioritize refugees who "had close ties to the United States," whose resettlement would further US foreign policy objectives and for whom the "United States has stood uniquely as a symbol of freedom from oppression" (Espiritu 2014; Tempo 2008). After the fall of the Berlin Wall in 1989, there was a decline in the numbers of refugees admitted to the United States from communist countries but no comparable increase in refugee admissions from noncommunist states (Waibsnaider 2006).

Prior to the resettlement of Iraqi refugees, there were two key instances where the United States admitted refugees in response to a sense of moral obligation. In both situations, those resettled were portrayed as refugees created by the United States as the direct result of unsuccessful interference in foreign countries: Hungarian refugees in 1956 and South Vietnamese refugees after the Vietnam War. In 1956, after the Soviet Union invaded Hungary to quash an anticommunist popular uprising, the United States sent military aid and the Central Intelligence Agency sent weapons to support the Hungarian resistance against the Soviet Army. Hungarian fighters were portrayed as "heroes" in the American media (Waibsnaider 2006; Bockley 1995). Once the revolt was put down, the United States had a more subdued response. It eventually admitted more than forty thousand Hungarian refugees, more than any other country. While to a certain degree one could understand the admission of Hungarian refugees as fitting part of the Cold War pattern of refugee admissions, there was a different logic at work here. The Hungarians were admitted not just because they feared a communist regime but also because they were the "victims of false expectations about US policy" (Loescher and Scanlan 1998, 54).

Somewhat similar to that of the Hungarian case, the rationale for the admission of South Vietnamese refugees was largely based in a sense of obligation to the former South Vietnamese allies who had fought alongside US forces and then were abandoned. In this case, the rationale for their admission was less an opportunity to score an ideological victory and more an admission of moral responsibility. President Gerald Ford explained resettlement following the war to the American public in terms of obligation when he said that "to do less would have added moral shame to humiliation." In some ways, the large-scale resettlement of South Vietnamese refugees who were associated with the United States following the end of the Vietnam War would be the inspiration and precedent for efforts to resettle so-called Iraqi allies.

In the first years following the US-led wars in Afghanistan and Iraq, the numbers of Afghan and Iraqis admitted as refugees to the United States were very low, despite the wars both creating new displacement and exacerbating existing displacement (Waibsnaider 2006). The rationale for the decrease in resettlement from these countries was explained in terms of security but may also have been related to a desire to show the American public that the United States was "winning hearts and minds." However, as the displacement crisis in the region worsened over time, and as stories emerged that demonstrated the threats facing the Iraqis who had worked with the US war effort (Johnson 2013; Packer 2007), public opinion and sustained advocacy led to policies to resettle Iraqis, especially those who had been harmed because of their support for the US-led occupation.

DIRECT ACCESS TO RESETTLEMENT

In the years shortly after the US invasion, high-profile advocacy campaigns (Johnson 2013) and media coverage (e.g., Packer 2007) publicized the cases of interpreters who worked directly with the American forces and were threatened, kidnapped, or murdered because of their affiliation. Iraqi labor was essential to the US military efforts. However, it soon became clear that the people who were supplying the expertise and labor were not being protected from retribution by those who saw their work as treachery. As a result of advocacy efforts, the US government passed the Refugee Crisis in Iraq Act in 2008, which included provisions for the resettlement of Iraqi allies who had been forced into hiding or exile as a result of their association with the American forces. The act was likewise described in terms of obligation. Sen. Ted Kennedy, who sponsored the bill, argued, "America has a special obligation to keep faith with the Iraqis who now have a bull's-eye on their backs because of their association with our government."[1]

For Iraqis, the implementation of the act created two parallel paths through which they might seek resettlement. They could seek it the traditional way by approaching the UNHCR, which might then refer them to one of about seventeen resettlement countries. I have written in other locations about how resettlement in this context is typically allocated to refugees who are the most vulnerable, such as those with severe medical issues, survivors of psychological trauma, and women and children at risk (El-Shaarawi 2015). Those who worked with the American forces and were persecuted as a result could have what is termed "direct access" and apply for resettlement to the United States through an intermediary, the International Organization for Migration (IOM), bypassing the UNHCR. Iraqis who applied through direct access had to prove affiliation with the Americans and then pass a number of interviews with the IOM and the Department of Homeland Security and undergo security and medical checks before being approved or denied for resettlement to the United States. The entire process could last months or years and was impenetrably bureaucratic. In itself, the resettlement process was a source of suffering for refugees (El-Shaarawi 2015), and its duration and difficulty were likely implicated in the conscious attention that refugees brought to the question of obligation.

The program to resettle Iraqis got off to a slow start. Section 1059 of the National Defense Authorization Act for Fiscal Year 2006 initially allowed for up to fifty special immigrant visas (SIVs) for Iraqi or Afghan translators/interpreters who worked with the US forces in Iraq or Afghanistan and their spouses and children. In 2007, President George W. Bush extended the law to authorize five hundred visas for fiscal years 2007 and 2008 only. SIVs are classified as permanent employment–based immigrants under the Immigration and Nationality Act, even though in this case they are not admitted for employment but rather to provide residence to individuals who worked with the Americans. While a separate category from refugees, the SIV holders would receive the same benefits as resettled refugees on admission to the United States. However, unlike refugees who must wait a year before they can apply for permanent residence, SIV holders are granted permanent-resident status immediately upon admission to the United States. The program expired in 2013, although the application process was extended into 2014. From 2007 through the end of 2015, 17,561 Iraqi individuals, including principal applicants and dependents, had been granted SIVs. A second immigrant classification was subsequently introduced in 2008 that provided the opportunity for individuals employed by, or on behalf of, the US forces to apply, providing that they had experienced "an ongoing, serious threat" as a result of their employment.

The burden of proof was onerous. In order to be eligible, applicants had to have worked with the US forces for at least twelve months, have received a favorable written recommendation from a general or flag officer from the US unit for which the applicant worked, have passed a background check, and not be otherwise inadmissible. For many Iraqis, this was an incredibly difficult standard to meet.

MUSTAFA'S CASE

Prior to 2003, Mustafa had been a police officer in Baghdad. The Coalition Provisional Authority did not disband the police after the fall of Baghdad, as it did with many other arms of government. However, in the period following the war, the police forces and the larger Interior Ministry became sites of unrest, with the desertion of large numbers of officers, the infiltration (and sometimes outright takeover) of forces by militias, and the crystallization of sectarian tensions within the force itself.

Mustafa recounted assisting the American forces in the early period following the invasion, when he felt optimistic that things would change in Iraq. When his branch of the police forces was taken over by Shi'a militants associated with the Mahdi Army, Mustafa, who was Sunni, quickly became persona non grata. At that time (2006), hundreds of police officers were being killed, more than members of the American and Iraqi forces combined. When Mustafa's own life was threatened, he decided to flee to Egypt. Bitterly he said, "I tried to help my country and because of that I had to leave."

The Refugee Crisis in Iraq Act presents a story of obligation to the Iraqis who supported the American effort and were persecuted by militias as a result. However, Iraqis had a much more complicated accounting of their affiliation with the Americans. While association with the Americans might bring with it access to the resettlement program, it was difficult to prove and also carried social risks. Iraqis had to verify their employment by providing a working email access for an American service member or employee of an American government organization who could vouch for their service. For Iraqis who were directly employed by the American forces, this information could be hard to procure, but for those whose affiliation was looser, the challenge was even greater. Mustafa, whose dealings with the American forces all took place while he was working as a police officer, this proof was even harder to establish. Mustafa spent a year acquiring a working email address of an American who could attest to his assistance, only to subsequently be rejected because he had never been directly paid by the Americans. My field notes and interviews are full of Iraqis who likewise felt that they had been persecuted because of their association with the Americans and who argued they should be eligible for resettlement as a result but who did not fit the specific criteria for resettlement. There is the man who helped Americans navigate his neighborhood but was never employed by them. There is the family whose home, used by American soldiers to pick off snipers along the main road to the airport, was identified as the place from which the American bullets came. And so forth. All of these individuals said that their association with the occupying forces put their lives at risk. To whom does obligation extend?

Service providers and adjudicators often told me that all refugees wanted to be resettled, but in my fieldwork I found that refugees expressed much more complicated, and ambivalent, ideas about resettlement to the United States. Iraqis often did not tell others, even good friends, that they had applied for resettlement. At times, this was because, even in Egypt, they did not want to be identified as being associated with the American effort. Those who were unsuccessful in their pursuit of resettlement, such as Mustafa, often felt stuck in between. As Mustafa said, "In front of Iraqi people I am now a traitor, having cheated my country, and in front of Americans I don't have a case." While many Iraqis sought resettlement, there were also those who found the idea of being resettled to the United States perverse. Iraqis routinely approached the organization at which I did much of my fieldwork asking to be resettled "anywhere but America," even if they might have worked with the Americans in Iraq and perhaps been eligible under the Direct Access Program. Some Iraqis felt deep ambivalence about resettling to the United States, a country that they held at least partly responsible for the fact that they had been forced out of their country. At the same time, other Iraqis accused some in the community of fabricating claims and affiliations in order to be resettled to the United States. While Iraqis' reasons for seeking resettlement and attitudes toward resettlement are topics I take up elsewhere, these examples illustrate the complexity of association. On the one hand, affiliation with the Americans created the space to make certain claims and possibly receive resettlement. On the other hand, there were concerns that working with the Americans might render one a "traitor" in the eyes of other Iraqis, as Mustafa feared, as well as some ambivalence about resettlement itself.

THE POLITICS OF OBLIGATION

Mustafa's case highlights both the challenges of proving obligation and his experience of feeling caught in between when his case was rejected. However, I would also like to briefly turn to questions of obligation beyond the Direct Access Program that emerged in fieldwork. Many Iraqis who had not worked with the Americans and so were not eligible for the program nonetheless used a rhetoric of obligation to argue for resettlement. In some cases, they argued that the United States' obligation extended beyond those who had directly assisted the Americans to all Iraqis who had been forced to flee their country because of the war. In other cases, obligation was extended beyond the United States and was understood in terms of justice. One man with whom I spoke repeatedly articulated a desire to be resettled in order to get what he "deserved." For him and others, resettlement as obligation was not about protection but about their ability to live what they determined to be good and fulfilling lives, lives that were not possible for them in Egypt.

In this chapter, I have considered an example of how one man, Mustafa, experienced and engaged with questions of obligation related to refugee resettlement. I also introduced questions of obligation as a way of adding nuance to our understanding of the solutions available to address refugee crises through attention to how processes of status determination are experienced by those who seek to be recognized. Resettlement, more so than other humanitarian goods, is limited and available to very few refugees. Also unlike other humanitarian goods, resettlement offers the possibility of permanent residence, and eventual citizenship, in the country of resettlement. It is often assumed that all refugees want to be resettled, an assumption that in some ways undergirds the suspicion and mistrust refugees face as part of the resettlement process. However, just as obligation is deployed as a rationale for resettling some refugees and not others, it is also redeployed by refugees as they understand, engage with, and experience the resettlement process.

The narratives of resettlement policy portray the United States as a nation of refuge, belying a more complicated, implicated geopolitical relationship between refugees, the conflicts that produce them, and the states where they ultimately settle. Attention to these complex and often unclear relationships troubles simple portrayals of resettlement as an unqualified good that all refugees desire. In this way, attention to the complex politics of displacement and resettlement may provide a different kind of corrective to the politics of suspicion in which refugees and asylum seekers find themselves. Instead of assuming that all refugees want to be resettled, an ethnographic lens helps us see how resettlement is influenced by complex local and geopolitical relationships.

A central tension in the literature on asylum, frequently discussed in terms of the tension between human rights and humanitarianism and security, is that between a state's obligation to its citizens and its obligations to noncitizens. However, the question of to whom states are obligated is a particularly difficult one to disentangle, depending as it does on time, position, who is understood as deserving of protection, and who is understood as a potential threat. On the face of it, the resettlement of Iraqis who worked with the US forces can be read as a simple morality tale. However, attention to the ways in which resettlement was administered and experienced suggests that questions of affiliation and obligation are much muddier in practice.

NOTE

1. See Johnson 2013 for a thorough account of the campaign to pass the Refugee Crisis in Iraq Act.

REFERENCES

Aleinikoff, T. A. 1995. "State-Centered Refugee Law: From Resettlement to Containment." In *Mistrusting Refugees*, edited by E. V. Daniel and J. C. Knudsen, 257-278. Berkeley: University of California Press.

Al-Mohammad, Hayder. 2010. "Relying on One's Tribe: A Snippet of Life in Basra since the 2003 Invasion." *Anthropology Today* 26 (6): 23–26.

Bockley, Kathryn M. 1995. "A Historical Overview of Refugee Legislation: The Deception of Foreign Policy in the Land of Promise." *North Carolina Journal of International Law and Commercial Regulation* 21, no. 1 (Fall): 253.

Boyle, Michael J. 2009. "Bargaining, Fear, and Denial: Explaining Violence against Civilians in Iraq 2004–2007." *Terrorism and Political Violence* 21 (2): 261–87.

Crawford, Neta C. 2014. *U.S. Costs of Wars through 2014: $4.4 Trillion and Counting*. Providence, RI: Watson Institute for International and Public Affairs, Brown University. http://watson.brown.edu/costsofwar/files/cow/imce/papers/2014/US%20Costs%20of%20Wars%20through%202014.pdf.

El-Shaarawi, Nadia. 2015. "Living an Uncertain Future: Temporality, Uncertainty and Well-Being among Iraqi Refugees in Egypt." *Social Analysis* 59 (1): 38–56.

Espiritu, Yen Le. 2014. *Body Counts: The Vietnam War and Militarized Refugees*. Berkeley: University of California Press.

Fagan, Patricia Weiss. 2007. *Iraqi Refugees: Seeking Stability in Syria and Jordan*. Qatar: Institute for the Study of International Migration, Georgetown University, and Center for International and Regional Studies, Georgetown University School of Foreign Service.

Fassin, Didier, and Estelle d'Halluin. 2007. "Critical Evidence: The Politics of Trauma in French Asylum Policies." *Ethos* 35 (3): 300–329.

Feldman, Ilana, and Miriam Ticktin, eds. 2010. *In the Name of Humanity: The Government of Threat and Care*. Durham, NC: Duke University Press.

Filkins, Dexter. 2008. *The Forever War*. New York: Random House.

Fischer, Michael M. J. 2003. *Emergent Forms of Life and the Anthropological Voice*. Durham, NC: Duke University Press.

Gibney, Matthew J. 2004. *The Ethics and Politics of Asylum: Liberal Democracy and the Response to Refugees*. Cambridge: Cambridge University Press.

Griffiths, Melanie. 2013. "Living with Uncertainty: Indefinite Immigration Detention." *Journal of Legal Anthropology* 1 (3): 263–86.

Griffiths, Melanie B. E. 2014. "Out of Time: The Temporal Uncertainties of Refused Asylum Seekers and Immigration Detainees." *Journal of Ethnic and Migration Studies* 40 (12): 1991–2009.

Haas, Bridget M. 2017. "Citizens-in-Waiting, Deportees-in-Waiting: Power, Temporality, and Suffering in the U.S. Asylum System." *Ethos* 45 (1): 75–97.

Horst, Cindy. 2006. "Buufis amongst Somalis in Dadaab: The Transnational and Historical Logics behind Resettlement Dreams." *Journal of Refugee Studies* 19 (2): 143–57.

Horst, Cindy, and Katarzyna Grabska. 2015. "Introduction: Flight and Exile—Uncertainty in the Context of Conflict-Induced Displacement." *Social Analysis* 59 (1): 1–18.

Jansen, Bram J. 2008. "Between Vulnerability and Assertiveness: Negotiating Resettlement in Kakuma Refugee Camp, Kenya." *African Affairs* 107 (429): 569–87.

Johnson, Kirk W. 2013. *To Be a Friend Is Fatal: The Fight to Save the Iraqis America Left Behind.* New York: Scribner.

Loescher, Gil, and John A. Scanlan. 1998. *Calculated Kindness: Refugees and America's Half-Open Door 1945–Present.* New York: Free Press.

Long, Katy. 2013. *The Point of No Return: Refugees, Rights, and Repatriation.* Oxford: Oxford University Press.

Ong, Aihwa. 2000. "Graduated Sovereignty in South-East Asia." *Theory, Culture and Society* 17 (4): 55–75.

Packer, George. 2007. "Betrayed: The Iraqis Who Trusted America the Most." *New Yorker,* March 19, 2007. https://www.newyorker.com/magazine/2007/03/26/betrayed-2.

Redfield, Peter. 2013. *Life in Crisis: The Ethical Journey of Doctors without Borders.* Berkeley: University of California Press.

Sadek, Sara. 2010. "Iraqi 'Temporary Guests' in Neighboring Countries." In *On the Move: Migration Challenges in the Indian Ocean Littoral,* edited by Ellen Laipsan and Amit Pandya. Washington, DC: Henry L. Stimson Center.

Sahlins, Marshall. 2011. "Iraq: The State-of-Nature Effect." *Anthropology Today* 27 (3): 26–31.

Tempo, Carl J. Bon. 2008. *Americans at the Gate: The United States and Refugees during the Cold War.* Princeton, NJ: Princeton University Press.

Thomson, Marnie Jane. 2012. "Black Boxes of Bureaucracy: Transparency and Opacity in the Resettlement Process of Congolese Refugees." *PoLAR: Political and Legal Anthropology Review* 35 (2): 186–205.

Ticktin, Miriam. 2011. *Casualties of Care: Immigration and the Politics of Humanitarianism in France.* Berkeley: University of California Press.

Van Selm, Joanne. 2014. "Refugee Resettlement." In *The Oxford Handbook of Refugee and Forced Migration Studies,* edited by Elena Fiddian-Qasmiyeh, Gil Loescher, Katy Long and Nando Sigona, 512–24. Oxford: Oxford University Press.

UN News Service. 2010. "Iraqi Refugees Regret Returning Home, UN Agency Finds." October 19, 2010. http://www.unhcr.org/refworld/docid/4cc51ce41e.html.

Waibsnaider, Meital. 2006. "How National Self-Interest and Foreign Policy Continue to Influence the US Refugee Admissions Program." *Fordham Law Review* 75:391–426.

Yoshikawa, Lynn. 2007. "Iraqi Refugees in Egypt." *Forced Migration Review* 29:54.

Zigon, Jarrett. 2008. *Morality: An Anthropological Perspective.* Oxford: Berg.

Chapter 2

Geographies of Aspiration and the Politics of Suspicion in the Context of Border Control

CHARLES WATTERS

At first glance, the right to seek asylum may appear unproblematic and unambiguous. Its genealogy can be traced back to the right of sanctuary in ancient Greece and similar practices in imperial Rome and early Christian civilization (Goldman and Martin 1983). It is enshrined in the Universal Declaration of Human Rights (UDHR). Article 14(1) provides that "everyone has the right to seek and to enjoy asylum from persecution in other countries." However, while signatory countries are normally keen to confirm their support for the principles behind the convention, this right has been steadily eroding as increasingly hard-line and restrictive asylum policies and practices have been introduced. The rapidity and diversity of new measures in the field recalls Giorgio Agamben's (2005) argument that a "state of exception" is present as a practice of government. He defines the state as "a point of imbalance between public law and political fact" that exists at an "ambiguous, uncertain borderline fringe between the legal and the political" (1). Commenting on the situation in Europe up to the present time, government "instead of declaring the state of exception prefers to have exceptional laws issued" (21). In the case of asylum seekers and refugees, a set of political considerations, not least those construed as linked to terrorism and security, routinely provoke the development and implementation of increasingly draconian laws and policies.

The present chapter examines the gap that has opened between the formal right to seek and enjoy asylum and the lived experiences of asylum seekers. Far from exercising a clear and legitimate right, those seeking asylum find their very quest for legitimacy called into question. To examine this gap, it is helpful to distinguish between entitlement and access and to examine asylum seekers' journeys in the context of what I have defined as "geographies of aspiration." Entitlement and access may be distinguished, with entitlement relating to formal conventions, laws, and policies applicable to those seeking asylum, while access relates to the lived experiences of asylum seekers within countries of reception, including opportunities for education, housing, legal support, and health care (Watters 2008). Moreover, while considerable volumes of literature have focused on legal dimensions of the so-called right to asylum, usually seen as the right to refuge or "to seek" asylum, little has been written about the correlative right "to enjoy" that asylum (Edwards 2005, 302). In emphasizing the right to enjoy asylum, the UDHR itself draws attention to a consideration not only of legal entitlements but also, arguably, to questions of access and the quality of the lived experiences of asylum seekers as they strive to realize these rights.

The questioning of the legitimacy of asylum seekers is often represented as underpinned by two primary concerns. Firstly, asylum seekers may raise the specter of a modern-day Trojan horse. Just as the mythological horse conveyed a benign image and was welcomed into the city, only for enemy combatants to appear in the dead of night to undermine the city's security, so present-day asylum seekers are seen as potential terrorists. US president Donald Trump described German chancellor Angela Merkel's decision to accept more than one million refugees from Syria as a "catastrophic mistake," adding that "people don't want to have other people coming in and destroying their country" (*Times* [UK], January 16, 2017). Thus, present-day asylum seekers may be constructed symbolically as a threat to Western interests and as potentially embodying primitive zealotry and barbarism antithetical to Western values (Morgan 2016). Secondly, while asylum seekers may not necessarily be viewed as would-be terrorists, they are often regarded as simply economic migrants using a pretense of persecution as an excuse to try to seek more prosperous lives elsewhere.

AGENCY, ASPIRATION, AND THE CIRCUMSCRIBED SPACE OF LEGITIMACY

As noted elsewhere in this volume, political discourse surrounding forced migrants in industrialized countries creates a sharp division between "genuine refugees" deserving of the support and protection of host countries and what are variously referred to as "economic migrants," "scroungers," or "queue jumpers," terms used to refer to migrants who are seen as arriving spontaneously and who may seek asylum. The first category and the one associated with the deserving poor who should be entitled to the host society's support, consists of those who are seen to have fled persecution. As such, they are viewed de facto as not exercising agency in choosing a country of destination. To suggest that they may have exercised a degree of rational choice has the potential to undermine their asylum claims. There is, as such, an overriding focus on the predominance of factors that have compelled the migrant to leave his or her home country, and this underpins the Dublin Convention within the European Union (EU), explicitly in place to deter economic migrants from "shopping around" to find a country in Europe with the best living conditions. The logic behind this convention is that if asylum seekers are genuinely fleeing persecution, they will be happy to have their claims considered by the first safe country they arrive in. They will be grateful to be free from persecution and not seek to pick and choose countries of destination. Within this context, to talk of those seeking asylum as having aspirations toward life in particular countries and not only preoccupied with questions of their own safety is to potentially undermine the arguments that are the basis of their asylum claims.

In my view, this polarization between a view of "genuine" refugees who lack agency and "bogus" refugees who are making choices with respect to potential destinations is deeply flawed. This dichotomy presupposes that clear distinctions can be drawn between those who flee persecution and simply aspire to reach any location that offers safety and those who aspire to better lives. To evoke a well-known theoretical model from migration studies, legitimate asylum seekers are driven completely by "push factors": real and present dangers that drive them from their homes, communities, and countries. The idea that asylum seekers may be making a choice in terms of safe destinations reveals a preoccupation with pull factors propelling them to particular countries and indicates lack of authenticity in asylum claims. A binary thus governs perceptions of the legitimacy of asylum seekers: they are seen as either passive victims or calculating opportunists. According to this logic, the manifestation of agency and aspiration among would-be asylum seekers discredits potential asylum claims. For example, the thousands of migrants congregating in northern France desperately seeking passage to the United Kingdom cannot be legitimate asylum seekers. Nor are those dissatisfied to remain in an EU country such as Malta while their claims are being assessed. A legitimate asylum seeker is, according to this view, one who is content to reach a destination that is "safe" and thus to have escaped danger.

Arguably this circumscribed view of the asylum seeker raises questions about the extent to which countries of reception support the right to seek *and enjoy* asylum from persecution enshrined in the UDHR. The reference to "enjoy" here suggests more than the realization of immediate safety and evokes the quest for a more fulfilled life. This quest is etched territorially into what I refer to as "geographies of aspiration," whereby routes are established to take asylum seekers toward destinations that are perceived not only as offering safety but also the potential for substantially enhanced lives. Routes are generated through intermingling of urgent needs for security and simultaneously aspirations to lead lives that are valued. The so-called Jungle in Calais is one example where in recent years around ten thousand migrants have been based at any given time, many from major refugee-producing areas such as the Horn of Africa, Iraq, and Afghanistan. Their journeys have taken them across many "safe" countries to the periphery of Western Europe to seek passage to the United Kingdom.

LEGITIMACY AND THE MORAL ECONOMY

While a shift away from a politics of compassion toward refugees can be discerned in Western Europe in the past two decades, what I have referred to as a dialectic of belongingness and otherness has a genealogy discernible in notions in medieval England of deserving and undeserving poor, with the latter legitimized through the wearing of "pauper badges" assigning them as appropriate subjects for charitable parish support (Watters 2007; Hindle 2004). The deserving poor exist in poverty through no fault of their own, either because of illness, accident, age, or lack of available employment. The undeserving poor are identified as able-bodied individuals who refuse to work and have no justification for doing so (Hindle 2004). The view of migrants as constituting a large body of undeserving poor is underpinned by ubiquitous representations of them wishing to enter Western countries to exploit benefits systems and to engage in criminal activities.

A contemporary shift toward a discourse of human rights in relation to forced migrants can be detected in reductions in the numbers of asylum seekers receiving full refugee status in many industrialized countries but simultaneously having enhanced opportunity to be allowed to remain in countries of asylum under very specific humanitarian provisions. For asylum seekers, the quest for legitimacy rests increasingly on a moral economy in which deservingness is associated often with medical, and specifically, mental health problems. Applications for full political asylum are rarely successful, but evidence of health and mental health problems may form the basis for the achievement of temporary leave to remain on humanitarian grounds. The moral economy is, in this sense, somewhat different from the Aristotelian idea of relationships between members of a group or community bounded by moral codes and mutual obligations. It is rather crucially linked to ideas of the "deserving" or "undeserving" (Watters 2007). Those seeking to support asylum seekers are often aware of the importance of emphasizing mental health and victimhood (Watters, 2001). Didier Fassin writing on the situation of illegal immigrants in France, observed the declining numbers receiving political asylum while noting that concomitantly similar numbers were receiving leave to remain on the grounds of ill health and in particular mental illness (Fassin 2001). Asylum seekers thus occupy specific "problem spaces" in which it is not their political bodies—the traditional route of legitimation—but their "sick bodies" that offer avenues of access toward legitimacy in receiving countries.

In this sense, the forced migrant represents what Agamben (1998) has termed "bare life." His or her rights are not those of a citizen but reside in the sphere of human rights. The rights thus accorded are viewed by Hannah Arendt as residual, only available as a result of the most fundamental of human attributes—being human (Arendt 2013). Those seeking asylum are not accorded legitimacy as potential citizens but as vulnerable and sick populations deserving of compassion only in circumscribed contexts where they are eligible for medical and psychological programs of support.

Within these circumstances, those working as advocates for would-be refugees adopt processes of "strategic categorization" in which they respond to these predefined opportunities for bio-legitimacy by highlighting the problems forced migrants face that are most likely to achieve successful outcomes (Watters 2001). In practical terms this may involve, for example, constructing legal cases in asylum appeals that point to the presence of mental health problems, specifically in many instances posttraumatic stress disorder (PTSD) in asylum seekers. It is important to point out that this should not be seen as an attempt to counter the politics of suspicion by inventing problems to enhance legal cases. Rather, those supporting asylum seekers are alive to the circumscribed and predetermined avenues to legitimacy available within a culture of mistrust and strategically categorize their problems to enhance their opportunities for support.

This is a dimension often missed by authors preoccupied by the political issues underpinning the ubiquity of diagnosis of PTSD and other mental health problems among refugee populations (Fassin and Rechtman 2009, Bracken, Giller, and Summerfield 1997; Summerfield 2001). Critiques have often focused on characterizing global mental health programs for forced migrants as manifestations of neocolonial dynamics of a medical model and of the power of psychiatry. However, the identification of mental health problems among refugees by psychiatrists and other mental health professionals may highlight the impact of policies of deterrence and serve as a powerful corrective to harsh regimes of detention and deportation. It can also act as a counter to the implementation of policies such as lengthy asylum processes (Silove, Steel, and Watters 2000; Steel and Silove, 2000).

ENTITLEMENT AND ACCESS

As noted above, it is important to be mindful of the potential distinction that may exist between entitlement and access. I have elsewhere defined entitlement in this context as referring to the right, enshrined in law and policy, to receive a service. Access here refers to the practical, on-the-ground reality of migrants' experiences in seeking and receiving services and support they are entitled to (Watters 2011). As such, the concepts have referents at a macro level at which law and policy are formulated and at a micro level at which they are implemented. European comparative studies have routinely failed to distinguish between these two concepts, leading to confused judgments to the effect that some countries may be doing well in terms of humanitarian responses to asylum seekers and refugees simply because they have good, explicit laws and policies in these domains. Stating simply that in country X all asylum seekers have a right to all forms of health care may tell us little about the real day-to-day experiences of asylum seekers presenting themselves at health clinics and trying to see a doctor. Access, in this sense, can only be properly analyzed with reference to firsthand experiences of local situations.

Methodologically, it suggests an integrative approach is essential, incorporating both documentary research into laws and policies and on-the-ground, lived engagement with the day-to-day realities of asylum seekers themselves. The ongoing situation in Zeebrugge, a port in Belgium through which undocumented migrants seek to pass en route to the United Kingdom, is illustrative. The issue of migration through the port came to international attention in June 2000 when fifty-eight Chinese migrants were discovered dead, having suffocated in the back of a Dutch-registered truck intercepted at the Port of Dover in England. The truck had passed through the port of Zeebrugge without detection. In another incident, in 2001, the bodies of eight Kurdish migrants were discovered in a freight container in Wexford, Ireland. Again the truck carrying it had passed through Zeebrugge, and according to an investigation by the Irish police, the migrants had arrived in Ireland "by mistake" as they had intended to go to the United Kingdom (*Irish Times*, December 10, 2001). The horror of these incidents added impetus for port authorities to implement measures to detect what those working at port authorities euphemistically refer to as "illegals."

I made the following record of the process following the detection of migrants in trucks in Zeebrugge:

> *Once discovered, the "illegals" were taken to an annex of three rooms close to the police headquarters. The immediate impression was of the dilapidated furniture and lack of decoration. One room had two or three desks with ripped coverings and a few uncomfortable wooden chairs that looked as though they may have been discarded by a local primary school, while in another there were two bedsteads covered with thin and dirty looking old mattresses and an old blanket. The walls were undecorated, grey and austere save for one which had a surprising and*

initially incongruous graffiti display that centred on the image of a frightened looking young bald figure with bloodshot eyes. The police explained that they had involved the local primary school in this, as they "wanted them to feel part of things." The rooms carried an almost tangible atmosphere of fear and sadness and the image of the figure seemed strangely appropriate. A third room was used for filming, photographing and fingerprinting the "illegals" and included some rudimentary equipment for these purposes. Thinking about the migrants' physical needs after a long an arduous journey I made an enquiry about washing facilities. The police advised that there used to be a shower but it wasn't practical to retain it. "Who would wash the towels?" one policewoman remarked drawing her hand over an imaginary pile of towels with a look of disgust. The minimal facilities did not include access to health care and the police experienced considerable difficulties in getting a doctor to attend to sick migrants. One migrant had recently arrived with an injured leg, and the police recounted spending all day on the phone trying to get help without success. Within the resources available to them, the police did try to give intercepted migrants a cup of tea and a little food, supplied by the Red Cross before they went on their way.

The police advised that if migrants asked for asylum, they were to be told that they would have to go to Brussels to apply, and they were given an address to go to. This situation had changed ten years later in 2016 when a much more formalized procedure had been established. Migrants were offered the necessary documents to apply for asylum in Belgium, but in interviews with police in 2016, they reported that migrants chose overwhelmingly to take their chances and to continue to seek some way of getting to the United Kingdom, no matter what the risks involved. Migrants were concerned about being "put on record" on the grounds that, if the application were formally recorded, this would show that they had made a claim for asylum in Belgium and consequently they could be returned to Belgium under the terms of the Dublin Convention. According to the convention, asylum seekers can be returned to the country in which they made their first application for asylum.

Initially the police could be characterized as exercising a "light touch" toward would-be asylum seekers to minimize the chances of an asylum claim being formally made. Indeed, the processes and physical environment appeared designed to convey the overall message to migrants and potential asylum seekers that there was nothing in Belgium for them and that they should get on their way to their anticipated destination. The minimal procedures adopted deterred migrants from claiming asylum, with all its legal and welfare implications, and indirectly encouraged continued attempts to reach the United Kingdom. While procedures at Zeebrugge have become more formalized in the past decade, this has, if anything, generated a more unwelcoming atmosphere. Migrants are held is stark, windowless cells, and the only facilities for rest is on gray concrete slabs. They are processed in authoritarian and bureaucratized ways in which they are given numbers that are called out when they are released from cells. Police dealing with them wear protective clothing to ensure there is no direct physical contact. Commenting on a parallel situation of apprehended undocumented children found by US Border Patrol officers, Jacqueline Bhabha and Mary Crock (2007) note, in a telling phrase, that "the children these officials meet are often physically located on US territory, but not considered legally present" (34). They note that some of those who do not have valid visas will be turned away immediately before ever being admitted to the country, while others will be given an option of voluntary return as an alternative to appearing in court. In the case of Zeebrugge, the migrants may be seen as present only in a sanitized and bureaucratized context of "bare life."

STRATEGIES, TACTICS, AND "PROBLEM SPACES"

Suspicion of migrants in border areas may be characterized as governed by processes of nonincorporation (Watters 2008). As indicated through the employment of a framework that distinguishes between entitlement and access, analysis of procedures and policies reveals only one dimension of this phenomenon. Nonincorporation is not only manifested in the tangible sets of rules and protocols governing the reception of undocumented migrants but also in the physical environments in which they are placed and in the bureaucratized manner of their processing. As argued above, they are governed by states of exception in which perceived threats of a mass influx of migrants from poorer countries leads to the introduction of specific rules aimed at deterrence (Agamben 1995). The desired position of "host" countries appears one in which the asylum seekers go through necessary procedures with a minimal impingement on welfare and social-care institutions and resources. To use a phrase adopted for a study of British immigration controls, they may be seen as such as being "governed at a distance" (Morris

1998). Moreover, suspicion is ubiquitous, and strategies of nonincorporation are linked to a view of migrants as untrustworthy. This perspective underpins the routine official skepticism accorded, for example, the claims for asylum made by undocumented children arriving at borders. As Nadine Finch (2004), a barrister working with child asylum seekers, has argued in her extensive study of the UK system:

> There appears to be an almost universal culture of disbelief within the Immigration and Nationality Directorate in relation to asylum applications from unaccompanied or separated children and there is no evidence of a liberal application of the benefit of the doubt to children's applications. For example, trafficked children and child soldiers are regularly refused asylum on the basis that their accounts of persecution are unpersuasive even when there is considerable corroborating evidence. (194)

While states of exception may be seen as governing strategies of nonincorporation, a governmentality approach is useful in the examination of processes of biolegitimacy and the attendant emphasis on the sick or damaged refugee. A broadly conceptualized governmentality approach suggests an investigative and methodological orientation that encompasses the processes whereby refugees are categorized and embedded in specific discursive formations. Its orientation is toward analysis of the ways in which refugee children *are* incorporated into societies through specific avenues of access and forms of legitimacy. This field of enquiry encompasses forms of incorporation identified by Aihwa Ong (2003) whereby refugees become "new kinds of subjects, mastering the codes and rules of bona fide refugees, compliant aid recipients" (65).

Central here is a focus on migrants and in the way they interpret and respond to the very problem spaces that they are placed within or, in terms employed by Michel de Certeau (1988), their use of tactics within the strategic spaces available to them. In doing so, they demonstrate that even within the most controlled and bureaucratized situations, manifestations of aspiration and agency are present. These may find material form through the setting up of informal networks of companionship and support, informal cafés, and artistic and educational outlets (such as libraries in the Jungle and a café in a large tented "open center" for asylum seekers in Malta). Not only migrants and refugees but also the various intermediaries—or what Stephen Castles and Mark J. Miller (2009) refer to as "meso"-level actors who represent migrants in various institutional contexts, be they health centers, social work offices, immigration courts, and so on—respond to and may resist political and economic structures. Like the Cambodian refugees in Ong's (2003) study of the interfaces between refugees and institutions in California, they do not simply absorb the designations and problems ascribed to them but also respond to them often in astute tactical ways to enhance their own opportunities. Accounts of the meanings migrants make of the circumstances they find themselves in are, of course, nothing new and are pervasive in the humanities and social sciences. In the case of refugees where a preponderance of research has focused on mental health status, such accounts are emerging belatedly owing to ubiquitous representations of forced migrants as passive victims of circumstances.

ENGAGING WITH ASPIRATIONAL DIMENSIONS OF FORCED MIGRATION

Is it not the case, however, that save for circumstances of immediate danger, such as just before or during an attack on a village, within processes of flight there is always an intermingling of fear and aspirations? Just as agencies such as the United Nations High Commissioner for Refugees seeks "durable solutions" to refugee problems, is it not the case that forced migrants seek both freedom from persecution *and* the chance of experiencing living conditions in which there are opportunities for education, jobs, and housing? As demonstrated here, what I refer to as this "aspirational" dimension of forced migration is present in the well-documented movement of migrants across Europe and, indeed, in the large-scale secondary migration to the United Kingdom of migrants who had received refugee status in Sweden, Denmark, and the Netherlands. It is also present in the highly controlled and bureaucratized environments of countries in which asylum seekers survive waiting to hear if they will be allowed to remain.

Thus, understanding the particular flows of migrants and refugees in contemporary Europe and, indeed, globally requires not only analysis of the politics of risk and of push factors, be they political and/or economic, but also what I would describe as a "geography of aspiration." Migrants experiencing ongoing destitution in camps in Calais or huddled in bus shelters and outside churches in Zeebrugge are driven by powerful aspirations of a better life elsewhere. To achieve this life, they will take extraordinary risks, including ongoing exploitation by gangs, being rounded up and imprisoned by police, and having their makeshift homes burned down. This endurance is in the context in which would-be asylum seekers are viewed as making choices to move from one "safe" European country to another "safe" European country. Rigorous research requires engagement with the texture of these aspirations and dreams. Commentators have noted that far from being ill-informed people duped by smugglers and traffickers, many of these migrants are well read and well informed (Yaghmaian 2005). Arguably, the desire to move from, for example, France or Belgium to the United Kingdom is driven by an astute sense that, as a person from a black and/or minority group, one has a better prospect of leading a successful and fulfilled life in the United Kingdom than in other European countries. In this context, it is notable that many former asylum seekers who have achieved refugee status in Nordic countries and the Netherlands have made subsequent moves to the United Kingdom in the hope of a better life. For example, Oxford University's Migration Observatory found that of 141,000 people, 7 percent of those who came to the United Kingdom under EU rules were born outside Europe. Somalis are one of the biggest such groups, with an estimated 20,000 coming to the United Kingdom from the Netherlands alone. Studies show that between one third and a half of the entire Dutch Somali community has moved to the United Kingdom (*Guardian*, January 28, 2013).

The movement to the United Kingdom had nothing to do with an idea of achieving improved welfare benefits, as the countries these migrants had initially settled in had generally better welfare provision than the United Kingdom. Rather, migrants were influenced by an idea that they could lead a more fulfilled life for themselves and their families there, including getting better employment and having better access to educational opportunities and social mobility. Migration to the United Kingdom shows a dynamic of push and pull factors, with an ongoing desire to improve circumstances. The ubiquitous politics of suspicion governing contemporary migration views evidence of undocumented migrants and asylum seekers having any desire beyond safety as pointing to their lack of legitimacy. Evidence that journeys may have also been taken to fulfill dreams and aspirations is seen as indicating that the initial grounds for leaving migrants' home countries are questionable. Until it is recognized that monumental forced movements across continents are governed both by desires to escape danger *and* dreams of a better life, appropriate responses to migrants' plights will not be achieved.

REFERENCES

Agamben, Giorgio. 1998. *Homo Sacer: Sovereign Power and Bare Life*. Stanford, CA: Stanford University Press.

———. 2005. *State of Exception*. Chicago: University of Chicago Press.

Arendt, Hannah. 2013. *The Human Condition*. Chicago: University of Chicago Press.

Bhabha, Jacqueline, and Mary Crock. 2007. *Seeking Asylum Alone: A Comparative Study of Laws, Policy and Practice in Australia, the UK and the US*. Annandale, Australia: Themis Press.

Bracken, Patrick, Joan E. Giller, and Derek Summerfield. 1997. "Rethinking Mental Health Work with Survivors of Wartime Violence and Refugees." *Journal of Refugee Studies* 10 (4): 431–42.

Castles, Stephen, and Mark J. Miller. 2009. *The Age of Migration: International Population Movements in the Modern World*, 4th ed. Basingstoke, UK: Palgrave Macmillan.

Certeau, Michel de, 1988. *The Practice of Everyday Life*, translated by Steven Rendall. Berkeley: University of California Press.

Edwards, Alice. 2005. "Human Rights, Refugees, and the Right 'to Enjoy' Asylum." *International Journal of Refugee Law* 17 (2): 293–330.

Fassin, Didier. 2001. "The Biopolitics of Otherness: Undocumented Foreigners and Racial Discrimination in French Public Debate." *Anthropology Today* 17 (1): 3–7.

———. 2005. "Compassion and Repression: The Moral Economy of Immigration Policies in France." *Cultural Anthropology* 20 (3): 362–87.

Fassin, Didier and Rechtman, Richard (2009) *The Empire of Trauma: An Inquiry into the Condition of Victimhood*. Princeton University Press.

Finch, Nadine. 2005. "Seeking Asylum Alone." In *The Asylum-Seeking Child in Europe*, edited by Hans Andersson et al., 57–66. Göteborg, Sweden: Centre for European Research at Göteborg University.

Goldman, Robert K., and Scott M. Martin. 1983. "International Legal Standards Relating to the Rights of Aliens and Refugees and United States Immigration Law." *Human Rights Quarterly* 5 (3): 302–26.

Hindle, Steve. 2004. *On the Parish? The Micro-Politics of Poor Relief in Rural England, c. 1550–1750*. Oxford: Clarendon Press.

Morgan, George. 2016. *Global Islamophobia: Muslims and Moral Panic in the West*. New York: Routledge.

Morris, Lydia. 1998. "Governing at a Distance: The Elaboration of Controls in British Immigration." *International Migration Review* 32 (4): 949–73.

Ong, Aihwa. 1999. *Flexible Citizenship: The Cultural Logics of Transnationality*. Durham, NC: Duke University Press.

———. 2003. *Buddha Is Hiding: Refugees, Citizenship, the New America*. Berkeley: University of California Press.

Silove, Derek, Zachary Steel, and Charles Watters. 2000. "Policies of Deterrence and the Mental Health of Asylum Seekers." *JAMA* 284 (5): 604–11.

Steel, Zachary, and Derek Silove. 2000. "The Mental Health Implications of Detaining Asylum Seekers." *Medical Journal of Australia* 175 (11–12): 596–99.

Summerfield, Derek. 2001. "Asylum-Seekers, Refugees and Mental Health Services in the UK." *Psychiatrist* 25 (5): 161–63.

Watters, Charles. 2001. "Emerging Paradigms in the Mental Health Care of Refugees." *Social Science and Medicine* 52 (11): 1709–18.

———. 2007. "Refugees at Europe's Borders: The Moral Economy of Care." *Transcultural Psychiatry* 44 (3): 394–417.

———. 2008. *Refugee Children: Towards the Next Horizon.* New York: Routledge.

———. 2011. "Towards a New Paradigm in Migrant Health Research: Integrating Entitlement, Access and Appropriateness." *International Journal of Migration, Health and Social Care* 7 (3): 148–59.

Yaghmaian, Behzad. 2005. *Embracing the Infidel: Stories of Muslim Migrants on the Journey West.* New York: Delacorte Press.

Chapter 3

A "Politics of Protection" Aimed at Mayan Immigrants in the United States

JOHN B. HAVILAND

Half a century ago, as a fledgling ethnographer, I started learning Tzotzil, a Mayan language spoken in the highlands of Chiapas, Mexico. I never imagined that I would spend part—sometimes all—of almost every year since then living in Chiapas and continuing to learn about the place, its people, and their social lives. By official count the absolute number of speakers of Indian languages in Chiapas continues to grow (from 809,000 in 2000 to about 1,142,000 in 2010[1]), of whom about a third are speakers of Tzotzil.[2] Chiapas, in the far southeastern corner of Mexico—the last place in the country before you hit Guatemala—is one of the handful of Mexican states whose population is a quarter or more Indian (although speaking an indigenous language is a less reliable marker of ethnic identification or ancestry than it might once have been).

I went to Chiapas first to study indigenous stringed-instrument music, and I continued to return "to the field" to learn about other things, from

Tzotzil grammar, gossip, and gestures to prices, "positionals," politics, processions, and places. I still spend about a week every couple of months in my adopted home in the community of Zinacantán. But the "field" I went to first in 1966 has, strikingly, now also come to me.

The present excursion into asylum research is hardly more than a footnote to activities with a quite different trajectory—namely, exploring the vicissitudes, both analytic and practical, of providing interpretation for speakers of Tzotzil, a large number of whom now live far from Chiapas throughout Mexico and the United States. Many are, indeed, my neighbors in California. When they run afoul of the law or other bureaucracies, they need interpretation—whether of words, gestures, experiences, or knowledge—and I have become one of the few people who can (at least try to) provide it. Interpretation, in turn, is almost always at the heart—although perhaps a routinely occluded heart—of pursuing and adjudicating asylum.

To anticipate briefly: the editors of this volume proposed that we consider a "politics of suspicion" that arises from a wider set of political ideologies and practices applied to the processes by which people seek, are granted, are denied, or are otherwise condemned to different sorts of immigration status, occasionally including political asylum. I intend, first, to show how "seeking asylum" is just one of the many interrelated sorts of activities, with associated legal and institutional ramifications, that my Tzotzil acquaintances must engage with as they traverse landscapes, cross borders, and search for places to live and work. More substantively, I mean to stand the notion of "suspicion" upside down by looking at those cases where, in a seeming contradiction, under the rubric of care or "protection" (in both its more and less benevolent senses—for the latter, recall the notion of "protection racket" associated with organized crime) asylum is coerced upon perhaps unwilling recipients. In the cases I have worked on, these reluctant asylum seekers are Tzotzil children. Very briefly, I will also relate these situations to a distinct but, in my opinion, ideologically closely linked bureaucracy, that of American family law and dependency courts, and in particular how Tzotzil immigrants are sometimes affected by them.

IMMIGRATION HISTORY OF TZOTZILES

Individuals from "my" village in Chiapas ventured sporadically northward several decades ago. The first man that I knew personally to emigrate, a godchild of mine, left in 1976 after a tumultuous marital drama. He was last heard from in Hollywood a little more than a decade ago, when his family dispatched me to Los Angeles to try, unsuccessfully as it turned out, to track him down. In the mid-1980s, two cousins from the village made their way to Oregon. One of these men immediately and inexplicably died, but the other remains in Oregon to this day. He brought his son to live with him in 2001, paying professionals to smuggle him into the country. (It took five tries.) By that time, a massive outmigration had begun from southern Mexico, with people from the poorest parts of the country coming north to cross the border in search of work: non-Indian *ladinos* (i.e., Spanish-speaking Mexicans) from throughout the state of Chiapas were joined by indigenous people, including Tzotzil speakers from many different Indian communities. Tzotzil speakers are now spread across the United States, with large pockets in perhaps unexpected places. Several thousand Chiapas Indians live semipermanently in Tampa, for example, not to mention in cities and towns on both coasts, and others are scattered just about everywhere in between.

Indians have a largely invisible place in the long and complex immigration history of Mexicans and other Latin Americans to the United States. Because this is true even at the level of academic scholarship on immigration (but see Cornelius, Fitzgerald, and Fischer 2007), one can only imagine how much more Indians are effaced in the day-to-day practices and bureaucracies surrounding immigration. Whereas for Mexicans in general the distinction between Indian (*indígena* being the preferred Spanish euphemism, as opposed to *indio*) and non-Indian (mestizo or ladino) is ever-present and usually salient, for most North Americans it almost never arises—a Mexican being simply a Mexican (and usually poor and presumed undocumented to boot).

Moreover, since with a few notable exceptions native North American Indian languages in the United States have been rubbed nearly out of existence, surviving largely in the revitalization and salvage efforts of the few, the fact that Latin American indigenous people speak many different robust first languages belonging to diverse language families totally unrelated to Spanish is even less familiar an idea than that there might be different "sorts" of people in the Mexican immigrant population. The rubrics of identity are complex and variegated, with different levels of resolution or granularity depending on how closely one cares to look.[3]

Since Tzotziles like other Chiapas Indians are relative newcomers among indigenous Mexican immigrants to the United States, the language is essentially unknown to American authorities. Because I am almost unique as a fluent Tzotzil speaker who also knows English, I have over the past decade moonlighted as a Tzotzil interpreter, motivated at first by a vague sense of responsibility to give a voice to Tzotzil speakers in contexts where they seemed, to their disadvantage, to lack one, and, as demand increased, taking on the new "profession" as an object of analytical attention in its own right.

INTERPRETING FOR TZOTZILES IN AMERICAN BUREAUCRATIC CONTEXTS

Although I did forensic linguistic consultation in Chiapas after the infamous Acteal massacre of 1997,[4] I came only gradually into formal interpreting in the United States, both in courts and in other contexts (such as emergency health calls from hospitals and other social service agencies around the country), to fill a growing need. I see from my records that I have interpreted for Tzotzil speakers on average once or twice a week continuously for most of the past decade. The great bulk of this interpretation is in courtrooms, interpreting for people accused of offenses related to their undocumented status in the United States, although there are criminal, civil, and dependency cases as well. Most Tzotzil speakers in the United States are not only "undocumented" but also condemned both to a legal shadow and to poverty, with associated liabilities. They are, furthermore, subject to unfamiliar norms of acceptable behavior. For example, and tangentially relevant to the main point of this essay, Tzotzil men and women are often completely ignorant of the existence of the American crime of "statutory rape," which involves even consensual sexual relations with underaged people, who are by American law legally incapable of giving consent in the first place.

A POLITICS OF "PROTECTION"

If I interpret telephonically and am thus invisible, my Tzotzil is just good enough that Tzotzil speakers can perhaps convince themselves that I come from some distant village where people talk funny. But no amount of linguistic training can be enough, in the moment, for rendering into intelligible Tzotzil the sorts of matters that routinely arise in most courts. My fragmentary, truncated, extemporaneous, and often stilted engagements with emigrant Tzotzil speakers—although sometimes frighteningly consequential—are also often riddled with gaps, confusions, missteps, and plain errors. But if this is true for me—an ethnographic old-timer—how much more true is it for the bureaucrats dealing with Tzotzil speakers before they get me on the phone? Interpreting provides a rich, if strange, source for ethnographic insight into other exotic folk: lawyers, judges, mediators, social workers, police, Border Patrol agents, professional translators—even doctors, nurses, insurance adjustors, prison guards, and agents of the Federal Bureau of Investigation (FBI).

Nonetheless, I rely on a peculiar and extraordinarily partial window onto the phenomena of interest, what as an ethnographer I consider a kind of binocular tunnel vision. (Imagine looking through binoculars turned around the wrong way.) It is "binocular" because, unlike other participants, I have access, albeit selective and imperfect, to both sides of the chasm that yawns between parties who have no shared language. But it is tunnel vision because it is randomly focused and anarchically incomplete: peering through a window rendered ever smaller by the fact that I do not choose my own cases or occasions but interpret only when I am asked to do so. What is more, most often my contact is limited to brief exchanges on the telephone.

With these caveats, let me introduce my main business in this chapter. Limits of space prevent me from presenting the cases of interest in more detail, so I will largely content myself with a plain narrative of the events and issues rather than indulge my normal linguist's inclination to overburden the reader with detailed interactional extracts.

Predictably, the grand bulk of the cases for which I am asked to interpret involve undocumented immigrants, and the results are simple and predictable. Charges are brought; threats are issued linked to the prescribed jail terms associated with those charges; a plea bargain is quickly struck between prosecutor and defender; the defendant, once he (and in almost every case it is a "he") understands his options, readily agrees, pleads guilty, serves out a term (which ranges from "time served" to several years in jail, usually with fines waived, depending on the charges and the criminal or immigration history); and he is subsequently deported to the border or to the interior of Mexico. Trials are almost unheard of in the courts that employ me, and my main function seems to be to lend a kind of procedural legitimacy to the massive incarceration and deportation of certain indigenous Mexicans (see Haviland 2003).

As almost the only "qualified" Tzotzil-English interpreter in the United States, however, I am sometimes recruited for more unusual cases. Transcript 1 is a fragment from a telephone call that came to me out of the blue one afternoon in 2011 from an Immigration and Customs Enforcement (ICE) agent located in Mississippi. After introducing himself and his co-present supervisor (lines 1–10) using a kind of familiar police-like bureaucratese, he invited me to open a conversation with "D," the "young man" in detention who had been tentatively identified as a Tzotzil speaker:

(1) D, initial call

1	ice:	if you care to . just engage a .
2		brief dialogue . to identify whether you can communicate with=[5]
3		[[6]
4	jbh:	I will do s-
5	ice:	= this . young man I would be most grateful
6	jbh:	I will do so
7		uh, can you hear me alright?
8		your volume is a little bit low but I can hear you
9	ice:	OK, I hear you just fine
10	jbh:	OK
11	(1.4)[7]	

As is my normal practice, I tried first to verify whether or not the person on the other end of the line was really a Tzotzil speaker by forcing him to respond appropriately to the ritualized salutation *mi li'-ot-e* (Q here-B2s-CL[8])—"Are you here?"—followed by what would be the correct address form given our relative ages, in this case the young man's first name (line 14). As often happens, my abrupt and contextually unexpected shift to Tzotzil took D by surprise, as evidenced by the long hesitation (line 15), even after my double repetition (lines 16 and 20)—the first of which I think the ICE agent, who had no idea what Tzotzil sounds like, thought to have been garbled by the phone connection. After another noticeable pause, D checked that he had heard me correctly (line 21), and then after another repetition (line 22) he responded normally in his own dialect of Tzotzil, *li'-un-e* (here-B1-CL)—"I am here" (line 23):

12 jbh: bweno
Alright
13 mi-
14 mi li'ote D
Are you here, D?
15 (2.2)
16 D, mi li'ote
D, are you here?
17 [
18 ice: uh, it was a little broken, try it again please
19 jbh: D, mi li'ote?
D, are you here?
20 (0.9)
21 d: uh?
Huh?
22 jbh: mi li'ote?
Are you here?
23 d: li'une
I'm here.

This was, of course, all I needed to establish that D was in fact a Tzotzil speaker, if a somewhat reluctant one. Because this was not a regimented courtroom interview, I began, as is also my custom whenever given license to do so, to converse informally with D to try both to find out more about the kid (as kid he was, at least judging by his voice) and to alert him conversationally to the possibility that, unlike the ICE agent, I might be some sort of normal, knowledgeable human being:

24 jbh: ali, buy nakalot che'e, buy lalik tal?
So, where do you live? Where have you come from?
25 (0.9)
26 d: ali ta:
Uh, from-
27 (0.8)
28 ta:
From-

29 ta mejiko
From Mexico
30 jbh: ji', jna'oj onoxe pero buy la-
Yeah, I know that, but where are you-
31 buy laparajele, buy lateklumale
Where's your village? Where's your town?
32 (0.9)
33 d: ali:
Um
34 (0.6)
35 chamula
36 jbh: pero bu junukal, buy parajele un?
But from which- which hamlet?
37 ta san juan chamula xkaltik
You mean from San Juan Chamula?
38 (0.9)
39 d: ja'
Yes.
40 jbh: a pero k'usi parajel un, buy nakal latot lame' un
Ah, but from which hamlet? Where do your mother and father live?
41 (1.4)
42 d: ta V**
*In V**.*
43 jbh: buy la
Where did you say?
44 d: V**
*V***
45 jbh: a bweno, pero te ta mero chamula un ma'uk ta
Ah, ok, but that's really in Chamula, not-
46 te- ma'uk ta jobel
not in San Cristóbal
47 (0.5)
48 d: ma'uk, ta mero chamula
No, in real Chamula.

D's responses were cautious and characteristically uninformative (Haviland and Haviland 1982, 1983), although I pressed him for details in part to let him know that I actually knew something about what sort of person he was and where he must come from. However, when I started to get into real identifying details—his full name and especially his age—he once again began to stonewall. Note the nearly two second pause following my question at line 50.

49	jbh:	a
50		k'usi ora latale ali-
		So when did you come? Uh-
51		k'usi lek labie, mi ja' onox k'u cha'al yaloj li vinik naxe?
		What's your real name? Is it as the man said earlier?
52	(1.8)	
53	d:	ja'
		Yes.

Once we actually launched the routine interrogation of personal information, D paused only briefly when calculating his age and birthdate:

54	jbh:	k'usi lek labie, mi ja' onox
		What's your real name, is it the same
55		k'u cha'al yaloj li vinik naxe?
		as what the man said earlier?
56	d:	ja'
		Yes.
57	jbh:	ali, k'usi sjol abie?
		So, what's your family name?
58	d:	D**** P. G.
59	jbh:	D. ma'uk domingo?
		D., not Domingo?
60	(2.2)	
61		Bueno, este...
		OK, so-
62	(0.5)	
63		i albon lek noxtok, k'usi ora vok'emot, jayib ajabilal?
		Tell me the truth, when were you born, how old are you?
64		(0.7)

65 d: beynte
Twenty
66 jbh: beynte?
Twenty?
67 d: jech
Right
68 jbh: pero mi ch'unbil, k'usi ta jabilal lavok' che'e?
But is that believable? What year were you born then?
69 (0.9)
70 d: ta 1990
In 1990.
71 jbh: a . bueno
Ah OK.
72 mala to
Wait a second.

The ICE agent, who had been waiting patiently for me to verify that I could speak with the kid and who was trying his best to pick out any familiar Spanish loans from the stream of conversational Tzotzil, had clearly at this point understood that I was asking about D's age. He stopped me, with a chuckle, when he heard the boy state his supposed birth year, saying that the boy had been "coached" to claim he was about five years older than computer databases—and his appearance—indicated. He then began to let me, the interpreter, in on a few details of his own investigation of the case:

73 ice: (hehh hehh)
74 (hhh) yeah, he's been— he's been coached
75 to say that, he originally gave
76 1994 as his date of birth
77 jbh: aha
78 ice: and he was previously arrested
79 um
80 uh, down on the border
81 where he gave 1995 as uh
82 date of birth
83 jbh: right
84 ice: but I believe he's
85 beginning to see

86 that this . uh .status as a juvenile is
87 beginning to cause him more headache than he cares for

The ICE agent—being observed by his superior—had a prepared script from which he must work. He also had a specific goal: to get D, who he thought was an undeportable minor child, onto an airplane to a holding facility within a matter of a few short hours. D was potentially "undeportable" because he was probably underage and had (as far as the agent had been able to determine) no responsible adults who could vouch for him in the United States or guarantee his safety should he be returned to Mexico. On the other hand, D had his own "agenda": to break through the coercive structure of his engagements with the *migra* (as the border-protection people are called in Mexican Spanish), who were forcing him to talk about his age and contacts in the United States. By contrast, what mattered most to him—at least when he finally began to talk to me (see transcript 2, line 9 below)—was his debt (money borrowed for his transport north, which had to be paid off to moneylenders in his community at 15 percent monthly interest), and his need to work to pay it off.

MULTIPLE ENGAGEMENTS AND ORDERS OF ENGAGEMENT IN INTERPRETING

The minimal interpreting context is necessarily one of multiactivity: it is logically triadic, involving minimally three bundled participants: a speaker in language 1, an interpreter, and a recipient in language 2. The interpreter is mechanically a kind of pivot, whose transparency as a ratified participant varies widely with the micropolitics of the institution in question. (Further decomposed roles in Goffmanian participant structure [Goffman 1979] are variably transformed in such engagements, with different roles sometimes erased, as can be seen in the play of pronouns in many of my extracts.)

All engagements, of course, alter or transform the entities engaged or call them into question—blunting or erasing distinctions (between persons and objects, for example) or enhancing or widening categorical differentiation. In the case of interpreting encounters, such transformations include converting Latinos into Mexicans and then into Indians, speakers into mutes, possible citizens into aliens, and persons into (various sorts of) nonpersons. Interpreting, paradoxically, sometimes renders speakers of a disadvantaged language totally deaf and dumb (as interactions between interpreter and speakers of the dominant language may begin to predominate, as we shall see).

There is a further conceptual multiplicity, since the people for whom the interpretation is required are usually not very much alike, neither with respect to their experiences and background nor their aims and purposes in the business at hand. For example, the immigration agent needed to confirm D's basic biography before sending him to juvenile detention. D, on the other hand, had quite different concerns that he was itching to put on the discursive table. Here is a further brief fragment, when the agent asked me to confirm when D had come to the United States:

(2) Feb 21, 2011–"when did you leave to come from there?"

1	jbh:	k'usi ora lalok'- lalok' tal te yo une? *What time did you leave there to come here?*
2	(0.8)	
3	D:	mu'yuk to jal *It hasn't been long.*
4	jbh:	mu'yuk to jal? *It hasn't been long.*
5	D:	ch'abal to jal *It's not yet long.*
6	jbh:	k'usi van- k'usi van k'ak'alil, *About what- About what date?*
7		k'usi van ta ual *About what month?*
8	(0.5)	
9	D:	mu'yuk to sutem o kil xtok, *Also, my debt hasn't yet been paid off;*
10		ep to kil ('o) *I still have a lot of debt (from traveling here).*

Here D, carefully avoiding my question about dates and the amount of time he had already been in the United States working, brought up the matter of his outstanding debt. Nonetheless, following the ICE agent's agenda, I pressed D about his birthdate.

11 jbh: aa
12 a bweno, pero entonse, k'usi- k'usi lek
Oh, OK. But so, what- uh – really what
13 ali:
Uh-
14 k'usi lek ali fechail lavok' un che'e
What date were you really born then?
15 (1.1)
16 D: ta mil novesyento noventaynweve . noventa
In 1999- uh, 90,
17 jbh: k'usi- k'usi k'ak'alil un?
On what- what day?
18 (1.9)
19 ice: ((laughs softly))

Once again, the ICE agent, able only to pick Spanish numbers out of the Tzotzil stream, inferred that D was continuing to give me an improbable birthdate.

20 D: ja', jna'tik une
Who knows?
21 jbh: mu xana' k'usi ta ual
Don't you know in what month?
22 (0.5)
23 D: mu jna'
I don't know.
24 jbh: a bweno pwes
Ah, OK then.
25 (0.6)

Of course, it is rarely the case that Tzotzil speakers know their exact birthdates—a highly irrelevant datum of information for Indian life, except in certain bureaucratic contexts. Asking someone for an exact age may often elicit an approximate decade instead. Because I had heard the ICE agent chuckle, I returned to the previous conspiratorial dialogue with him.

26 jbh: so he continues to say-- he was born in a - in a -
27 community called X***

28		of Chamula which is right -
29		very, basically right next to San Cristobal
30		and he's uh-
31		he says that he doesn't know his-
32		date or month of birth
33		and continues to give the year of 1990
34	(0.5)	
35	ice:	OK, um
36		that's consistent with the uh
37		the uh coaching,
38		however he provided his date and month of
39		birth twice correctly
40		uh, according to our records which
41		was 11/13 of ninety-five
42		when he was arrested by the border patrol

Notice how this particular "engagement" between the immigration agent and D, mediated by my own somewhat different engagement with D, is also informed by multiple previous encounters which in Bakhtinian fashion shadow the present one.[9] So, there are the ICE agent's previous conversations with D (in Spanish) and those of Border Patrol agents in previous encounters documented in ICE and other computer records, when this same boy was allegedly detained on earlier occasions while attempting to cross the border. In similar fashion, D's mention to me of his debt conjures a series of well-known scenarios in which Tzotzil speakers borrow money from one another, with a frighteningly familiar set of expectations about repayment, interest, and the likely consequences of default.

Here we encounter what (borrowing a metaphor from Silverstein 2003) could be called different orders of engagement: a first-order engagement between principals and interpreter builds upon second-order past engagements—some directly experienced, others narrated, others only alluded to in the shadows—which in turn build upon still higher orders of remove. As an ethnographically faithful translator trying to manage the interactive exchange of meaningful information between interlocutors, I may need to reimagine and (at least provisionally) render prior engagements between narrators and narrated protagonists, and so on, for indeterminate further orders of engagement.

A PROPER "ASYLUM" CASE

Let me temporarily leave D as I left him that afternoon, in the clutches of the migra in Mississippi and move back in time about four years, to when I was originally induced to become a "certified" Tzotzil interpreter for the Department of Homeland Security (DHS) and the agencies that provide all official interpreters for US immigration courts.[10]

My first official immigration case involved a then fifteen-year-old girl who had been detained by immigration authorities in Florida, where she had been reported to the Immigration and Naturalization Service for working illegally as a domestic servant in a private home. From Florida she had been sent to a women's detention center in Arizona to await deportation, and there she had come to the attention of a legal nongovernmental organization (NGO) that specializes in immigration law and minor children. One of the lawyers had befriended the girl, "R," and determined that she had limited Spanish and was probably a native speaker of Tzotzil. An Internet search turned up my name, and the lawyer called to ask me whether I would consider pro bono work on the girl's case, explaining that because R had apparently been the victim of sexual trafficking, and given what she could learn of the child's family circumstances, the NGO hoped to apply for protection and legal status for R by having her declared an "unaccompanied alien child" under US law, thus coming under the purview of the Convention on Rights of the Child, which puts issues of a child's safety before any considerations of his or her legal status. It was imperative, if I were to be able to interpret for R in immigration court, that I become certified for DHS work. After meeting the girl (and engaging her in probably the first more or less normal conversation she had been able to have in several months), I started the convoluted certification process, at the same time helping the lawyers flesh out more of her story.

The NGO had already begun to assemble a narrative to help R obtain legal status. It involved a rather horrific history of childhood abuse, sexual exploitation by older men (including her father and uncles), flight from home to the United States, and continued exploitation in Florida by a further chain of men—including the man twice her age, also originally from her remote village in Chiapas, who had secretly had her reported to the immigration authorities when she refused to become his child bride.

R herself, little by little, told me a rather different story—a not uncommon tale of teenaged couples whose liaison is disapproved by strict parents and who elope from home, only to end up impoverished in a strange and hostile environment in exile north of the border. It was fairly clear that her initial preference would have been to find and be reunited with her childhood boyfriend, with whom she had originally escaped her village, or, failing that, with her own older brother (who she thought was also in Florida). Nonetheless, having been provisionally placed in supervised foster care in Arizona and enrolled in a local high school with a largely Spanish-speaking student body, she started to feel strongly attracted to the scenario the lawyers had painted for her: obtaining legal status first as a ward of the state in Arizona and then as a legal resident (able to study nursing, as she once mused, or to become a lawyer in her own right). Several legal procedures were required to implement such a plan. First and most important was to demonstrate that R was, indeed, an abused and abandoned child in need of "protection," who could thus legally be declared a ward of the state. As her eighteenth birthday approached, achieving such status in turn became ever more urgent for her lawyer.

As has happened in other cases in which I have been involved, the lawyer quickly realized that as a long-time ethnographer with continued close ties to friends and fictive kinsmen in Chiapas, I could do much more to advance the plans for R than simply give her an authoritative "professorial voice" as her interpreter in immigration court or serve as a pro bono investigator. She thus recruited me to attempt, on one of my periodic trips to Mexico, to track down R's parents, to explain to them the plan, and to bring back their witnessed signatures on crucial documents to be presented to the juvenile division of the local family law court. This was a task the NGO had none of the necessary resources—linguistic, ethnographic, financial, or practical—to undertake. The relevant declaration, for each of the parents to sign, included the following language:

> I am unable to care for my Child at this time and I do not object to the court granting custody of her to the Arizona Department of Economic Security. . . I understand that . . . a future hearing may result in further proceedings for permanent guardianship or in termination of my parental rights. . . . I understand . . . [this declaration] . . . may result in the Child being adjudicated dependent and in further proceedings for permanent guardianship or termination of our parental rights. If my parental rights are terminated, all my rights to the Child, including the

> rights to custody, care, control and visitation, will be completely ended. I understand that my obligation to pay support and the Child's right to inheritance will continue until the entry of a final order of adoption, if any, of the Child.

R said that she spoke by telephone with her mother regularly a few times a month, and she had alerted them to expect me. Following her instructions, I ultimately undertook the journey to the lowland jungles of Chiapas where R's parents lived in a community of evangelical Protestant converts (cf. Nash 1995; Eber 1999; Kovic 2005; Rus 2005; Rus and Vigil 2007) exiled from their original home villages in the highlands. Despite considerable suspicion in the village, I finally tracked the parents down and explained the situation to them as best I could. (As the reader can imagine, rendering the English legalese of the document cited into idiomatic Tzotzil was no straightforward matter.) After what became a cordial visit (during which my Zinacantec companion bought some of their chickens), the parents gave me yet another Rashomon-like version of the history of R's "escape" from the village almost a year earlier. They remembered her dissatisfaction with opportunities in her tiny, impoverished village and blamed her being lured into trying to travel north across the border on the urging of an unscrupulous neighbor lady.

Ultimately I brought back the legal documents with the parents' signatures (which my wife and I witnessed). I also brought R a short videotaped message her parents had composed for her, with her siblings sitting on their laps. Both urged her to be happy and to consult with *kajvaltik* ("our Lord") for guidance and solace in whatever was to come, hoping that at the very least she would soon come back to visit them. The father's language echoed the formal, parallel phrasing of Tzotzil ritual language and prayer (Haviland 1994, 1996, 2000), a kind of Tzotzil analogue of the legalese of the documents he had willingly signed, evidently intended to soothe and reassure his wayward daughter:

(3) **R's dad sends her his advice**—*lek oyan, junuk avo'on*

1 ja' . lek oyan, i junuk avo'on
Be well, be content

2 i xamuyibaj un, mu me xavat avo'on
And rejoice, please don't worry

3 ja' lek me chamuyibaj
It's better to rejoice

4 atimi chavat avo'one i a veses
If you worry, then sometimes

5 xk'uxub ajol i
Your head will hurt

6 cha'ipaj, mi o k'usi ep chanope
You will get sick, if you think too much

7 muk' i xanop i junuk avo'on cha'abtej
Don't think about it, and be content. Work

8 chano jun
And study

9 chapas kanal uk
You will succeed, too

10 espesyal para jo'ot i mu k'usi yan ya'el
It's special just for you, not for anything else

11 chavil ma ti yo'e
You will see that over there

12 a yan xa ech'el akuxlajel (apas xa un)
You will made a different kind of life

13 ja' yu'un, ja' mu xach'un lo'loel
So don't be tricked

14 mo'oj much'u k'usi chal
Not about what someone might say

15 ma'uk k'u batenot spasel i:
That's not what you have gone to do

16 i oy k'usi ti avo'ontanoj ti labat ya'el
There is something your heart has desired that you have gone for

17 te chka'i
I will hear

18 chk'otik ta pasel va'i un, mu jna'
if it comes to pass, I don't know

19 parake jech chijmuyibajkutike
so that we may rejoice

20 este yu'un mu xkat ko'onkutike
Uh, so that we don't worry our hearts

21 ja' chopol ti mi k'usi anop

It would be bad if you thought too much

22 k'usi lik apas

If something bad started to happen to you.

23 yec chkat ko'onkutik

Then we would be worried

24 chka'uk ti ja' yech chbat ti ja' yech chapas

If I thought that it would turn out that way, that something happened to you

25 jech xichikutik mi yech chapas

if we thought something bad happened to you.

26 mu k'al lek jmoj jun avo'one, ke: chijmuyibajkutik ek

But when you are fully content, then we, too, will rejoice

27 chka'ikutik ek

We, too, will feel that way

28 i ja nox jech chakalbe un, cha' ox p'el lik'opoj i

And that's what I want to tell you, just two or three words I have spoken.

29 tee, koman, junuk avo'on, chamuyibaj i chijmuyibakutik ek

So stay there, be content. Iif you rejoice we, too, will rejoice

With the parents' voluntary agreement to terminate their parental rights in hand, the lawyers were able to petition for R's legal status as a ward of the court, which in turn began a long and somewhat tortuous path to regularize her immigration status in the United States. In the end, R's case in immigration court was heard with just Spanish interpretation (and by that time she was almost ready to graduate from an English-speaking high school), and she was granted asylum. I last spoke to her when she was attending junior college, and I have been told that she ultimately married a man who had also been helped to legal status by the same NGO. I do not know whether she has ever been back to her village in Chiapas.

The striking contrast between how most of the Tzotziles for whom I interpret fare (intercepted, incarcerated, and deported with a record of felonies) and R's "successful" outcome is what originally pushed me to reflect on whether such cases are exceptional or whether they are, instead, consistent with the underlying policies governing immigration in this country. Selecting a particular "protected" category of individual—in this case, a minor female who may very well have been sexually victimized by other immigrants from her own community—itself relies upon a stereotyped view (of sexual relations in general, of migrant Mexican males as sexual predators, and of the presumed social circumstances of minors in Mexican society) as the narrative background to any particular individual's history. But in this sort of case, the background, more than any demonstrable facts, provides the narrative framework on which bureaucratic decisions are based. These decisions, in turn, freeze and reify the stereotyped narrative and the background assumptions on which it rests.[11] As usual, the narratives of the powerful are by definition themselves powerful narratives, able to refashion facts to suit their narrators.

D'S CASE: SECOND DAY

Let me return to D. When I hung up the telephone where we met him in Mississippi that first day, I thought I had heard the last of the matter. However, the Chamula lad quickly resurfaced. In addition to doing pro bono work with hospital emergency rooms and other sorts of health-related interpreting, I have interpreted for a lateral part of the justice system that involves the special protections afforded to minors in the United States, often the province of private or charitable child-oriented psychological and social work services. The day after I conversed with the ICE agent and D, I received—quite independently and via a different private interpreting service that had contracted my services principally for such health-related work and that charged its clients by the minute—a call from a child-protection center in Texas. I thus by happenstance continued to trace D's distressing history through to what was the end (at least at the time) of my own engagement with his case.

As I was soon to discover, D had been transferred to a (private, Christian) home for juvenile offenders on an island off Galveston, Texas, where he was now in the hands of the US Department of Health and Human Services. I learned that the young man had, indeed, been provisionally deemed undeportable, as a minor child whose history and possible risks of abuse and exploitation (at home and in the United States) had not yet been established. The new call was from a woman in Texas who told me she needed to interview a Tzotzil-speaking child. Having at first no idea that this was the same boy I had spoken to the day before, I as usual tried first to confirm that I could speak to the child in question (transcript [4], lines 7–17):

(4) D's second day

1 int: OK, I'm going to do an interview and I just-
2 need a - jmmmm
3 yeah, I just need translation
4 jbh: maybe you should just let me confirm that I can actually speak to him, no?
5 (0.6)
6 int: ok
7 jbh: OK, mi li'ote D**?
*OK, are you here, D**?*
8 (0.6)
9 D: li'une
I am here.
10 jbh: ali:
Uh-
11 mi lek, mi ja' yec onox ti D abie
*Is it really the case that your name is D**?*
12 (0.9)
13 D: ja'
Yes.
14 jbh: a
15 bweno li vo'one Xun jbi
OK, my name is John
16 li vo'one Xun jbi ta jelubtas li k'ope
My name is John, and I'll translate the language
17 (0.8)

It seems clear that D immediately recognized that I was the same person he had spoken to the day before, in what was probably his first Tzotzil conversation since he had been detained and separated from his Chamula relatives some weeks previously. However, for me the penny had not yet dropped, and perhaps because the interpreting context and the agency calling me were so different, it took me a while to accept his insistence (odd to me at the time) that we had already spoken and his clear exasperation that I kept asking him the same questions he had answered twenty-four hours before, which was to become a theme in our conversations, as one "expert" after another dragged him through the same interrogative litany:

18 D: ali vi vo'ot une chak'opoj to ta stz'el bu makalun to'oxe?
Are you the one who spoke there near where I was shut up before?
19 jbh: e jna'tik
Eh, who knows?
20 ali buyot lavie, mi ali volje onox ti jk'opon jbatike?
But where are you now, if we actually did speak to each other yesterday?
21 (0.7)
22 D: ma'uk xa
Not any longer.
23 jbh: ma'uk xa
Not any longer?
[
24 D (?)-em xa (?)
(I've been moved) already
25 jbh: e jna'tik, jna'tik mi o bu j-
Eh, who knows, who knows if we-
26 jk'opon jbatike, bu lalik tal, buy a-
have spoken together. Where have you come from, where's your-
27 buy la- laparajele?
your village?
28 (1.4)
29 D: ja?
Huh?
30 jbh: bu lalik tal, buy aparajel
Where do you come from, where's your village?
31 (1.1)

This time around, after a long pause, D skipped the hedging preliminaries and told me directly from what village he hailed. It was only then that I realized he must be the same child I had talked to previously (lines 36–37):

32 D: te ta v***
*There in V****
33 jbh: a ta v***
*Ah, ta V***

34 mi ma'uk ti ali-
Isn't it uh-
35 D: te
There
36 jbh: mi ja' li- pero ja' nan ij-
Are—But yes, perhaps
37 jk'opon jbatik volje
we DID speak to each other yesterday
38 (0.6)
39 D: ja' lajk'opon jbatik volje, vo'ot lajka'i xun abi mo'oj
Yes,. We spoke yesterday, I think you're the one called John, no?
40 jbh: ji' vo'on a'a
Yeah, that's me
41 bweno, malao to, buyot xa lavie, ta tejas xa?
OK, but wait, where are you now, already in Texas?
42 (1.0)
43 D: ta tejas
In Texas
44 jbh: a bweno, mala to, yu'un ta jk'opon xa li antze
Ah,, OK. Wait a bit, while I talk a bit to the woman.
45 (0.6)
46 D: bweno
OK.

Once I discovered that I was speaking to the same kid as the day before, I so informed the Texas social worker, who took a few moments to assimilate this idea—quite unexpected for her, given that she had just dialed in to an on-demand telephonic interpreting service to get an interpreter in the first place. (I am not sure how the ICE agent had tracked me down the previous morning.) She emphasized that the child was now in a children's center and that he should be more forthcoming and, for example, admit his real age (lines 61–54):

47 jbh: ah, ma'am, yes in fact I know this guy, I've spoken to him before, so you should go ahead
48 (1.5)
49 int: you've spoken to him before?

50 jbh: yeah I spoke to him yesterday in Jackson Mississippi I believe
51 (1.3)
52 int: OK, with immigration?
53 jbh: yes that's right
54 (1.2)
55 int: OK
56 (0.9)
57 umm
58 (1.2)
59 I need to:
60 I need to know
61 OK, first I just want to make sure that he understands that this place
62 is for minors
63 and I know that he keeps saying that he's twenty years old, but
64 I hope he trusts me that we're trying to help him
65 jbh: OK
66 (0.8)
67 D
68 (0.5)
69 D: ow
I'm here
70 jbh: lek me tze'ano achikin chk li'e
Open your ears well now
71 ali komo ali antze le' ali s-
Uh, like this woman
[
72 D: sale
OK [in Spanish]
73 jbh: ma'uk skwenta migra ali
She not from the migration people
74 te la ta jun centro
She says she's in a "Center"
75 pero li sentro taje skwenta li much'u kremotike
But this "Center" is for people who are boys
76 tzebetike, ma'uk li muk'ta krixchano xkaltike
or girls; not for grown up people, let's say

77 (0.5)
78 entonses
Therefore
[
79 D: mmm
80 jbh: komo sike to chaval noxtok ti chaval noxtok ti ali-
Since you continue to say, as well- to say that um
81 ti jtob ajabilale, pero mu- xu x-
that you're twenty years old, but you're not-
82 mu xach'unbat, mu xch'un onox yiloj onox lavunale
-you're not being beleived, they'll never believe it, they've seen your papers
83 (0.9)
84 komo ilok'
Since it came out
85 la ta komputadora lavunale, iyal onox ti k'usi ora la'ayane
on the computer, your documents, they always tell what time you were born
86 li k'usi ora vok'emote
what time you were hatched, as you say
87 D: ja' jech taj une
It's that way (i.e., what I say is true).
88 jbh: ja' yech une
It's that way?
89 entonse
In that case-
90 D: ja' jech
It's that way.

Reading through the transcript, I realize that my previous engagement with the same child now shadowed our conversation in this second different context: I dredged from memory (rather than from the current exchange) his previous claims about his age and birthdate:

91 jbh: entonse mu xa xch'un ti ayanemot ta:
In that case, they won't believe that you were born in-
92 ta 1990 komo ma'uk la yech ali
in 1990 because that's not how it

93 ali chlok' ta komputadora la
comes out on the computer, according to them

94 (0.8)

95 pero mu la—
But don't-

96 D: ma'uk?
It isn't?

97 jbh: pero mu me xaxi', mu me xaxi', batz'i junuk me avo'onton un
But don't be afraid, don't be afraid, be cheerful

98 le' chaskolta li antz taje, ma'uk la migra, ma'uk xa li polisiya
That woman will help you, she's not from immigration and not from the police

99 polisiya xkaltike
She's not police.

And in response to my interpreted reassurances—doubtless irrelevant to D himself—about the person interviewing him, the frustrated child immediately started again to put his own agenda on the table, in ways that could not be followed up as the social worker pursued her own script. He repeated his desire to be set free:

100 D: yu'un chilok' xa nox
But I feel I just want to

101 chka'i ne
Be released already

102 jbh: mu jna' ta- ta jak'betik ta jlikel
I don't know, we'll- we'll ask her about it in a moment

103 (0.6)

104 D: mm, mi chiyak' nox ech'el ta jna onox
Mm, will she send me back to my own house

Following her own priorities, the social worker at the juvenile home had suspicions about D's past and his likely intentions, based on her experiences with other juvenile inmates. She disregarded his pleas for release—not part of her brief, in any case—wanting instead to know about where he was living, with whom, and what sort of relationship he had with his housemates in Mississippi (transcript 5):

(5) D's living arrangements

1	int:	uh, who were you living with in Mississippi?
2	jbh:	bweno k'al teyot ta Mississippi, buy nakalot?
		OK, when you were in Mississippi, where were you living?
3	(1.8)	
4	D:	ta partamento
		In an apartment
5	jbh:	ta partamento, much'u achi'in un?
		In the apartment, who did you accompany
6		much'u xchi'uk un
		With whom?
7	D:	ali jun kamigo
		Uh, with a friend of mine
8	jbh:	amiko un, mi ma'uk achi'il, amigo no'ox?
		A friend, not a relative, just a friend?
9	(0.6)	
10	D:	amigo nox
		Just a friend
11	jbh:	ja' a'a
		Yes
12	D:	ja' ti xkojtikin jbakotike
		We know each other
13	jbh:	buy- buy ti avojtikin abaike?
		Where- where did you become acquainted?
14	(0.9)	
15	D:	te nox te, nopol-
		There, just there, nearby
16		yo' ech'el chamula
		Down in Chamula
17		sankre de chamula stuke
		He himself is of Chamula blood

D's use of an uncharacteristic (and noncommittal) Spanish expression, "*sankre* [sic] *de chamula*" [line 17], is particularly notable to me now, in retrospect, both because it suggests that his Spanish was perhaps better than he let on to his interviewers and because it continued a pattern of avoiding the specifics of his relationships with his Chamula companions, some of whom had been arrested along with him (and in most cases were already deported), but others of whom remained unidentified, still at large, and probably still at work in Mississippi (see line 25).

18 jbh: A bweno pwes pero xavojtikin onox
Ah, OK, so it was someone you already knew
19 (0.8)
20 D: xkojtikin
Yes

As is the standard for such interpreting encounters, I rendered this little conversation into a first-person answer (lines 21–24) to the social worker's original question (line 1). D broke in (line 25) to give me a bit more explanation, which I then interpreted (line 32).

21 jbh: so I was living in apartment with a friend
22 the friend is not a relative and I met him
23 uh, in my hometown in Chamula
24 (0.6)
25 D: ja' te komen, mu'nuk buy bat une
He remained there, he didn't leave
26 jbh: ali-
Uh-
27 D: te oy to
He's still there
28 jbh: a buy- buy ti oye
Ah, where- where is he?
29 mi tey to ta jlumaltike o mi te ta missisippi to?
Is he in our country [Chiapas] or is he still in Mississippi?
30 (0.7)
31 D: Mississippi to, te oy o to
Still in Mississippi, he's still there
32 jbh: so and that friend is still in Mississippi, he hasn't been
33 arrested as far as I know
34 (2.5)
35 int: did you come- when did you come to the US?

The social worker also wanted to probe the nature of D's border crossing, particularly why and with what resources he had paid his coyote. Both her institutional vocabulary (for example, her use of the word "smuggler," whose connotations in English are considerably more complex, and negative, than Spanish loans such as *coyote* or *pollero* and especially than more ordinary Tzotzil labels for the role, which are often reasonably positive, such as *j'ik'vanej* ["guide"] or *jelubtasvanej* ["person who crosses people over" or, indeed, "interpreter"]), and her special preoccupations also contributed to my own problems in the triangular rendering of mutual trust and comprehension:

(6) Smuggling [D2a-3]

1 int: who paid for you to come over here to the US, who paid for your smuggler?
2 jbh: bweno k'alal lajelav tal ta desyerto, kusi mi tojbil mi-
So when you crosssed the desert, was it paid for?
3 min atojoj onox avaj-
Did you pay for your-
4 ali jelubtasvanej
for the person who crossed you over?
5 (0.9)
6 D: k'usi van?
What was that?
7 jbh: k'alal ajelav tal min tojbil, min a-
When you crossed over this way, was it paid, was it--
8 min atojoj onox li much'u ali
Did you pay whoever
9 poyero xkaltik li much'u chasjelubtas-
aas the smuggler, as we say, the one who crossed you over?
10 D: tojbil
It was paid for
11 jbh: tojbil
Paid for?
12 much'u istoj un
13 D: jmm
Mmmhmm
14 (1.2)

15 jtoj jtuk porke . ep me kil ne
I paid for it myself because .. I have a lot of debt
16 jbh: ah, ji' pero bweno ali k'alal atoj...
Ah, yes, but, OK, when you paid-
17 D: yu'un me, yu'un me li'ipaj k'uxi xkaltik un
Indeed, because- because I had gotten sick, as we say,
18 epaj ti kil une ja' telon o
My debt grew large, I was wiped out by it
19 ja' taj ch'om tak'in o
By borrowing money
20 jbh: aa
21 pero ti vo'ot atoj un k'usi van yepal atojbe
But what you paid, how much was it you paid?
22 yo' chajelav oe
In order to cross over
23 (0.5)
24 D: diez
Ten
25 jbh: diez
ten
26 (0.5)

I again tried to render the gist of this first-person response from D's mouth into an exchange for the interviewer.

27 jbh: ah so he- ah
28 jmm
29 so lemme just uh-
30 tell you what he was saying to me, he said he paid
31 himself
32 uh ten thousand pesos to the coyote to cross the border
33 he had borrowed money at home because he has
34 many debts
35 that are a result of a previous sickness
36 (2.3)

In a direct echo of Miriam Ticktin's (2011) observations about French asylum-seeking strategies and French rules for serious illness as a justification for "care," the social worker (after absorbing his answer during a long pause at line 36 and then switching to her native Spanish at line 37) pounced on D's reported sickness as a possible motive for his immigration to the United States and a potential strategic ploy for a possible future revised immigration status:

37 int: ¿de qué estabas enfermo antes?
[Switches to Spanish] With what were you sick before?
38 jbh: ali k'usi ip chava'i to'oxe?
What sickness did you have before?
39 (1.2)
40 D: a?
Huh?
41 jbh: k'usi ip chava'i to'oxe?
What sickness did you have before?
42 (1.2)
43 D: yu'un k'ak' jutuk kok yu'un jech xa no'ox?
It's that my leg got burned a bit, that's all

The social worker asked me to repeat that her institutional interests and affiliations were unlike those of the immigration authorities in whose hands she thought D imagined himself to be. She wanted him to understand the procedures established for undocumented minor children: to allow them to be placed with certain relatives in the United States, regardless of their immigration status, while the mandated determinations were carried out about possible risks and dangers should a child be repatriated. As an interpreter I was obliged to try to render her words, despite the fact that D himself was trying to push his own concerns: he wanted neither protection nor asylum but out:

(7) **Trust**

1 int: I know that you have been here for less than a day
2 and that you don't trust us
3 but we don't work for immigration
4 we do get contracted by the government
5 but it's

6 through the Department of Health and Human Services,
7 not Immigration,
8 cause you are younger
9 so please don't be scared to tell me
10 if you have other relatives here,
11 I don't need to know where they live
12 I just want you to contact them
13 and let them know that you're OK
14 (0.5)
15 jbh: OK, uh
16 uh, N***, let me just tell you
17 that I have already told him that you're not
18 working for immigration,
19 because I understood that from the people who contracted me,
20 but let me just-
21 tell him again just to make it a little clearer
22 (0.5)
23 D
24 (1.2)
25 D
26 ali tzotz me chayalbe li antz taje
So that woman wants to tell you strongly
27 komo li yabtel taje une,
That her work
28 ma'uk skwenta migra,
Has nothing to do with immigration
29 ma'uk skwenta polisia un
Nothing to do with police
30 ali j-
31 jtos xa li yabtel une skwenta—
She has a different kind of job
32 D: te-
There-
33 jbh: skwenta li- ja' k'u cha'al salubridad ta jlumaltik
Something like "public health" in our country
34 ali skwenta salud un, ma'uk ja chas-
It's about health, not for -

35 chask'el un, chaschabi
She wants to watch you, to take care of you
36 chask'elulan
They want to keep watching out for you

A basic misrecognition of the situation of this Tzotzil teenager made the social worker's words sound, I expect, completely hollow (as well as requiring me to dance around her own particular bureaucratic and social understanding of the situation to try to reassure young D). She did not, for example, appear to recognize that despite his tender age, D had contracted debt and set out as an adult to *sa' tak'in* ("look for money"), as one says in Tzotzil.

DAYS 3–10: LAWYER, SHRINK, COUNSELOR

Over the next days (and, in fact, weeks) at the children's home, D was assigned three more professional case workers, all of whom called me for translations periodically: an immigration lawyer, a clinician who administered psychological evaluations, and another social worker, D's "counselor" or therapist at the juvenile home, who tracked his behavior and adjustment to the new surroundings, asking me to probe the boy's state of mind and to comment on his cultural background. Transcript 8 is drawn from an exemplary conversation with the latter from D's fifth day in the home. It is clear that D had by now realized that his hopes for immediate release were for naught. In extremely lethargic Tzotzil, with long pauses (lines 5, 9, 11, etc.) preceding his responses, D reported that he did not feel like eating, a characteristic Tzotzil symptom of illness. When I pressed him about whether it was just a matter of unfamiliar food—for example, whether or not he was being given tortillas, a food without which no Tzotzil meal is considered complete (lines 22–23)—he responded with another classic expression of Tzotzil unwellness: "I just eat one or two" (line 25):

(8) Depressed

1 int: aquí está D
(In Spanish) Here is D (to JBH)
2 jbh: bueno
OK

3 (0.60)
4 jbh: bweno D k'u xa'elan un?
Well, D, how are you doing?
5 (2.01)
6 D: li'une
I am here.
7 jbh: bweno
OK
8 jbh: mi ja' to yechot
Are you well?
9 (3.34)
10 jbh: mi ja' to yechot, mi lek lavay, mi lek chave'?
Are you well, are you sleeping well, are you eating well?
11 (2.19)
12 D: m'm
No
13 jbh: k'usi, k'usi li i'i
What? 'No' what?
14 1.62)
15 D: mu'yuk chive' tajmek
I'm really not eating
16 jbh: muk' chave' ta jmoj?
Are you not eating at all?
17 (1.68)
18 D: tana, pero mu'yuk,
Yes, but not really;
19 mu onox jk'an ya'ele,
I don't feel like it,
20 mu jna' k'u cha'al
I dunno why
21 jbh: a pero muk' bu nopem xava'i
Ah, but you're not used to it
22 mi'n chayak'be onox lavote
Are they at least giving you your tortilas?
23 mi ch'abal vaj mi oy vaj
Are there no tortillas, or are there tortillas?
24 (2.00)

25 D: pero k'ajom jun chib, chib no'ox
But only one or two, just two
26 jbh: a mu xak'an lek
Ah, so you don't really want them
27 pero mu me xa'ipaj un che'e
But please don't get sick
28 mas nan lek batz'i k'elo me aba
It woud be better for you to take care of yourself
29 (0.68)
30 ali malao to te
Just wait a bit
31 chka'itik k'usi xi li- ali senyor taje une
Let's hear what the gentleman there says

Still more telling, when I signaled that I was about to return my attention to the counsellor, D again immediately brought up his most central desire—to return home:

32 D: ta jk'an chisut ech'el un
I want to return home from her
33 jbh: an ji', jna'oj
Why, yes, I know.
34 te chka'itik k'usi xi li vinik taj une
Let's hear what the man says
35 (1.20)
36 jbh: I***, nada mas le saludé,
*(In Spanish) I**, I just greeted him*
37 así de la forma normal, este
38 le pregunté que es lo normal en estas
And I asked him, as one normally would in these
39 este tipo de caso,
circumstances,
40 pués, cómo ha dormido,
How he's been sleeping
41 si está comiendo
If he's eating
42 y me comenta y eso también me lo comenté ayer,
And he remarked, and he made the same comment yesterday,

43 que no está comiendo, que no:
That he's not eating, that he doesn't
44 (0.85)
45 que no sabe porqué pero como que no tiene apetito
That he doesn't know why but that he has no appetite
46 no le dan ganas de comer
That he has no desire to eat

Unsurprisingly, the therapist diagnoses "depression" and begins to inquire of me (as an anthropologist—a further sort of engagement implicit in my interpretation work with some American authorities) about young D's "religious beliefs" as a potential therapy.

47 int: OK
48 está deprimido
He's depressed
49 (1.79)
50 sí, sí está deprimido
Yes, yes, he's depressed
51 pregúntame si él asiste a una-
Ask him for me if he attends a-
52 si él tiene alguna . creencia religiosa
If he has any . religious beliefs

The therapist went on after this on to ask me whether in D's culture they "go to church" and whether it is "a Christian church"—something this particular children's home was especially concerned about. The ultimate goal of the personnel at the children's home was to convince D that his best course of action was to ask for provisional asylum in the United States as an "endangered minor," to accept foster parents, and to continue his schooling. D, on the other hand, insisted that what he wanted (and was in fact obliged) to do was to get work to pay his debts before returning home to Chamula—a place he could not go empty-handed while title to his father's lands was being held as collateral by local usurers (who also expected at least 10 percent monthly interest on the 15,000 pesos of principal).

It became clear, to me at least, that D's situation was basically unresolvable until he could both prove his age and identity and cooperate sufficiently with the authorities to convince them that he could "safely" return home. I spoke with D's father by telephone and on one of my periodic fieldtrips to Chiapas met with both parents. His parents gave me photocopies of D's birth and sixth-grade school certificates, and I also copied a photo that showed him with his godparents at his primary school graduation ceremony, which had taken place less than a year before.[12] Putting these in the hands of his immigration lawyer back in Texas meant that D ultimately was able to force his way in front of an immigration judge to express his own urgent desire to be repatriated, despite repeated efforts by the brigade of lawyers, social workers, counsellors, and psychologists to convince him that he would be better off (and likely successful) if he were to accept "unaccompanied alien child" status and apply for asylum.

After two more months of twists and turns, psychological pressures, and delays in therapy and immigration court, D was finally repatriated back to Mexico after seventy-one days in custody. (Ironically—and perhaps appropriately—I was never assigned to interpret in the relevant hearings in immigration court, and I assume that D was represented there by his Spanish-speaking lawyer.) In late 2014, when I last stopped by the village to visit his family, D was away doing construction work in central Mexico, still trying to pay off his debts from that initial disastrous trip to the United States four years earlier. His brother confided to me that D speaks now with some regret about not taking American authorities up on their proposal that he seek legal residence in Texas, where he could have continued to go to school and grown up a gringo, thus at least partially ducking his current state of debt-peonage. This has been the result in the cases of a few others for whom I have interpreted, although the results have been at best ambivalent when individual and family interests are taken into account.

A POLITICS OF "PROTECTION" AND ITS FLIP SIDE(S)

Although I cannot develop the argument here, I am convinced that the notion of "coerced protection" that motivates American authorities to try to force asylum on certain categories of children has another chilling institutional expression. There is an obvious irony in the fact that while adult "economic refugees" are routinely excluded from the ranks of legitimate asylum seekers, their children may be coerced into "protective custody."

These same "protected" children are usually, in the view of their home communities, old enough to leave home, although admittedly in often extremely precarious circumstances and not necessarily with their parents' blessings. They are also able to seek gainful employment in the vast marketplaces of gray and black labor in their own countries, if not elsewhere. Under American law and given American sensibilities, the state must instead protect such children from exploitation, regardless of their own wishes. This is why R was officially "removed" from the care of her father and mother, whose "parental rights" were officially terminated more than a year after she had actually run away from home. It is why D was kept in custody for months after his older brothers had been summarily deported and gone back to work, either in Mexico or, illegally, back in the United States. In this chapter, I have illustrated the role(s) that a hapless and initially naive interpreter/ethnographer plays in such proceedings and the complex social and interactive engagements in which such specialized encounters occur. As I mentioned at the outset, the resulting perspective is by necessity partial and selectively limited.

There is, however, another implementation of the same ideology: the fact that US courts routinely take children away from immigrant families on the grounds that such children, too, are "not safe" in their families and thus need "protection." This is what has happened in some of the most distressing Tzotzil cases on which I have worked. The category "felony child neglect"—prominent on the list of the legal difficulties in which Tzotziles for whom I have interpreted sometimes find themselves—refers to cases in which the state "removes" children from their Tzotzil-speaking families. Hard as it may be to imagine, in one such case a Tzotzil father was deported and his wife had her infant child legally removed from her care for more than one year because of an extreme case of diaper rash that, once brought to the attention of authorities, was never forgiven. In another, a Tzotzil woman whose husband had been accused (but was never charged) with inappropriate behavior with their eight-year-old daughter lost not only that daughter but also her other younger children—aged five, three, and one, and, ultimately a year later, her two-month-old infant as well—first to foster care and then to permanent adoption because she could not meet the court's plan for "reunification" (which included mandatory sexual abuse survivor courses and having to learning the Spanish or English in which she would have been able to take them).

I continue to do Tzotzil interpretation, to help courts locate interpreters for other Mesoamerican Indian languages, and to have hopes for the potential usefulness of these complex and officially consequential engagements between languages, mediators, and bureaucracies. Nonetheless, because of their partiality, their ordered histories, and the engagements, reengagements, and disengagements that they disguise, I have no illusions about the efficacy of the interactions I have as a Tzotzil interpreter and especially about the ultimate effects of such interpreting work on the lives of the Tzotzil speakers whom (in my own mind, at least) I am trying to help. The notion that it is worthwhile to help otherwise silenced speakers of indigenous languages in such proceedings should probably be replaced by a more cynical view. As I have argued elsewhere (Haviland 2003), far from giving a few Tzotziles a voice where they are voiceless or lending them at least a whisper of my own "power" and prestige as a professor (who is sometimes accorded at least a snippet of recognition from judges and lawyers, as opposed to most interpreters, who are usually entirely effaced as transparent nonpersons in the courtroom), these interpreting engagements, complex as they are, often work not to enhance justice and equality, or even to serve the best interests of the speakers, but rather to lubricate and legitimize the wheels of bureaucracy itself, including its systematic and structural injustices. The appearance of "full and true" translation and, thus, linguistic transparency is little more than a pretext for imposing ideologically driven legal resolutions on sociopolitical conundrums.

In a parallel way, the rare cases of "coerced asylum" that emerge from the vast parade of summary deportations and incarcerations sanctioned by the courts and other agencies I sometimes work for are exceptions that prove the rule. If a "politics of suspicion" (and the concomitant blindness it derives from and reproduces) holds sway not only over asylum petitioners but essentially over all migrants, such suspicion can be suspended only for individuals who, for other ideological reasons, can be considered by definition to be morally pure and ethically blameless: prototypically infants and children. It is thus a corollary of the same "suspicion" of immigrants that renders imperative "protection" for the blameless among them. Surrounded by morally contaminated adults, the blameless require isolation and protection, and coerced asylum (if not removal from families and termination of parental rights or the institutionalized conversion into minigringos of unwilling adolescents) is one vehicle for achieving it.

NOTES

1. Counting people five years or older, the percentage of that age segment of the Chiapas population that speaks an indigenous language is 24.3 percent. In the 2010 census, only Oaxaca had a larger total population of speakers of indigenous languages, which represents almost 34 percent; Yucatán has about 30 percent but less than half as many speakers. (Source: http://www.inegi.org.mx/.)

2. Another third are speakers of Tseltal, a close cousin, with the rest divided unevenly between half a dozen or so other languages, most of them also Mayan. Tzotzil and Tseltal each share fifth place in the list of most spoken Mexican Indian "languages."

3. Many lawyers approach me for help interpreting for their clients knowing only that they come "from Mexico"—and in this they may even be wrong, as I have been asked to interpret in Tzotzil for people who turn out actually to hail from rural Guatemala or farther south. Employers or contractors in Oregon sometimes told me they preferred to hire the hardworking "*oaxaquitos*"—"little people from [the state of] Oaxaca." They thus themselves lumped together quite a patchwork of different languages and regions. And speakers of Amuzgo, a tiny Oto-Manguean language with which I have worked in my own neighborhood in California, suffer from a kind of triple-whammy: for North Americans they are lumped together with other "Mexicans," for most Mexicans they are just more *inditos* from Oaxaca, and for the much more populous speakers of dialects of the related Mixtec family of languages they are those strange neighbors whom you cannot understand even a little bit when they speak in their own tongues. (Among themselves, Amuzgos also distinguish carefully between people from their own communities and people—even Amuzgo speakers—from other places.)

4. After the brief but widely publicized rebellion against the Mexican state and its "bad government" by the Zapatista Army of National Liberation in Chiapas that began on January 1, 1994, there followed a period of "low-intensity" warfare between largely indigenous Zapatista groups and progovernment paramilitaries. A particularly violent confrontation involved the murder of around forty-five mostly women and children in a church in the Tzotzil village of Acteal (Ajte'al in Tzotzil) in December 1997, a crime for which more than one hundred Tzotzil-speaking people were ultimately charged and imprisoned.

5. A final equals sign (=) and a similar sign in a subsequent transcript line indicates a "latch"—i.e., the fact that two lines follow each other with no apparent pause between them. In this case, for example, the latch connects the current line #2 directly to line #5 in the transcript.

6. Square brackets like this one indicate overlap between the line above and the succeeding line of transcribed speech. That is, they mark the place where the preceding line in the transcript begins to be overlapped by the subsequent line.

7. Parenthetical numbers show audible pauses, in seconds.

8. I here write Tzotzil with a highly simplified Spanish-based practical orthography, in which *ch* = *tʃ*, *j* = *h*, *x* = *ʃ*, *tz* = *ts*, ' = *ʔ* (glottal stop) when following a vowel; otherwise it indicates an ejective or glottalized version of the preceding consonant. Where I present morpheme-by-morpheme glosses, I use the following abbreviations: Q = interrogative sentential proclitic; A1–3 = ergative proclitics in first, second, and third persons; B1–3 = absolutive suffixes in first, second, and third persons; and CL = phrasal clitic.

9. See Bakhtin (1986) (and, e.g., Irvine [1996] and her notion of "shadow conversations") for the theoretical grounding of a useful perspective that finds in all talk echoes, allusions, and virtual responses to previous conversations, real or imagined, to show that people's words are, far from being monologic, inherently linked to those of past (and future) interlocutors.

10. There are several ironies here, not the least of which is that only a handful of people in the world could possibly "certify" the linguistic qualifications of a Tzotzil-English interpreter, and I am one of them.

11. Another case, too complex to detail here, illustrates the kind of ideological cleansing that takes place of actual biographies. A Tzotzil-speaking man who had been jailed by the state of Florida for alleged child abuse (itself a long and contorted story) was later released and provided with state-funded housing for both himself and his two teenaged daughters after the daughters—rescued by the FBI—denounced another Tzotzil-speaking man from another village, who had claimed to be their "uncle," for trying to sell them into prostitution.

12. Until recently, at least many, if not most, Tzotzil-speaking children go no further in school than sixth grade, often "graduating" in their mid to late teens. The number of boys reaching this level far exceeds that of girls.

REFERENCES

Bakhtin, Mikhail M. 1986. *Speech Genres and Other Late Essays*, edited by Carol Emerson and Michael Holquist. Translated by Vern W. McGee. Austin: University of Texas Press.

Cornelius, Wayne, David Fitzgerald, and Pedro Lewin Fischer, eds. 2007. *Mayan Journeys: U.S.-Bound Migration from a New Sending Community*. La Jolla: Center for Comparative Immigration Studies, University of California, San Diego.

Eber, Christine E. 1999. "Seeking Our Own Food: Indigenous Women's Power and Autonomy San Pedro Chenalho, Chiapas (1980–1998)." *Latin American Perspectives* 26 (3): 6–36.

Goffman, Erving. 1979. "Footing." *Semiotica* 25 (1–2): 1–30.

Haviland, John B. 1994 [1992]. "Lenguaje ritual sin ritual." *Estudios de Cultura Maya* 19:427–42.

———. 1996. "'We Want to Borrow Your Mouth': Tzotzil Marital Squabbles." In *Disorderly Discourse*, edited by Charles L. Briggs, 158–203. Oxford: Oxford University Press.

———. 2000. "Warding Off Witches: Voicing and Dialogue in Zinacantec Prayer." In *Les rituels du dialogue, promenades ethnolinguistiques en terres Amérindiennes*, edited by Aurore Monod-Becquelin and Phillipe Erikson, 367–400. Nanterre, France: Société d'ethnologie.

———. 2003. "Ideologies of Language: Some Reflections on Language and U.S. Law." *American Anthropologist* 105 (4): 764–74.

Haviland, John B., and Leslie K. Haviland. 1982. "Behind the Fence: The Social Bases of Privacy in a Mexican Village." *Estudios de Cultura Maya* 14:323–52.

———. 1983. "Privacy in a Mexican Indian Village." In *Public and Private in Social Life*, edited by Stanley I. Benn and J. Gaus, 341–62. London: Croom Helm.

Irvine, J. T., 1996. "Shadow Conversations: The Indeterminacy of Participant Roles." In *Natural Histories of Discourse*, edited by Michael Silverstein and Greg Urban, 131–59. Chicago: University of Chicago Press.

Kovic, Christine. 2005. *Mayan Voices for Human Rights: Displaced Catholics in Highland Chiapas.* Austin: University of Texas Press.

Nash, June. 1995. "The Reassertion of Indigenous Identity: Mayan Responses to State Intervention in Chiapas." *Latin American Research Review* 30:7–41.

Rus, Jan. 2005. "The Struggle against Indigenous Caciques in Highland Chiapas." In *Caciquismo in Twentieth-Century Mexico*, edited by Alan Knight and Wil G. Pansters, 169–200. London: Institute for the Study of the Americas.

Rus, Jan, and Diego Vigil. 2007. "Rapid Urbanization and Migrant Indigenous Youth in San Cristóbal, Chiapas, Mexico." In *Gangs in the Global City: Alternatives to Traditional Criminology*, edited by John Hagedorn, 152–84. Champagne-Urbana: University of Illinois Press.

Silverstein, Michael. 2003. "Indexical Order and the Dialectics of Sociolinguistic Life." *Language and Communication* 23 (3–4): 193–229.

Ticktin, Miriam. 2011. *Casualties of Care: Immigration and the Politics of Humanitarianism in France.* Berkeley: University of California Press, 2011.

Part II

Technologies of Suspicion

Chapter 4

Asylum Officers, Suspicion, and the Ambivalent Enactment of Technologies of Truth

BRIDGET M. HAAS

> How can we tell the difference between a bogus and a genuine asylum seeker? It is always possible that we may not be able to tell, and that the bogus may pass their way into our community. . . . Indeed, the possibility that we may not be able to tell the difference swiftly converts into the possibility that *any* of those incoming bodies may be bogus.
>
> *(Ahmed 2004a, 122)*

> Our job, it's an impossible job.
>
> *(US asylum officer, 2010)*

This chapter takes as its point of departure the simultaneous claims that any asylum seeker may be a fraudulent one and that discerning who is a genuine asylum claimant versus a "bogus" one is marked by indeterminacy, if not impossibility. How, then, do adjudicators perform this "impossible job"? Using data collected from interviews with asylum officers who adjudicate affirmative asylum claims, I explore how asylum officers engage with various "technologies of truth" (Merry and Coutin 2014), revealing these adjudicators' often ambiguous enactment of these technologies and forms of authoritative knowledge. I argue that while the asylum seeker emerges as the central figure of suspicion, adjudicators approach bureaucratic technologies and, ultimately, their own judgments of claimants with mistrust as well. Finally, I consider the ways in which asylum officers mediate, both intersubjectively and intrapersonally, the weight of the challenge of confidently adjudicating cases.

THE ASYLUM PROCESS

The data for this chapter are drawn from a larger project that focused on the lived experiences of asylum claimants in an urban, Midwestern area of the United States. While the primary data collection was with asylum claimants, for part of this project I also conducted interviews with fifteen asylum officers, as well as interviews with numerous immigration attorneys and advocates.[1] Asylum officers are employed by the United States Office of Citizenship and Immigration Services within the Department of Homeland Security (DHS) and are trained to conduct interviews with individuals who have filed an affirmative asylum claim: an appeal to the government for protection owing to "a well-founded fear of persecution" in his or her country of origin (see the introduction to this volume). A person may file an affirmative claim regardless of legal status (i.e., whether they maintain a valid nonimmigrant visa, such as a tourist or student visa, or have either overstayed their visa or entered the country without being processed by an immigration official), provided that he or she has not been apprehended by DHS.

The division between "deserving" and "undeserving" migrants typically maps onto the presumptive distinction between political refugees and economic migrants, a division that is reinforced by current immigration discourses and policies. In this framework, economic migrants are understood not only as a threat to the human rights of "genuine" asylum seekers but also to the moral fabric of the United States.

It is now well recognized in the scholarly literature that the distinction between economic and humanitarian migrants is an untenable one and that categories of mobility are socially and politically constructed (Dauvergne 2004; Holmes and Castañeda 2016; Yarris and Castañeda, 2015; Zimmerman, 2011). Yet the distinction between these categories of migrants remains the primary lens through which asylum adjudication occurs, as this chapter illustrates. Moreover, the putative distinction between "right" migrants (humanitarian/political migrants) and "wrong" ones (economic migrants) relies on a conceptualization of them as inherent and self-evident categories, thus dangerously obscuring the fact that it is the asylum system itself that constructs these categories of subjecthood. Indeed, it is in the adjudication of asylum claims that categories of mobility and personhood are made legible and meaningful.

At the heart of the asylum process—and of this chapter—is the stark fact that it is an institutional actor and not the asylum seeker himself or herself who decides if his or her story of suffering is truthful or sufficient enough to be considered deserving of asylum status. Though the claimant is the only person with firsthand knowledge of the events discussed in the asylum interview, it is in the interactions between adjudicators and claimants that a persecution narrative emerges (Puumula, Ylikomi, and Ristimäki 2107). Yet, ultimately, "epistemic authority is positioned to the asylum officer who can determine how the narrative will eventually be interpreted" (Puumula, Ylikomi, and Ristimäki 2017, 16). This fact of inequitable power distribution is made additionally problematic given the broader lens of suspicion that informs the everyday micropolitics of asylum adjudication. As Olga Jubany (2011, 2017) has argued, the asylum screening process is "informed by a meta-message of disbelief and denial" (2017, 6). This, in turn, shapes the everyday interactions between claimants and adjudicators and critically circumscribes how asylum claimants are understood and assessed during their interviews. Thus, this chapter is concerned with the "evaluative *gaze*": the "ways in which [asylum] employees [are] engaged in processes of judgment, hierarchization and moralization" and aided by particular technologies of truth and suspicion (Codó 2011, 738).

ASYLUM OFFICERS: PROTECTING WHOM?

Sara Ahmed (2004a) posits the bogus asylum seeker as evoking the figure of the "bogey man": someone who "could be anywhere and anyone" (123). In this way, all asylum seekers emerge, at least initially, as suspect. From the standpoint of both policymakers and the adjudicators I discuss here, the threat that the bogus asylum seeker poses, however, often has less to do with the potential for actual physical destruction in the form of terrorist or criminal acts and more to do with the moral destruction of the integrity of America's generous and compassionate "humanitarian benefit" of asylum. Here, as Ahmed argues, the bogus asylum seeker comes to be aligned with the burglar: he or she is "taking something" (123)—in this scenario, a benefit reserved for the truly deserving—to which he or she does not have a legitimate claim.

While concerns over terrorism and threats to national security were a significant impetus for increasingly restrictive immigration measures (particularly after 9/11), the asylum officers with whom I spoke seemed confident that the numerous screening measures to which asylum applicants were subjected would prevent terrorists or other persons who posed a national security threat from getting through the system. In other words, once asylum officers ran the necessary background checks on asylum applicants (conducted by other branches of DHS, such as Immigration and Customs Enforcement), officers did not feel the need to probe within interviews for these kinds of national security concerns or potential terrorist threats. Rather, the threat of granting asylum to fraudulent applicants—namely economic migrants posing as humanitarian refugees—emerged as the key concern for asylum officers, as the following narratives reflect:

> My biggest concern was, you know, that I was referring or denying somebody who was a true refugee. . . . Likewise, I was very concerned that I was granting somebody who was getting one over on me. You know what I mean? Because I don't like the system being abused. I really don't. (Asylum officer ID07)

> We do get the embellishers. We get the liars. We get the people with fraudulent intent. Um, we have a, we're very generous, and we try to be very fair. . . . But the reality is we deal with a lot of economic refugees, and that separates them from other refugees as a group. So, we get a lot of people that, in my opinion, are without a doubt, economic refugees who are trying to convert that into a claim that will pass muster. (Asylum officer ID12)

Here asylum applicants who are not "true refugees" but rather "economic migrants" trying to "get one over" on officers are framed as a kind of cancer on the system: morally suspect individuals who need to be identified and labeled as such.

Asylum officers framed the task of "weeding out" undeserving asylum seekers as a critical effort in ensuring the integrity of the US asylum system, as well as protecting the state from hosting such morally suspect figures. In this way, "the asylum determination process is a way of enacting the biopolitical practice of the border" (Puumula, Ylikomi, and Ristimäki 2017, 1). On a broader scale, the discourse of protecting the nation from the bogus asylum seeker—who could be anyone and anywhere—serves at best to justify and routinize the increasing policing and criminalization of asylum seekers (Squire 2009; De Genova and Peutz 2010); at worst, it justifies "the repetition of violence against bodies of others" (Ahmed 2004b, 47; see also Ticktin 2011). While such discourse justifies overt and brute forms of violence on migrants deemed undeserving of incorporation into the state, I focus in this chapter on what Cécile Rousseau, Marie-Claire Rufagari, Déogratias Bagilishya, and Toby Measham (2004) have referred to as "clean violence": acts of violence associated with technocratic organizations and bureaucracies that are less overt but just as damaging as other modes of organizational violence (1095).

ASYLUM OFFICERS AS MORAL GATEKEEPERS

Given the specter of the "bogey man" in the form of the bogus asylum seeker, asylum officers very much framed their role as a balancing act between protecting the state and protecting applicants. Asylum officers described themselves as what I refer to as "moral gatekeepers": caught between the humanitarian imperative to grant refuge to those in need, on the one hand, and the duty to protect the security of the nation, on the other. A central question thus emerges: Who is it that asylum officers are supposed to be protecting? Asylum officers seemed to struggle with this dilemma, reflecting a broader "ambivalence about our moral obligations to the people who make claims" (Bohmer and Shuman 2008, 263). As asylum officers described it:

> You know, you just hope that you do right by the applicant. And you hope you do right by your country. Because, you know, we were hired by the country to protect the citizens of the United States. And so, at the same time we want to be humanitarian and extend the helping hand of the country to the people that deserve it. You're just constantly

> doing a balancing act, and you're hoping you're getting it right. (Asylum officer ID03)

> Certainly [you] don't want to make a decision where you're sending someone into harm's way, but at the same time you don't want to disrupt the integrity of the program and just kind of find everybody eligible that may not need the same kind of protection as somebody else. So it's just kind of hard balance sometimes. (Asylum officer ID09)

The "hard balance" of protecting the nation and "doing right by the applicant" is predicated on asylum officers' ability to discern between genuine and undeserving claimants, a task they view as central to their job. The stakes here are high. To be sure, many officers used the metaphor of "opening the floodgates," evoking images of the nation being overwhelmed by the "wrong" kind of migrants.

Key to the positioning of oneself as a moral gatekeeper is the understanding of asylum seekers as already constituted subjects with regard to their deservingness of legal protection. In this way, asylum officers view the forms of knowledge and "technologies of truth" (Merry and Coutin 2014) that they bring to bear on the adjudication of asylum cases as a kind of archaeological method, with the claimant's identity ("genuine" or "bogus") being the object of investigation—hidden but discoverable by a trained eye. Again, such a view obfuscates the ways that the asylum officers, through the application of these techniques and technologies, actually produce asylum seekers as particular kinds of subjects.

And yet, asylum officers underscored the indeterminacy, if not impossibility, of confidently making such judgments, of discerning between genuine and fraudulent claimants. As one senior asylum officer summed up, "You just never know if you've ever made the right decision." Moral gatekeeping appears to be on tenuous ground. How, then, do asylum officers engage in moral gatekeeping when it is both a necessary and impossible job? More specifically, how is "deservingness" and "undeservingness" (of legal recognition) "locally reckoned" in the context of asylum adjudication (Willen 2012)?

In exploring how asylum officers make judgments about what is genuine and what is fraudulent within asylum seekers' narratives, I am interested in the moral conceptions and the technologies of truth and suspicion that are deployed in the adjudication process. These technologies "produce and reinforce hierarchies between what is 'knowable' and what is not" (Merry and Coutin 2014, 1). While asylum officers attempted to construe these technologies of knowledge as neutral and "objective," a more fine-grained analysis reveals their acknowledgment of the interpretive and ambivalent nature of asylum adjudication. In contrast to the ideal of asylum adjudication, the process is slippery and highly fraught, and asylum officers find themselves caught up in an endless cycle of suspicion.

CREDIBILITY AS KEY: DID THIS *REALLY* HAPPEN?

To a large extent, "deservingness" within the asylum process is predicated on perceived credibility, the idea that an asylum claimant's story of suffering is authentic—that it *really* happened to him or her. As legal scholar Michael Kagan (2003) argues, though credibility is not an explicit criterion for refugee protection, "in practice, being deemed credible may be the single biggest substantive hurdle before applicants" (368). Indeed, credibility has been shown to be "the core of the asylum process" (Thomas 2006, 79; see also Coffey 2003; Rempell 2009).

In my interviews with asylum officers, the issue of credibility was the single most salient issue. Without exception, all asylum officers spontaneously highlighted credibility—more specifically, credibility assessments—as a central concern in their work. While the asylum office does not collect data regarding the reasons for denials or referrals of asylum claims and was therefore unable to report how many cases were referred or denied due to adverse credibility findings, officers stressed that the most challenging cases were the ones in which a claimant's credibility was suspect. As I have noted, all asylum seekers were viewed as suspect since anyone could be a fraudulent claimant, and asylum officers viewed their biggest threat to be an applicant trying to "pull one over" on them. Thus, the integrity of the asylum system and, by proxy, the nation as a whole is pitted against the asylum seeker who lies in order to gain access. Credibility, then, was often the key factor in discerning genuine asylum seekers from so-called bogus ones.

However, asylum officers expressed a high degree of ambivalence about credibility assessments:

> Credibility determinations are horrible. They're just impossible to tell if someone's telling the truth. . . . Or know for sure they're lying. You know, and you can't ever really know. In rare times, you can know for sure that someone's lying, and it's like "Yeah!" [laughs]. "Cause I have proof. I got them!" But most of the time you might just have a feeling they're lying, but you can't catch them on anything. . . . So we don't want to grant them until we believe them. And then we don't believe them, so we don't want to grant them. (Asylum officer ID010)

> People can make up their stories just to gain the benefit. So that is probably the most difficult just because none of us are necessarily psychologists or . . . have that background where you can just look at someone and know they're lying. (Asylum officer ID05)

The above excerpts make clear the crucial link that adjudicators made between credibility and deservingness. Lying, from the perspectives of asylum officials, is a manipulative strategy employed by asylum applicants to gain access to a benefit to which they, as "liars," should not have the right to claim. And while research has shown that what may be identified as lying or withholding of information, particularly among refugees, is culturally and socially variable, such factors are not routinely taken into account by adjudicators (Bohmer and Shuman 2008). Furthermore, the conflation of lying with undeservingness fails to recognize the "moral economy of lying" that asylum regimes evoke, whereby successful testimonies often necessitate a recrafting or rearranging of biographical details and other elements of asylum seekers' stories (Beneduce 2015).

These excerpts also reveal a critical paradox: credibility assessments are simultaneously necessary and impossible. Asylum officers understand their own capacity to discern between truthful and fraudulent claimants to be tenuous at best. While he or she may "just have a feeling" one way or the other, officers lack the expertise of a psychologist, for example, who would presumably be able to more confidently apprehend truthfulness or other "subjective" phenomena. There is, then, a danger inherent in this paradox of necessity and impossibility. To be sure, the highly subjective nature of credibility assessments has been criticized in the literature, pointing to adjudicators' abuse of credibility assessments, wide discrepancies in adverse credibility decisions, and the interference of cultural bias with credibility determinations (Coffey 2003; Vedsted-Hansen 2005; Floss 2006; Thomas 2006; Rempell 2008; Schroeder, 2017). The asylum officers with whom I spoke seemed quite aware of the dangerous murkiness of credibility assessments because of their subjective elements. Emotional display, in particular, emerged as a particular focus of suspicion.

CREDIBILITY, EMOTION, AND NARRATIVE PERFORMANCE

Asylum officers cited identifiable aspects of narrative performance that contributed to a sense of credibility: adequate use of detail, telling a linear story but able to "jump around," and, importantly, the consistent use of proper names and dates. For the most part, however, asylum officers did not explicitly cite demeanor as a factor in credibility assessments, although they often alluded to an intangible quality that accompanied compelling accounts of a story. Thus, part of an applicant's ability to "convince [the officer] that this happened to them" rested on his or her ability to evoke from the officer an empathic understanding, to make an affective connection. In this sense, it was the job of the asylum claimant to "elicit compassion" and engage in the act of "*selling* one's suffering" (Ticktin 2011, 139, 127). Emotional display, though, could be tricky for asylum officers to read. If, as Fred Myers (1979) has argued, emotional talk can be a genuine reflection of inner states *and/or* strategic assertions of what is emotionally expected in a particular context, asylum officers were charged with discerning whether or not a claimant's expressions of fear or sadness were "real" or strategic forms of self-objectification—and, of course, they could be both. Asylum officers reported that they often mistrusted claimants' acts of crying, for example, knowing that it could be "real" emotion or it could be strictly performative.

Yet even if asylum officers were confident that the emotional display of a claimant was "real"—that is, that the emotion the claimant expressed was a genuine reflection of his or her inner state—this was not enough to establish credibility in the eyes of these adjudicators. Another layer of suspicion was added: it could be the case, asylum officers told me, that the emotion is real, but the *source* of that emotion is suspect. For example:

> It's kind of hard [to assess emotions] because you don't know when somebody's crying why are they crying. They could be crying 'cause

> their mom just passed away and they didn't get to go to the funeral. Or they could be crying because they're recounting something bad or they left their kid, so it's kind of hard because you *can see the emotion, but you don't know the source.* And it could be anything. (Asylum officer ID06; emphasis added)

Here, although this asylum officer may not discount the veracity of the claimant's emotion, her crying was not necessarily effective in establishing credibility because the source of the sadness could not be identified. And yet because of the subjective nature of phenomenon such as emotion, its source, of course, can never be definitively identified or proven. The asylum claimant remains a suspect figure, and evidence of her authenticity must be found elsewhere.

If asylum officers then look to aspects of a claimant's testimony and narrative performance that can be more readily identified and measured, such as level of detail or the use of names and dates, these elements, too, can become gray areas. In practice, the demarcation of what constitutes "subjective" and "objective" becomes ambiguous. In the course of discussing what kinds of "evidence" or signs asylum officers are trained to look for to determine credibility and authenticity, one officer recounted the following case:

> And one time I had a man, this poor guy, he was getting his dates all confused, and he was, like, just all over the place, and it was very . . . and I was like, Gosh, this guy is sooo making up this story on the fly, whatever. And then he described going to jail, and I asked what they do to you, and he said, "They hooked me up to some wires." And I said, "Then what happened?" And then he said, "Then I got really hot." And I was, like, Oh my God, you were electrocuted. Your brain's scrambled eggs. You can't, you can't give me dates, whatever. But unfortunately, because the guy was not represented and had no medical evidence at all, I couldn't say he was credible because his dates were a mess. (Asylum officer ID05)

This narrative brings into relief many problematic aspects of the asylum interview and highlights the ambiguity that imbues so much of the adjudication process. If we trace the narrative arc in this short passage, we see the asylum officer moving from suspicion ("I was like, Gosh, this guy is sooo making up this story") to belief ("Oh my God, you were electrocuted") and back to suspicion ("I couldn't say he was credible"). This officer's final judgment of denying credibility comes not from her *subjective* disbelief of the claimant's story but rather from the institutional disciplining of adjudicators that requires "subjective" evidence (e.g., personal testimony) to be corroborated by "objective" data (e.g., medical evidence, legal argument, consistent use of dates). Importantly, we see in this narrative passage an (inter)subjective moment of understanding in which the asylum officer realizes that something *really* did happen to her interviewee, despite his inability to offer a narrative that aligns with the cultural expectations of the politico-legal logic of asylum. It is from the inconsistencies and the untellability of the narrative that the asylum officer apprehends what she recognizes as the truth: the claimant was tortured. Furthermore, the officer understands this to be the reason for his inconsistencies: "Your brain's scrambled eggs. You can't . . . give me dates." And yet this intersubjective moment of understanding through absences, through what was not said, was quickly rendered invisible given the lack of "objective" evidence that could support his perceived credibility. The asylum seeker's inconsistencies of dates quickly shift meaning from being a credible indicator of past persecution (an effect of torture) to the very justification in rendering that episode of persecution invisible as a legitimate claim for recognition.

While this ultimately results in an act of bureaucratic violence—a denial of asylum to a survivor of torture—it is important to note the moment, though fleeting, in which the techniques of knowledge and decision-making typically deployed in the adjudication process fail. Here it is in this moment of the failure of these technologies of truth that the asylum officer understands the claimant's story. However, the authoritative weight given to "consistency" in asylum narratives delegitimizes alternative technologies of knowledge and decision-making that asylum officers may employ. Ultimately, in rendering silent her own (inter)subjective understanding of the claimant's authenticity and credibility, this asylum officer reproduces, albeit ambivalently, the forms of authoritative knowledge that have been previously established (i.e., inconsistencies in dates = lack of credibility). This move exposes the adjudication system, and the credibility determination process in particular, as a method not of getting at the truth but as "a means for constructing what the Truth is" (Beard and Noll 2009, 457).

CORROBORATING CREDIBILITY

Merry and Coutin (2014), in their discussion of technologies of measurement (e.g., census, audit), suggest that "interior, relatively subjective phenomenon" often confound classification and are therefore "gauged by something more objective" (12). Likewise, asylum officers reported that they sought out "objective" measures to corroborate—or refute—"subjective" phenomena such as emotional displays. Throughout my conversations with asylum officers, they attempted to frame credibility assessments as an objective and analytic process, even as they simultaneously acknowledged their highly interpretive and subjective nature. To this end, they stressed the need to "verify" a claimant's testimony with "factual evidence" provided by external documents such as State Department reports on country conditions. Given adjudicators' perception of oral and written testimony as too subjective, they often searched for external ways to discern credibility. While the use of resources such as the State Department reports could be seen as a way to triangulate data, officers instead framed this as the need to affirm or negate a claimant's *subjective* testimony of suffering and persecution with a putatively *objective* source (see Lawrance, this volume). This echoes arguments made by Miriam Ticktin (2011) and Didier Fassin and Richard Rechtman (2009), who have traced the historical and cultural trajectory by which asylum seekers' own testimonies carry increasingly less legitimacy in the legal and political arenas and are often subordinated to other forms of expertise or evidence (see also Lawrance and Ruffer 2015).

In my interviews with asylum officers, all of them stressed the importance of country conditions research, particularly State Department reports, for testing and establishing an applicant's credibility. Recent legal scholarship, however, has pointed to the "wildly varying degrees of deference" given to State Department country reports by immigration judges (Walker 2007, 4). Critics argue that the reports are often "used as a crutch" in the legal arena (Floss 2006, 250) and that they have been problematically used "as dispositive rejections of the asylum applicant's admittedly credible personal testimony" (Walker 2007, 4). Another source of (putatively) "objective" data used to corroborate credibility by adjudicators was external documentation that could constitute "evidence," such as political membership cards, affidavits from witnesses or family members attesting to the applicant's persecution, police records, and so forth. This was the case despite the fact that, in theory, asylum may be granted based solely on a claimant's testimony. In practice, however, both asylum officials and lawyers and legal advocates told me that this is rarely the case. Indeed, as one asylum officer told me, "anything that corroborates a story will help."

Despite officers' attempts at framing external documentation as "objective," in practice the assessment of documentation, like the assessment of written and oral testimony, was fraught with paradoxes and ambiguities that made this a much more slippery domain for adjudicators:

> It's more challenging to be from a country where fake documents are readily accessible, because you just can't believe them. And they might have perfectly nice documents, and we're going to be like, "Yeah, but you're from Cameroon." You know. It's more suspect. So I think they have a harder time proving their case. (Asylum officer ID13)

> I mean, sometimes the more documents you have the less likely it might be to believe a story. I mean, if someone says that the militia came and set fire to her house but then you have all these documents. "Well, how'd you get these documents if your house was on fire, and it was this really quick thing that was happening?" (Asylum officer ID08)

If material evidence such as identification documents was met with suspicion, evidence attesting to trauma was an even more significant source of mistrust and ambivalence.

"YOU DON'T KNOW WHAT'S REAL AND WHAT'S NOT": TRAUMA, CREDIBILITY, AND SUSPICION

Fassin and colleagues (2005, 2007, 2009) have examined the devaluation of asylum seekers' personal testimonies within the political asylum process in France. In the French asylum context, Fassin and Rechtman (2009) argue, the diagnostic category of posttraumatic stress disorder (PTSD) marks "an end to suspicion," and a medical certificate attesting to an asylum seeker's past trauma may constitute "proof" of persecution (77). The concept of trauma and its related diagnosis of PTSD were certainly salient themes in my interviews with asylum officers. However, in contrast to Fassin and Rechtman's (2009) argument, trauma and PTSD emerged as much more contentious issues in my research site. Asylum officers were ambivalent about the use of psychiatric and psychological evaluations and their ability—or not—to corroborate claims of credibility and assist in discerning genuine asylum seekers from fraudulent ones. Some officers articulated giving more weight to these evaluations. For example, one officer told me, "It's almost sickening that the more trauma the better in a weird sense—the more obvious their eligibility." Other asylum officers articulated their perspectives on psychiatric evaluations:

> I find it [a psychiatric/psychological evaluation] very helpful because it gives me something to kind of hang my hat on. I mean it gives me one more legal tool that I can say look here, you know, they may be telling me the truth even though they can't tell me the story. (Asylum officer ID04)

> [Psychological/psychiatric evaluations] are helpful for showing how much injury they've suffered, how bad the harm has been to them. Also, kind of, it bolsters credibility in that, you know—they're telling a psychologist the same thing they're telling me. (Asylum officer ID09)

While these narratives suggest that some officers made a connection between psychological evaluations, psychiatric diagnoses, and both credibility and eligibility, they do so for various reasons. The idea that "more trauma" allows eligibility to become more evident echoes Fassin (2005, 2007) and Ticktin (2006, 2011) in positing the subjectification of a suffering and traumatized body as an authentic, legitimate, and hence deserving body. The officer who suggested that psychological evaluations give her "something to kind of hang [her] hat on" does not necessarily link trauma with credibility. Rather, this officer frames the evaluation as "one more tool" in which to interpret demeanor within the asylum interview. Other officers reiterated this aspect of the evaluations, arguing that while the evaluations may not bolster credibility, being aware of trauma or PTSD allows them, as adjudicators, to adjust their style of interviewing, including taking more time, being sure to have extra tissues available, speaking in a softer voice, or, as one officer put it, "trying to have a little bit more sensitivity."

Finally, the asylum officer who claimed that a psychological evaluation helps to bolster credibility (ID09) points to the ways in which an evaluation may be approached as evidence in which to compare and test for inconsistencies or omissions of information. In other words, this officer did not claim that the trauma diagnosis bolsters a claimant's credibility per se but rather that the possibility of finding consistent testimony between the psychiatric evaluation and what he hears in his interview with the claimant is helpful in credibility determinations. However, there can be detrimental unintended consequences from the submission of these evaluations: a psychiatric evaluation can also be source of inconsistencies and thus used as a way to weaken or even disprove credibility.

Overall, asylum officers expressed suspicion regarding claims of trauma during their interviews and had mixed feelings about how much weight to accord to trauma and psychiatric diagnoses in assessing applicants' eligibility and credibility:

> I don't know, it seems like everybody says they have PTSD and depression. . . . So, it's kind of like "meh." You don't know what's real, what's not. (Asylum officer ID08)

> I think it's [submission of psychological evaluations] helpful to some extent. Like, we'll get things [psychological evaluations] from [a local human rights organization]. I think it's helpful to know, too, that a lot of times, at least with those types of organizations, there's a level of vetting that goes on too. So that could be helpful or not helpful, because either the person has been vetted and is clearly credible to these people the whole time, or they've gotten more time to practice their story. So it's kind of a mix. (Asylum officer ID02)

> Well, if I have read their statement . . . I can compare what they're telling me now to what they've written before, and most of the time people stay consistent, but sometimes it's like "You say here you were arrested three times, and you're telling me it was only twice." And they'll go (in exaggerated voice), "Oh, yeah, I forgot" or something like that. And you're like, "Hmmmm. Why did you forget?" And they say (in a sarcastic voice) "The trauma," and I'm like, "Oh, okay" (speaking in sarcastic, skeptical tone and rolling eyes). (Asylum officer ID03)

The first exchange related above (with ID08), in which the asylum officer wonders whether or not an applicant's claim to PTSD or depression was "real" perhaps reflects the "PTSD fatigue" that a local attorney claimed to affect adjudicators. A PTSD diagnosis here is approached dubiously. And though the frequency with which asylum seekers report PTSD and depression is reported in the psychological and psychiatric literature, in practice the perceived ubiquity of such diagnoses actually seems to lessen the importance of these categories within the asylum interview.

WHAT AND WHERE IS THE "REAL"?

While some officers consider psychological evaluations as a way to "bolster credibility," the second narrative presented above (ID02) demonstrates that this is a contested stance. As this officer asserts, "vetting" by psychological organizations can either support credibility claims or can be indicative of a rehearsed (i.e., fraudulent) testimony. The final narrative presented above (ID03), while not speaking directly to the issue of submitted psychological evaluations, nonetheless reflects an overall skepticism or ambivalence on the part of asylum officers regarding the veracity of the concept of trauma as it is employed—here by an asylum claimant herself—within the asylum interview. What this officer hints at, with her sarcastic and skeptical tone, is that assertions of trauma may be a tool to be manipulated by asylum claimants in justifying inconsistencies. Thus, implicit in this officer's narrative is the same ambiguity regarding the realness of claims to trauma and trauma-related diagnoses.

Even for those adjudicators who did not deny the veracity of trauma-related psychiatric disorders, evaluations and psychiatric records attesting to this did not represent an unquestioned form of "proof" of an applicant's eligibility or credibility. The case of Ruth, a Cameroonian asylum seeker and former political activist with whom I worked closely, painfully highlights this. During Ruth's court hearing, her lawyers presented psychological and medical evaluations attesting to the long-term trauma she had suffered in her home country. The evaluations attributed her PTSD, depression, and anxiety, as well as her traumatic brain injury (TBI), to Ruth's reports of detention and torture in Cameroon, claiming that such injuries and disorders were consistent with her testimony. However, immigration officials denied Ruth asylum based on negative credibility findings, primarily based on inconsistencies regarding dates of her injuries as well as an allegedly altered membership card for a political party (the Southern Cameroons National Council [SCNC]). Upon appeal, Ruth's volunteer legal representatives drew attention to the fact that, according to medical records, Ruth suffered from "cognitive deficits, including memory loss, secondary to TBI," as well as PTSD, both factors that could significantly contribute to inconsistencies in testimony.

Ruth's lawyers also stressed that her application included alternative evidence regarding her political party membership (the central aspect of her claim), including an affidavit from the SCNC chairperson in her hometown in Cameroon and receipts from membership dues. The Bureau of Immigration Appeals (BIA) was not persuaded and upheld the original adjudicator's claim that "the fact that [Ruth's] SCNC card is not believable casts major doubt on the whole of her claim." With regard to the psychiatric diagnoses and TBI, the BIA stated, "The fact that the respondent has suffered a traumatic brain injury does not establish that she was credible about the source of that injury, or her alleged political affiliations."

Ruth's case suggests two important factors regarding how concepts of trauma and credibility are interpreted and assessed within the legal process. First, Ruth's case demonstrates that PTSD—or even a TBI—does not represent an end to suspicion in asylum cases (Fassin and Rechtman 2009, 77). Even if the veracity of "trauma" or psychiatric diagnoses were not questioned, many adjudicators nonetheless viewed these categories as too subjective, precisely because the source of trauma or disorder was, to some extent, open to interpretation. Stuart L. Lustig (2008) has argued this point, positing that the difficulty in discerning the source of trauma for adjudicators (e.g., does PTSD result from political persecution or the act of flight and/or culture shock?) leads to less of a reliance on psychological or psychiatric evidence.

Second, because of the perceived subjective nature of psychological evaluations and psychiatric diagnoses offered as evidence, inconsistencies in asylum seekers' interviews or hearings (either inconsistencies within oral and written testimony or inconsistencies between testimony and country conditions documents) seemed to trump psychiatric evidence. That is, inconsistencies in testimony appeared to serve as greater evidence of a lack of deservingness than did trauma and trauma-related disorders in indicating deservingness.

MEDIATING THE WEIGHT OF AN IMPOSSIBLE JOB

Asylum officers ultimately conceded, either explicitly or implicitly, that assessing credibility and adjudicating claims were fluid, subjective, and fallible procedures, despite attempts to make it as "objective" a process as possible. The technologies of knowledge deployed in the adjudication process were often engaged ambivalently by asylum officers, setting in motion a cycle of paradox and mistrust. Documents represented concrete, "objective" evidence, yet these could be fraudulent. Emotions could reveal to adjudicators the authentic interior states of claimants, but such affective displays could be merely strategic performances, and their sources could be unknown. Psychiatric diagnoses and invocations of "trauma" could add legitimacy to a claim or be dismissed as "too subjective." Indeterminacy characterized myriad elements of the adjudication process, and yet the credibility assessment as a technology of truth works to "produce certainties out of ambiguous and contested situations" (Merry and Coutin 2014, 2).

ADJUDICATORS' AMBIVALENT POSITIONS OF POWER

Attention to moments of ambivalence in the adjudication process illustrates that the object of suspicion is not limited to the asylum claimant. Though often reluctant to admit it, asylum officers also viewed their own judgments with mistrust as well:

> You know, I've come to realize that I don't really know, bottom line. Bottom line, I don't *really* know. I believe I'm a perceptive person and I'm intuitive, but, you know, I can't read a person's mind. . . . I'm not infallible. So I live with it. And, um, well, I live with it. (Asylum officer ID14)

So how do asylum officers "live with it?" How do asylum officers mediate, both inter- and intrapersonally, the demands of their position: discerning between genuine and bogus asylum seekers? In closing, I highlight some ways in which I observed asylum officers responding to the impossibility of certainty in evaluating stories of profound suffering and pain.

In my interviews with these asylum officers, I noted that they readily owned their decisions to grant asylum, especially to those whom they felt were "genuinely deserving." Declarations such as "saving somebody's life" or "helping somebody in a very real sense" were common when officers described their jobs. However, they would often distance themselves from cases that they denied, thus demonstrating an ambivalent relationship to their own authority and power. For example, asylum officers emphasized repeatedly that claimants get "two bites of the apple." Here, they are referring to the fact that most asylum seekers can have their case heard by an immigration judge if an asylum officer denies them. While highlighting the power of immigration judges may have served to undermine asylum officers' authority as decision-makers, it simultaneously abdicated them from the ultimate responsibility of denying someone legal status.

The language that asylum officers used performed the social and moral work of both emotional detachment and the abdication of ultimate responsibility. More specifically, asylum officers would often frame asylum as a "benefit" or "service" to which an asylum claimant must prove his or her "entitlement," with one asylum officer explaining succinctly, "It's our job not to bestow a benefit on somebody that's not deserving." In echoing this sentiment, another officer insisted that asylum "is not a charity . . . this is not a hand-out" and that applicants must "demonstrate that they qualify for the benefit that they seek." An additional, senior asylum officer summed it up in this way:

> You know, in the final analysis, my take is, um, there's a community that we work for. Yeah, we work for the applicants, okay, but they're just applicants. Until they've demonstrated they're true refugees, then we will accord them the benefits they seek. Until then, they're coming to us, and they want something from us. When they demonstrate they deserve it, then they become, from my point of view, a customer. . . . They're an applicant until they become a customer. . . . I will extend every courtesy and cordiality and all the rights that they're entitled to. But I don't believe that I'm dealing with customers. I mean . . . we are a *service*, but we provide the service to those who have demonstrated they are *entitled* to that service. So my biggest challenge has always been granting somebody who ought not to be granted and referring or denying somebody who should be granted. (Asylum officer ID04; emphasis added)

While the language of "benefits," "services," and "customers" is perhaps not surprising given the neoliberal American context, I am interested in the moral value of such a framework. This rhetoric allows for an affective distancing of the asylum officer from the claimant. For example, the following quote from a senior asylum officer demonstrates how the asylum-as-benefit framework was invoked in light of the emotionally charged exchanges with asylum claimants:

> They [applicants] beg—they're begging you, "Please, please." I want to be like, "I'm not the queen, you know. I have to follow the rules and whatever. It's not *me* giving it to you. It's *you* qualifying." (Asylum officer ID08)

Here, using the implicit framework of asylum as service or benefit supports the asylum officer's emphasis that the burden is on asylum claimants to prove their case. This effectively shifts responsibility of a denial from the adjudicator to the claimant, who was purportedly unable to convince the officer of his or her deservingness or qualification of status. The following, final quote from a senior asylum officer illustrates the struggle officers engage in to distance themselves from claimants while acknowledging that the reality of their decisions are, truly, matters of life and death:

> A lot of times I'll tell the new officers when they get here it's like you have to be able to divorce yourself if you want to be able to sleep at night. You make a decision—the best decision you can based on the information you have at hand. And you let it lie. You know, our job is to try to help the people. But we're not the ones who are harming them. So, you know . . . they still have the burden to make their case. And if we decide against them . . . all right, you can't sit there and second-guess yourself that they're going to be deported and go back and be killed. Because certainly that may happen. But you're still not the one killing them. You're not the one doing this to them. Somebody else is. (Asylum officer ID15)

Cécile Rousseau and her colleagues (2002) have examined the refugee determination process in Canada and suggested that adjudicators may suffer from "vicarious traumatization," a process parallel to countertransference in the therapeutic setting, where denial of refugees' testimonies is one response. Adjudicators' vicarious traumatization contributes to a collective "culture of disbelief" in which refugee claimants are denied at high rates because of a perceived lack of credibility. While I am not arguing here that asylum officers in my research site suffer from such vicarious traumatization (though they may), Rousseau et alia's work (2002, 2004) is instructive here in underscoring the thoroughly intersubjective nature of asylum interviews and the impact that such encounters have at an institutional level.

The asylum interview is an intersubjective activity in which both asylum officers and asylum claimants attempt to make meaning of narratives of suffering and pain. Asylum claimants must struggle to be understood as worthy and legitimate subjects. Meaning here is cocreated, though in a highly inequitable exchange. To be sure, asylum officers wield a tremendous amount of power, and my research data show that a denial of asylum status (re)shaped not only the material circumstances of asylum seekers' lives but also profoundly mediates their experiences of self and social world.

The language of "benefits," "customers," and "entitlements" may serve to divorce asylum officers from the visceral pain of asylum claimants and the powerful impact that their decisions have on claimants' lives. Yet what are the consequences of such distancing? When asylum seekers become "customers" and the asylum interview a transaction, there are various aspects of asylum seekers' experiences that become muted or effaced. Within the performance and evaluation of asylum claims at stake is the power to define the very contours of claimants' identities and social realities.

Because "any incoming body could be bogus" (Ahmed 2004a, 123), asylum officers adopt a "lens of suspicion" (Bohmer and Shuman 2008) for the adjudication of claims, with the goal of identifying the "bogus." Yet following Ahmed (2004a), because the bogus asylum seeker has no reference (it could be anyone), the adjudication system and the technologies deployed by asylum officers must "stick" to bodies certain social identities and categories. While asylum officers attempted to frame this as an objective process where the true identities of claimants—genuine or fraudulent—are to be uncovered through the "rigor" and "order" of the adjudication process, a closer look at the narratives of asylum officers reveal cracks in this framework. This is most evident in asylum officers' claims that ultimately adjudication relies on one's "gut" or is ultimately "always a judgment call." And yet this subjective core is elided by the insistence that "objective" evidence be brought to bear on elements deemed "too subjective" (affective displays, psychological affidavits, etc.). The cruel irony here is that while emotions of asylum seekers are often deemed too subjective—and hence suspect—to be counted as evidence, it is ultimately often the emotions of asylum officers that serve as a technology of constructing the "truth" about an asylum applicant. Asylum adjudicators use emotion both to dispel and create suspicion (Kobelinsky 2015). Asylum officers' use of their gut or their intuition is problematic in that such modes of apprehending claims represent "hidden practices of decision-making that remain beyond scrunity" (Puumula, Ylikomi, and Ristimäki 2017, 16). Moreover, the routinization of such hidden practices (e.g., the use of one's intuition or the reading of nonverbal cues) ensures that over time these practices gain legitimacy and are uncritically viewed as part of professional knowledge (Jubany 2011, 2017; Puumula, Ylikomi, and Ristimäki 2017).

Close attention to the ambivalence that asylum officers express about their work and the embedded technologies of knowledge and suspicion provides a glimpse into aspects of the performance and interpretation of testimonies that get hidden or rendered silent. (The story of the claimant whose "brain is scrambled eggs" provides an important case in point.) For it is in the breakdowns of knowledge and decision-making that we can better understand the (often invisible) power of technologies of truth—even if enacted and reproduced ambivalently—and the symbolic violence that these technologies may effect. Throughout this process, what goes unacknowledged is the way in which these technologies for getting at the truth actually construct the truth and create social categories and social realities. Confronting this necessitates a consideration of the social and personal injustices that are consequences of the "impossibility" of asylum adjudication.

NOTE

1. This research was generously supported by the National Science Foundation (grant SES 0921535) and the Wenner-Gren Foundation (grant 8026).

REFERENCES

Ahmed, Sara 2004a. "Affective Economies." *Social Text* 79 (22): 117–39.

———. 2004b. *The Cultural Politics of Emotion*. New York: Routledge.

Beard, Jennifer, and Gregor Noll. 2009. "Parrhesia and Credibility: The Sovereign of Refugee Status Determination." *Social and Legal Studies* 18:455–77.

Beneduce, Roberto. 2015. "The Moral Economy of Lying: Subjectcraft, Narrative Capital, and Uncertainty in the Politics of Asylum." *Medical Anthropology* 34 (6): 551–71.

Bohmer, Carol, and Amy Shuman. 2007. "Producing Epistemologies of Ignorance in the Political Asylum Application Process." *Identities: Global Studies in Culture and Power* 14:603–29.

———. 2008. Rejecting Refugees: Political Asylum in the 21st Century. London: Routledge.

Codó, Eva. 2011. "Regimenting Discourse, Controlling Bodies: Disinformation, Evaluation, and Moral Categorization in a State Bureaucratic Agency." *Discourse and Society* 22 (6): 723–42.

Coffey, Guy. 2003. "The Credibility of Credibility Evidence at the Refugee Review Tribunal." *International Journal of Refugee Law* 15 (3): 377–414.

Dauvergne, Catherine 2004. "Making People Illegal." In *Critical Beings: Law, Nation and the Global Subject*, edited by Peter Fitzpatrick and Patricia Tuitt, 83–100. Aldershot, UK: Ashgate.

De Genova, Nicholas P., and Nathalie Peutz, eds. 2010. *The Deportation Regime: Sovereignty, Space, and the Freedom of Movement.* Durham, NC: Duke University Press.

Fassin, Didier, and Estelle D'Halluin. 2005. "The Truth from the Body: Medical Certificates as Ultimate Evidence for Asylum Seekers." *American Anthropologist* 107 (4): 597–608.

———. 2007. "Critical Evidence: The Politics of Trauma in French Asylum Policies." *Ethos* 35 (3): 300–329.

Fassin, Didier, and Richard Rechtman. 2009. *Empire of Trauma: An Inquiry into the Condition of Victimhood.* Princeton, NJ: Princeton University Press.

Floss, John R. 2006. "Seeking Asylum in a Hostile System: The Seventh Circuit Reverses to Confront a Broken Process." *Seventh Circuit Review* 216: 216–71.

Herlihy, Jane, Peter Scragg, and Stuart Turner. 2002. "Discrepancies in Autobiographical Memories: Implications for the Assessment of Asylum Seekers; Repeated Interview Study." *British Medical Journal* 324 (7333): 324–27.

Holmes, Seth M., and Heide Castañeda. 2016. "Representing the 'European Refugee Crisis' in Germany and Beyond: Deservingness and Difference, Life and Death." *American Ethnologist* 43 (1): 12–24.

Jacquemet, Marco. 2011. "Crosstalk 2.0: Asylum and Communicative Breakdowns." *Text and Talk* 31 (4): 475–97.

Jubany, Olga. 2011. "Constructing Truths in a Culture of Disbelief: Understanding Asylum Screening from Within." *International Sociology* 26 (1): 74–94.

———. 2017. Screening Asylum in a Culture of Disbelief: Truths, Denials, and Skeptical Borders. Cham, Switzerland: Palgrave Macmillan.

Kagan, Michael. 2003. "Is Truth in the Eye of the Beholder? Objective Credibility Assessment in Refugee Status Determination." *Georgetown Immigration Law Journal* 17:367–415.

Kobelinsky, Carolina. 2015. "Emotions as Evidence: Hearings in a French Asylum Court." In *Of Doubt and Proof: Ritual and Legal Practices of Judgment*, edited by Daniela Berti, Anthony Good, and Gilles Tarabout, 163–82. New York: Routledge.

Lawrance, Benjamin N., and Gayla Ruffer, eds. 2015. *Adjudicating Refugee and Asylum Status: The Role of Witness, Expertise, and Testimony.* Cambridge: Cambridge University Press.

Lustig, Stuart L. 2008. "Symptoms of Trauma among Political Asylum Applicants: Don't Be Fooled." *Hastings International and Comparative Law Review* 725:729–33.

McKinnon, Sara L. 2009. "Citizenship and the Performance of Credibility: Audiencing Gender-Based Asylum Seekers in U.S. Immigration Courts." *Text and Performance Quarterly* 29 (3): 205–21.

Merry, Sally Engle, and S. B. Coutin. 2014. "Technologies of Truth in the Anthropology of Conflict." *American Ethnologist* 41 (1): 1–16.

Myers, Fred (1979). "Emotions and the Self: A Theory of Personhood and Political Order among Pintupi Aborigines." *Ethos* 7 (4): 343–70.

Puumula, Eeva, Riita Ylikomi, and Hanna-Leena Ristimäki. 2017. "Giving an Account of Persecution: The Dynamic Formation of Asylum Narratives." *Journal of Refugee Studies* 31 (2): 197–215.

Rempell, Scott. 2009. "Credibility Assessments and the REAL ID Act's Amendments to Immigration Law." *Texas International Law Journal* 44:185–232.

Rousseau, Cécile, François Crépeau, Patricia Foxen, and France Houle. 2002. "The Complexity of Determining Refugeehood: A Multidisciplinary Analysis of the Decision-Making Process of the Canadian Immigration and Refugee Board." *Journal of Refugee Studies* 15 (1): 43–70.

Rousseau, Cécile, Marie-Claire Rufagari, Déogratias Bagilishya, and Toby Measham. 2004. Remaking Family Life: Strategies for Re-establishing Continuity among Congolese Refugees during the Family Reunification Process." *Social Science and Medicine* 59:1095–108.

Schroeder, Jeanette L. 2017. "The Vulnerability of Asylum Adjudications to Subconscious Cultural Biases: Demanding American Narrative Norms." *Boston University Law Review* 97 (315): 315–48.

Squire, Victoria. 2009. *The Exclusionary Politics of Asylum*. London: Palgrave Macmillan.

Thomas, Robert. 2006. "Assessing the Credibility of Asylum Claims: EU and UK Approaches Examined." *European Journal of Migration and Law* 8:79–96.

Ticktin, Miriam. 2006. "Where Ethics and Politics Meet: The Violence of Humanitarianism in France." *American Ethnologist* 33:33–49.

———. 2011. *Casualties of Care: Immigration and the Politics of Humanitarianism in France*. Berkeley: University of California Press.

Vedsted-Hansen, Jens. 2005. "The Borderline between Questions of Fact and Questions of Law." In *Proof, Evidentiary Assessment and Credibility in Asylum Procedures*, edited by Gregor Noll, 57–66. Leiden: Martinus Nijhoff.

Walker, Eliot. 2007. "Asylees in Wonderland: A New Procedural Perspective on America's Asylum System." *Northwestern Journal of Law and Social Policy* 2 (1): 1–29.

Welch, Michael, and Liza Schuster. 2008. "American and British Constructions of Asylum Seekers: Moral Panic, Detention, and Human Rights." In *Keeping Out the Other: A Critical Introduction to Immigration Enforcement Today*, edited by David C. Brotherton and Philip Kretsedemas, 138–60. New York: Columbia University Press.

Willen, Sarah S. 2012. "Migration, 'Illegality,' and Health: Mapping Embodied Vulnerability and Debating Health-Related Deservingness." *Social Science and Medicine* 74 (6): 805–11.

Yarris, Kristen, and Heide Castañeda. 2015. "Introduction to Special Issue: Discourses of Displacement and Deservingness: Interrogating Distinctions between 'Economic' and 'Forced' Migration." *International Migration* 53 (3): 64–69.

Zimmerman, Susan E. 2011. "Reconsidering the Problem of 'Bogus' Refugees with 'Socio-economic Motivations' for Seeking Asylum." *Mobilities* 6 (3): 335–52.

Chapter 5

Country of Origin Information, Technologies of Suspicion, and the Erasure of the Supernatural in African Refugee Claims

BENJAMIN N. LAWRANCE

In 2009, the adherents of a vodou priest (*bokono*) kidnapped Dopé in Cotonou, Benin, and brought her to the *atikevodou* (healing vodou) shrine of Sakpata near Cové, where she was imprisoned and raped.[1] After several weeks, Dopé, an educated, married mother, escaped to her husband and then fled to the United States to seek asylum. She believed her experiences were the result of her childhood betrothal as *trokosi*, a form of inheritable religious debt slavery, exacted as punishment for her mother's infidelity. Dopé's supernatural narrative troubled her lawyers, who feared no judge would consider it credible. They reframed her claim by documenting misogynistic forced-marriage practices, sexual assault, child abuse, child slavery, and the widespread belief in levirate (widow remarriage to husband's kin) in Benin. Her lawyers chose gender-violence arguments coupled with established precedent pertaining to slavery and trafficking as a strategy to avoid foregrounding the discussion of vodou, often considered a form of witchcraft by adjudicators.

Dopé's experience, like those of other women whose testimonies I have been asked to evaluate, is emblematic of legal strategies unfolding in response to the increasing securitization of migration (Squire 2009) and new technologies of adjudication (Lawrance and Ruffer 2015a). Until the 1980s, refugee and asylum legal procedures operated within an informal climate of trust, and applicants were generally presumed to be telling the truth. Customized research—such as expert testimony from scholars or professionals (Lawrance et al. 2015) or medical reports (Lawrance 2013, 2015; Wylie and Wallace 2014)—was almost unheard of. Since the 1980s, however, significant global geopolitical changes—including, but not limited to, the end of the Cold War and the expansion of globalized transnational technologies—have conspired to turn the refugee experience upside down. The refugee status determination (RSD) process is now overshadowed by a "climate of suspicion, in which the refugee or asylum seeker is seen as someone trying to take advantage of the country's hospitality" (Fassin and D'Halluin 2005, 600).

A "hermeneutics of suspicion" (Ricœur 1970; Gadamer 1984; Stewart 1989; Kessler 2005) characterizes asylum and refugee proceedings and gives rise to new technologies (Lawrance and Ruffer 2015a). One such technology, data referred to as "country of origin information," or COI, has become central to "testing" asylum narratives (Good 2015), and increasingly it features in so-called "credibility assessments" (Cohen 2002; Thomas 2006). Adjudicators increasingly emphasize the importance of empirical research in establishing claimant credibility (UNHCR 2013; CREDO 2013). Claims and counterclaims must be anchored by objective data (such as verification of party membership) or publicly sourced information (such as verification of a riot or bombing), and arguments substantiated by scholarly evidence (such as plausibility of forms of persecution). This dramatic transformation in asylum procedure partly explains why lawyers reshape their clients' narratives, as they are seeking to interface with the increasing reliance on expertise (see Lawrance and Walker-Said 2016).

COI has emerged as a specialized knowledge category that attempts to answer, with empirical data, the central matter of refugee law—namely, who is a refugee? As Jean-François Lyotard (1983) explained, the burden resting on individual asylum seekers to prove claims that often cannot be documented is a "wrong" but one that is "accompanied by the loss of means to prove the damage" (5). The temptation to stretch, embellish, or invent narratives that conform to asylum law is thus enormous. Cross-cultural and cross-linguistics communication barriers coupled with physical and psychological traumas add considerable complexity (Einhorn and Bertoldt 2015; Smith, Lustig, and Gangsei 2015), making inconsistency part and parcel of the process of narration (Cohen 2002). Indeed, the borderline between "political" and "economic" refugees is very difficult to determine (Derrida 2001,12).

This chapter explores how one particular technology of suspicion, when applied to supernatural narratives embedded in the asylum claims, disrupts prevailing refugee practices with unsettling consequences for claimants and their capacity to narrate their own truth. The disjuncture between the initial narration of the experience by the refugee on the one hand and the process of translation via lawyers and expert witnesses appearing before adjudicators on the other has opened a space for the growth of "credibility assessments" and a proliferation of COI research methods and practices. Here I explore the relationship between credibility and COI and consider why COI has come to occupy such a prominent role in the context of supernatural narratives. Constraints of refugee-convention definitions of protection compel lawyers to marginalize witchcraft, vodou, and related supernatural practices and to foreground other elements of the claims, which, they opine, may be more effectively supported by expert evidence and COI. But, in so doing, the strategies of lawyers, the prejudices of adjudicators, and the refugee conventions broadly understood subject terrified individuals to further bureaucratic violence.

CONTEXTUALIZING SUPERNATURAL ASYLUM CLAIMS

Recent scholarship on the supernatural in Africa—including but not limited to practices described as magic, sorcery, and witchcraft—has returned to the distinction, first articulated by E. E. Evans-Pritchard (1976), between external and somatic supernatural power. Witchcraft, the preeminent folk terminology for the supernatural, is much more public in Africa today (Geschiere 2008) and features in political and social debate (West 2007). Witchcraft-driven violence challenges sociopolitical order with a variety of political and legislative outcomes (see Comaroff and

Comaroff 1993; Geschiere 1997; Ashforth 2005; Luongo 2011). Witchcraft and sorcery "denote a continuum ranging from supernatural malevolence to supernatural healing" (Luongo 2015, 186). Harry West (2005) describes Mozambique's Muedan Plateau as a "world of sorcery filled with shades of gray" (77). By contrast, however, in the "global arena of asylum," according to Katherine Luongo (2015), "no ambiguity about witchcraft or witches exists" (186, 187). Witchcraft operates as an "embodied capacity" to "harm" (Luongo 2011, 9). And in asylum claims, witchcraft has "an uncomfortable ahistoricity and an awkward detachment from institutions" (Luongo 2015, 187).

Supernatural allegations are as complex a site for refugee adjudicators as they are for scholars but for different reasons. As Luongo (2015) explains, claims for protection from "the threat of violence driven by witchcraft" often appear "extraordinary" at "first glance" (183). Immigration authorities "struggle with" witchcraft as a "unit of analysis," viewing both allegations of *and* expert testimony about sorcery "with institutionalized incredulity" (185). Claims from Nigeria and Tanzania, for example, assessed by the Immigration Review Board in Canada were rejected throughout the early 2000s because the violence described by the refugees was not considered a convention-anchored basis for protection. Notwithstanding these early rejections of claims, increasing numbers of refugee claims in Canada, Australia, the United Kingdom, and elsewhere describing "witchcraft as an engine of violence" (183) strongly suggest that African asylum seekers "have engaged the official rhetoric of refugee protection" and are developing a sui generis "particular social group" jurisprudence to enable protection (184).

Asylum seekers are often uncomfortable divulging the full details of the supernatural realm, but generally speaking it is my experience that many are confident that their experiences mark them as constitutive of a protected "particular social group" (Millbank 2009). Luongo's analysis examined cases in which witchcraft is front and center. I have received solicitations to write about cases that mirror some of those she has analyzed. In one recent example from Nigeria, addressed directly to me by email, an individual from Nigeria described himself as "a witch" and described his fear that he was to be "killed with black magic." But in contrast with the published cases analyzed by Luongo, here I examine asylum claims in which the supernatural is only one facet in a multidimensional case. By selecting such cases, I seek to sidestep the ongoing debate concerning the evolution of the definition of the "particular social group" basis for asylum (see Helton 1983; Graves 1989;

Musalo 2003) and the position of the supernatural (Schnoebelen 2009; Bruynell 2012) and instead to focus on how and under what conditions African spiritual practices are viewed as lacking credibility and rendered insufficient for refugee protection. Examples from Ghana, Togo, Burkina Faso, and Benin, from at least ten represented to me by attorneys, illustrate several dimensions of this bureaucratic violence.

CREDIBILITY AND COI

Before considering credibility in the context of supernatural asylum claims, how credibility became the shibboleth it currently is merits some consideration. Assessing credibility has emerged as site of administrative and governmental attention because it reveals the unbounded, unanchored dimensions of the legal predicament of the refugee. Refugee law draws on criminal (Byrne 2005, 180), administrative, and civil law, and unevenly so; it is not simply human rights practice or international humanitarian law. The measurement of consistency and plausibility of refugee narratives can never be an exact science, and "how much" (Sweeney 2009) of one or the other depends on a variety of factors. RSD operates within an unbounded legal domain and in a constant state of flux, the unanchored nature of which is revealed by policies, procedures, standards, and practices, many of which are themselves the subject of legal challenges, judicial review, and international mandates and criticism.

The central elements of credibility, as discerned by Michael Kagan (2003), may be separated into "positive" and "negative" factors that are accorded probative weight in adjudication. The positive factors consist of detail, specificity, consistency, furnishing all facts early in the proceeding, and the general plausibility of the account. The negative factors are vagueness, contradiction, delayed revelation of details and facts, and general implausibility. These powerfully probative criteria, however, may not be divorced from the multiplicity of contexts of production, beginning with the first interview upon arrival or detention, via multiple rounds of statements and court and appellate testimony. As Rosemary Byrne (2005) observes, asylum seekers "must deliver their testimony credibly, and must be found credible in differing contexts" (179).

Credibility assessment speaks to a central tension embodied in asylum seekers, insofar as they are thrust between the imagined and idealized protections of refugee law and national realities and arbitrariness of domestic immigration control. Credibility draws attention to the "intensely narrative mode" (Millbank 2009, 1) of the adjudicatory power of RSD and central importance of communication (Doornbos 2005). Robert Thomas (2006) explains the central tension thus: On the one hand, recognizing "genuine claimants is to fulfil the humanitarian objectives of the convention and protect fundamental human rights" (80). On the other hand, "the decision-maker" is also "concerned to ensure that non-genuine applicants are refused in order to maintain ordinary immigration control" (80). But as Kagan (2003) has observed, assessments of credibility, "often the single most important step" in adjudication, are "frequently based on personal judgment that is inconsistent from one adjudicator to the next" (367, 378).

Decisions about a "well-founded fear of being persecuted," as required by the United Nations' 1951 Convention Relating to the Status of Refugees, increasingly depend on COI about an applicant's origin country's history and prevailing situation (UNHCR 2013). For the purpose of RSD, external consistency necessitates that adjudicators evaluate new claims against COI (Good 2015). Adjudicators must decide not only whether an uncorroborated story appears *internally credible* but also that it is *externally consistent* with available COI (Weston 1998; UKBA n.d., para. 4.3). Novel or unusual claims are subject to additional scrutiny, and they provoke COI requests from refugee officers or judges to COI directorates. The United Nations High Commissioner for Refugees requires that COI be publicly accessible to all parties.

Despite the increasing prominence of COI data in RSD globally, limited attention has been paid to the definition of and practices surrounding its emergence, collection, and use. The European Country of Origin Information Network, for example, defined COI merely as "information on conditions in countries of origin of asylum seekers" (ecoi.net 2013). The UK Border Agency (UKBA, replaced in 2013 by UK Visa and Immigration), while giving an equally broad definition, explains that its focus is on COI concerning "human rights issues and matters frequently raised in asylum and human rights claims" (UKBA n.d.). It is now widely recognized that COI figures importantly in RSD globally (ARC 2013), yet how the specific research practices, mechanisms, and standards contribute to a definition remain unexplained. Isolated national processes have been described (Rousseau et al. 2002; ACCORD 2013), but the national differentiation in terms of production and employment (Gyulai 2011, 7) remain undocumented.

COI appears to have emerged domestically and unevenly from international law. Contemporary refugee and asylum law, defined in the wake of World War II, rests on the 1951 refugee convention and its 1967 protocol. Only with the protocol was "refugee" status expanded to include populations outside Europe and to events occurring after January 1, 1951. These instruments have been domesticated with varying degrees of success throughout the globe (Goodwin-Gill 1999; Barutciski 2002; Kagan 2006). While these guidelines may appear straightforward, apart from the challenges of verifying the stories of events that occurred thousands of miles away, other aspects of the law also leave room for ambiguity: how to define a "well-founded fear of persecution" or "membership in a particular social group" and what constitutes "political opinion."

A commitment to empiricism resides at the heart of COI, but its compilation, indexing, databasing, storage, and ultimately its implementation in adjudication is complicated by national anxieties about the volume of migration (see Gibney 2008; De Genova and Peutz 2010; Kanstroom 2012). Whereas each asylum seeker's claim is considered on its merits, decisions based on COI may become "precedent-setting" and influence other decisions (Good 2015). Attempts to investigate and prove aspects of one particular case may subsequently become the benchmark and determine the parameters of ensuing claims (Kassindja and Bashir 1998; Musalo 1998; Piot 2007), seemingly regardless of the domestic legal system in operation. Embedded within asylum and refugee narratives and their successive iterations in rulings, judgments, COI information, appeals, and precedents are analytical categories, constructed identities, and personal narratives of fear, trauma, and jeopardy.

COI operates within the constraints imposed by national legal processes, but these limitations are opaque at best. COI operates as an "institutional setting" for complex "transnational connections" (Radcliffe 2001, 20) that "reproduce" state power (Stevens 1999) and functionality. Research on expert testimony offers some insight into how to locate COI's limitations. Expert testimony seeks to render refugees recognizable according to social and political norms configuring the present-day rule of law and thus to lead to the courts' recognition of claimants as worthy of asylum (Good 2004a,

2004b). In the United Kingdom, courts routinely seek to "constrain the expert's influence, through such means as the 'hearsay rule' . . . and the 'ultimate issue' rule, which prevents witnesses from giving opinions on the main issues at stake" (Good 2008, sec. 48). The parallel is especially cogent because COI, like expert testimony, contributes to the reframing of asylum seekers' narratives as legal evidence in order to fit them into the host country's applicable rules of law. In so doing COI decontextualizes the claimant from his or her social and political subjectivity, erases personal experience, and subjects the refugee to bureaucratic violence.

SUPERNATURAL REFUGEE NARRATIVES

Asylum claims in which the supernatural is only one facet in a multidimensional case enable us to avoid entering into the rich but frustrating debate about what constitutes a particular social group basis for asylum. Four examples illustrate four particular dimensions of how African spiritual practices are rarely viewed as religion per se for the purpose of refugee protection. Akosua from Ghana draws attention to whether or not magic is an external extrafamilial force. Konda's narrative from Togo further unsettles the line between family and community in supernatural narratives. Dopé's experience in Benin, with which I began this chapter, highlights how supernatural belief is not confined to lower socioeconomic echelons. And Aliyah's story from Burkina Faso draws attention to how documenting the materiality of the supernatural realm subversively destabilizes the legitimacy of supernatural religious practice.

Akosua

The first supernatural story troubles common perceptions that magic is an external extrafamilial force. Akosua, from Ghana, fled in the mid-2000s to the United Kingdom and claimed asylum. She was a young woman in her late teens and the youngest of several siblings. In her first statement, she described the immediate cause of her flight from a village in the Volta Region via Accra to London as an attempt to force her into a marriage to an elderly man (*afeto*) several years earlier, while she was still a child. In her fuller subsequent narrative, however, she described how she was first conveyed to the man who lived either by or in a vodou shrine. Upon closer scrutiny, it became apparent that her forced marriage began as an act of trafficking, insofar as her parents sold her for a previously negotiated bride-price, and they then paid a third party to have her physically conveyed to the afeto. Her experience then became one of enslavement to a shrine in a manner akin to trokosi in southeastern Ghana.

Whereas her description of her experience in the shrine was consistent with scholarly and media accounts of victims of trokosi enslavement and trafficking for labor and sexual exploitation, subsequent events explain how her narrative became more problematic. Before the attempted marriage ceremony, the afeto fell ill. Akosua assumes that the afeto's family took him to a shrine outside their village and that the shrine's bokono deduced that his illness was the result of black magic performed by Akosua because the young woman was disinclined to marry. Akosua was physically conveyed to the same shrine, where she was accused being a witch and of causing his illness and also of killing her own father and aunt by magic (she used the word "juju"). Her head was shaved (common both for trokosi initiates and those accused of juju) in the presence of male and female elders; the female elders also performed a cleansing ceremony (*dodédé*). Akosua's asylum claim was rejected at the first-tier tribunal as unfounded because the UKBA contended that such "witch camps" only existed in the north of Ghana, and she was in the southeast where there was no evidence of witch camps.

Konda

A second case concerns a young girl, Konda, who fled Togo while still a minor, blurs the line between magic and the family but in a different way. Konda initially grounded her claim in political activity. In her first adjudication, her opposition political involvement was not believed by the UKBA. Her description of protests, beatings, arrests, imprisonments, rape during detention, and her parents' attempt to coerce her into a union against her will, was rejected in whole as "fallacious." But a second dimension of her case was considered particularly troubling by the UKBA. Konda explained that after some time in Togo, she fled to Benin to reside with her uncle. She then returned to Togo because her uncle's wife (her aunt) performed "black magic." Konda was initially hesitant to divulge this information. She did not provide any information about her aunt in her initial interview. But in a subsequent interview with a Home Office adjudicator, Konda's fear of her aunt was explained as one reason she returned to Togo. Konda was never asked to provide a detailed account of what happened or details about her aunt's threats. Because she had failed to inform the UKBA at the outset about the supernatural dimension, they concluded that the "entire claim" was unbelievable. And because Konda would not divulge the details of the supernatural threats, her fear of her aunt was also not believed.

In response to the UKBA as part of a new appeal, Konda conveyed a much more detailed allegation against her aunt. She explained:

> My Aunt was capable of killing me. She is a witch and people have died mysteriously and there was no reason identified for their deaths so it was decided that she must have been responsible for their deaths. She has killed people and that is why she is a witch. I think that she was a practitioner of voodoo, which is illegal in Togo. She was well known in our area. The police do nothing but people of the villages sometimes chase out people like my Aunt. If I was returned to Togo my family would know where I was and I would be found by my Aunt. She can know what is going on in my head, what I am thinking and feeling and she can know what is going to happen in my future. I believe that my Aunt has in the past been the reason why I may have become ill. She does not practise any good magic only bad magic.[2]

Whereas the UKBA continued to disbelieve Konda's entire narrative, she was granted temporary protection, as a minor, and her case was reheard several years later.

Dopé

The third case, Dopé, with which I opened this chapter, demonstrates how in contrast with many adjudicators perceptions that "primitive beliefs" are the realm of poor and illiterate, the supernatural is not confined to lower socioeconomic echelons. Dopé, an educated, married mother living in the economic capital of Benin, Cotonou, but originally from the village of Cové, fled to the United States after her traumatic experience. Dopé claimed she was kidnapped as an adult in her late twenties by adherents of a bokono and brought to his atikevodou shrine of Sakpata, where she was imprisoned and repeatedly raped. Dopé believed her experiences *as an adult* were the result of her childhood bonding as a trokosi, part of a punishment for her mother's infidelity. Dopé interpreted her predicament to be the result of her public disavowal of the trokosi obligations when she reached maturity. She had been raped and abused by her kidnapper's brother multiple times as a child.

But when she reached maturity, she simply walked from the compound and moved to Cotonou to begin a new life. Whereas the individual to whom she was betrothed had made no attempt to entice her to the shrine, after his death his brother dispatched men to kidnap her, consistent with his understanding of levirate.

In her initial interview, the US asylum officer rejected the idea that educated, literate women practiced vodou. The Bureau of Immigration and Citizenship Services (BCIS) held that only the poor, rural, and illiterate would be involved in sorcery and magic. Drawing on various scholarly and media materials, the BCIS noted that the primarily Yoruba settlement of Cové, in the Zou Department, is the location of a powerful religious community called Egungun. The many religious communities in the area are all tied to variants of the Yoruba religion. These communities share many practices, preeminent among them being the honoring, cultivating, and worship of spirits (*vodou*). Cové is the site of multiple sects and most famously the Gélédé secret society. Ritual enslavement for punishment (trokosi enslavement) is a form of female religious bondage necessitated by debt obligations that is of decreasing prevalence in parts of Ghana, Benin, Togo, and Nigeria, particularly among the Ewe-speaking communities. Trokosi, literally "wives of the spirit Kosi," (see Akyeampong 2001, 221) is one form of *vodounsi* (Brand 2001). While the origins of the institution are somewhat unclear, purportedly egregious cases of exploitation in the 1990s highlighted by local and international human rights organizations brought renewed attention to this form of slavery and sexual abuse.[3]

Aliyah

A final anecdote, from Burkina Faso, highlights the materiality of the supernatural realm, providing substance to claims but also adding additional layers of complexity. Aliyah, a woman in her mid-twenties from a small village near Bobo-Dioulasso, is a survivor of attempted forced genital cutting at the hands of her father and his family and of forced prostitution, trafficking, and attempted forced marriage at the hands of her erstwhile protector, a "madam" in Ouagadougou, the nation's capital. Aliyah's father had informed her at the age of sixteen that she was to be subjected to genital cutting. She subsequently fled her village and became destitute in Ouagadougou. Miriam, an individual who knew Aliyah's late mother, befriended her and took her in. But Aliyah was unaware at the time that she was being groomed for a prostitution network that Miriam ran with the consent of and for the benefit of many highly influential Burkinabe politicians. Miriam sent Aliyah to the United States to marry one of her former clients. But once in the United States, Aliyah claimed asylum. Ever since Aliyah's rejection of the proposed union, Miriam has sent small boxes of strange objects from Burkina Faso in the mail. Aliyah believes she is being subjected to a form of black magic.

Aliyah's boxes of supernatural oddments had the potential to derail an otherwise compelling and multivalent narrative of persecution for several reasons. After spending some time in the southern United States awaiting her adjudication, Aliyah had taken to referring to the boxes of items as "voodoo." Precisely why she adopted this term was never explained to me. But in an exchange with her attorney, I explained that it might make sense to avoid using the word voodoo (or the variants *vodou* and *vaudou*) because these terms are not traditionally associated with Burkina Faso. I explained that if I were trying to translate the experience, I would call it animist practice and animist objects, "black magic" (in quotes), witchcraft, or occult supernatural practice. These suggestions were informed by several considerations. Claims about black magic can often unsettle adjudicators, as Luongo argues. Indeed, the US immigration judge viewed the objects with noticeable discomfort and waved them aside with his hand when they were presented only several feet away. Vernacularization of indigenous terminology can also raise potential red flags. On the one hand, the asylum seeker and his or her counsel are attempting to convey in comprehensible, and perhaps palatable, language meanings that would otherwise be lost on adjudicators with little to no familiarity with a specific region or country, such as Burkina Faso. But on the other hand, adopting a term such as voodoo (perhaps as a result of conversations with African Americans in the South or with other francophone African immigrants) could be interpreted as evidence that Aliyah was lying about her national origin in Burkina Faso.

Assembled together, these four examples reveal several critical dimensions in asylum claims invoking the supernatural as they pertain to credibility. First, from a narrative standpoint, the supernatural is all-encompassing; it can enter conversation at any point, seamlessly, and without warning. The question thus arises: How does the credibility assessment attempt to contain supernatural narratives? Second, the supernatural realm unites and divides families; asylum seekers identify supernatural causes within the family and outside, and equally they can be part of, or thrust from, families as a result. Another question thus arises: How should adjudicators interpret the persecutory context of family supernatural dynamics against the refugee convention's mandate? Third, the supernatural realm knows no social or economic boundaries; it is not confined to asylum seekers of lesser education or with limited exposure to Western, secular, Christian, or other beliefs. A question emerging from this is how to account for the credibility of belief systems vis-à-vis the refugee convention? And finally, the supernatural can present itself as oral testimony but also in a physical and material context. From an evidentiary standpoint, adjudicators are used to examining political party affiliation cards and arrest warrants, but they may now be presented with boxes of seemingly random objects delivered as curses, weapons, or threats. And from this issue, the question emerges of how to weigh evidentiary matters within the wider context of credibility determination. In summary, supernatural asylum claims raise a host of credibility matters that do not easily find solutions.

But what precise elements of supernatural claims are evaluated in credibility assessments? What details are tested? And against what are they tested? When, in the case of Konda, the UKBA held her narrative of her aunt to be fallacious, how was the evaluation or test conducted? What evidence was brought to bear? When Akosua's narrative of being in a camp or enclosure was rejected as not supported by objective evidence, what data was used, and what was its probative value? When Aliyah's box of oddments was pushed aside by the immigration judge, how did his discomfort alter her narrative and her capacity to seek protection? And when Dopé was told to her face that it was implausible that she, as an educated mother and business owner, would be involved in vodou, what assumptions were embedded in the adjudicator's statement? Each of these cases speaks to the various ways in which COI research enters into the adjudicatory process.

COI AND THE ERASURE OF THE SUPERNATURAL

COI is a uniquely national, applied iteration of "global knowledge" (e.g., Mahajan 2008; Rothstein 2009; Keim, Çelik, Ersche, and Wöhner 2014). In response to the expanding evidentiary burdens of RSD, national directorates, independent research centers, nongovernmental organizations

(NGOs), and for-profit companies operating under a spectrum of mandates, self-regulation, national policies, and ideologies have proliferated in the industrialized Global North. COI operations consist of research networks (Riles 2000) employed by government ministries, professional contractors, court clerks, on-the-ground technicians, embassy staff, and contracted freelance academic professionals. COI is a dynamic "science-lay hybrid assemblage" (Delgado 2010, 564) of global knowledge, wherein refugee subjectivities and expert knowledge intermingle on the path toward a determination.

Lawyers ultimately reshaped each of the four cases described here as part of an intentional strategy as the vicissitudes of the adjudicatory process unfolded. Various lawyers, independently of one another, deemed it necessary to downplay the supernatural and elevate established grounds and matters supported by COI. Akosua was a victim of a form of internal (i.e., domestic) human trafficking and domestic violence whereby she was first forced into a marital arrangement against her will with the afeto and subsequently bonded to a fetish shrine for punishment for alleged criminality, an experience that is not uncommon in the region of southeastern Ghana populated by the Ewe ethnic group. While Akosua's story is not representative of the majoritarian trokosi experience, it is nonetheless consistent with practices. Whereas the vast majority of individuals bonded to shrines are bonded for a fixed period or in perpetuity, are prepubescent, and undergo a ceremony in the presence of a bokono and become trokosi, Akosua entered the shrine as a young woman for an unspecified amount of time and as a punishment for her alleged actions—actions that had caused spiritual pollution and shame to her family.

In the case of Dopé, whereas ritual enslavement and vodou may have puzzled an adjudicator, defensively resisting slavery, kidnapping, rape, and imprisonment—in a country where vodou is publicly sanctioned and where the state has designated a "National Voodoo Day"—enters established grounds for particular social group persecution.[4] The constitution and the statutes of Benin prohibit many practices attendant to slavery but importantly make no mention of trokosi and vodounsi, sexual slavery, forced marriage (*mariage forcé*), and sexual assault in the context of marriage. Revisions to the Family Code (Code des Personnes et de la Famille) in 2004 repealed many discriminatory aspects of *Le Coutumier du Dahomey*, the 1931 collection of customs and rules codified during French colonial rule. But while "customary law," as it appears in the *Coutumier*, no longer has the status of law and is no longer recognized by the courts, it remained the case that many "women continue[d] to be subject to the 'Coutumier du Dahomey' which treat[ed] them as legal minors and accord[ed] them limited rights in marriage and inheritance."[5]

At the time of Dopé's hearing, the practice of levirate was documented in Benin.[6] Aspects of Dopé's forced-marriage narrative may have been illegal under the 2004 revision of the Family Code, but the practice of levirate remained quasi-legal insofar as it was not specifically prohibited.[7] The 2004 Family Code explicitly prohibited forced marriage, but there was no evidence of enforcement.[8] And whereas from the mid-1990s the governments of Ghana and Togo made concerted efforts to stamp out the remaining vodounsi, including trokosi, and mediate the relocation and retraining of individuals, Benin passed no similar law.[9] Dopé's legal team thus successfully reassembled her narrative as that of a woman fleeing multiple backward traditional misogynistic practices, at the center of which was a very violent form of forced marriage for which there was no plausible expectation of state protection.

In Konda's case, after attaining maturity, she again petitioned for asylum but included previously omitted components predating and postdating her flight, notably her parents' attempt to lure her back to Togo in order to coerce her into marriage, and her aunt's witchcraft. Whereas the political grounds for the first ruling still held true, Konda's second attempt to remain permanently in the United Kingdom was reframed by the new information about the attempted forced marriage, and her fear of her aunt, the alleged witch, was downplayed. The jeopardy of forced marriage was more or less set aside in Konda's original claim because she was a minor. Moreover, the man's three existing unions were viewed by immigration officials as an indication that he was a morally and legally upstanding citizen, thus diminishing Konda's credibility. After she reached legal maturity and her case was again reviewed, her lawyers considered her political activities to be important but likely insufficient for asylum.

Konda's lawyer made a calculated decision to abandon the supernatural because of the abundant nature of the COI pertaining to forced marriage and a sense that the authorities would treat the black magic dimension with skepticism. Konda wanted to describe her aunt's supernatural powers, and in interviews she explained in depth her aunt's capacity of black magic. Unexplained deaths, unexplained illnesses, and a variety of other tales underscored why Konda was willing to leave her temporary refuge in Benin and return to the threat of coerced marriage in Togo. But her lawyers saw things differently. Instead, her parents' attempt to coerce her into a union was presented as a mechanism with which to ameliorate the damage her political actions had allegedly caused her family. In their attempt to coerce Konda into marriage, her parents arranged for a story to be published in a Togolese biweekly newspaper that gave the impression that she was "lost" (*perdu*) and needed "help" (*assistance*). Konda's parents' narrative portrayed her as a misguided girl who had fallen into bad company and needed rescuing. It was carefully and intentionally designed as a mechanism of entrapment whereby an unwitting bystander or resident seeing Konda might possibly take pity on her and bring her to the authorities. Together the newspaper article and photograph conveyed an unmistakable message to an urban Muslim readership—namely, that she was a runaway bride. Because of the detailed and abundant information about coercive marriage practices in Togo, her lawyer effectively excised the supernatural in its entirety from her narrative.

In Aliyah's case, the absence of concrete rules of evidence in US immigration courts was a cause for concern. When documents such as passports and party membership cards are produced as evidence, BCIS will often subject them to what they refer to as "forensic tests," although the nature of the test, method, and comparative evidence is never provided. Document fraud is an area of acute concern for immigration ministries globally, and document "verification" can be a long and drawn-out process. I am also frequently asked to comment on the type of documentation produced as evidence of identity. Precisely what sort of tests birth certificates or passports can be subjected to, however, is a matter of debate beyond the scope of this chapter. But against what data or comparative materials boxes of purported supernatural objects can be compared and evaluated is unclear. Aliyah's mailed threats were never scrutinized for content, nature, or origin. No expertise on charms, magic, or witchcraft reported on their form and nature. The legal team that successfully represented Aliyah's asylum claim embraced the judge's discomfort and permitted the materials to be set aside. She prevailed in her claim because of the merits of her experience of attempted genital cutting, forced prostitution, trafficking, and attempted forced marriage.

BUREAUCRATIC ERASURE

Supernatural narratives are routinely viewed as neither credible nor verifiable. This is problematic on many fronts, not the least of which is the ethnocentricism of the adjudication process that is inherently hostile to African religious and spiritual practice. Scholars, practitioners, and activists ought to be concerned, not simply because entire realms of knowledge and practice are dismissed but also because of the deeply biased quality of information and research conducted when claims and narratives are framed as lacking in credibility from the outset.

But more importantly, asylum claims invoking the supernatural draw attention to the bureaucratic violence of the RSD process by highlighting how a climate of suspicion creates and entrenches new technologies such as COI that erase the lived experiences of refugees. Whereas refugee law is structured by international conventions and protocols, it is implemented domestically by national governments. The practices surrounding COI are complex and multivalent, but the productive contexts appear uniformly national. A far cry from the "cosmopolitan" (Cheah 1998, 2006; Appiah 2007), "postnational" (John 2014), or "glocalized" (Livingston 2001; Köhler and Wissen 2003) iterations of global knowledge diffusion, the empirical context of COI has a robust national imprimatur. As a consequence, asylum seekers with supernatural dimensions to their claims experience intense pressure to reframe and resituate their claims according to ideologies that routinely position African supernatural realm as outside conventional religious paradigms.

The bureaucratic erasure of the supernatural by COI is hardly surprising. COI reflects the ideological and moral compasses of its producers. COI agents may be researchers employed directly by ministries, licensed professionals, tribunal clerks, technical or embassy staff, or freelance academics. Many are new migrants or former asylum seekers. They may operate as gatherers and collators or synthesizers and interpreters of knowledge. The information comprising COI data ranges from the narrow and personal to broad national or regional questions: it encompasses questions tailored to a specific refugee narrative and general research and "fact-finding" (Swift 2008). The majority of COI researchers are, at best, likely leery of black magic or any references to supernatural forces.

And as COI is produced and applied within hierarchical legal systems, the paradigmatic bias is amplified at higher levels. Individuals with morals, ethics, and ideological outlooks run COI agencies. More established COI agencies appear to cloy to the science of *témoignage* (witnessing) (Binet 1905), at least in the manner in which Médicins Sans Frontières revitalized the concept in the 1970s (Fassin 2008; Brauman 2010), as a vital conduit of otherwise inaccessible knowledge. But more often than not, COI agents operate with what might best be described as a form of "foreknowledge" and an instinct of what claims are "expected to look like," in the sense that they understand the novelty of claims must be situated within an "already existing, generic template" (Mahajan 2008, 585).

COI is a slippery amalgam because of the diversity of COI practices and practitioners. It may contain accounts of interviews with activists, politicians, scholars, or others conducted firsthand by COI agents. It can include secondhand research, gleaned from scholarly articles or "parascholarly" (Claybaugh 2010) summaries, introductions, or thought pieces. Newspaper articles, press releases from NGOs, and empirical, qualitative, quantitative, and anecdotal data collated from governmental or NGO reports are its bedrock. But COI agents may even solicit opinions from scholars, former diplomats, military officials, and even itinerant tourists who have been in a particular region or witnessed an event. And importantly, as the social media revolution has transformed the circulation of knowledge and proved pivotal in political crises, more nimble COI agencies have developed mechanisms and protocols for the collection of information about claimants from publicly accessible Internet sites, such as Facebook, Twitter, or LinkedIn. The collection of what is often regarded by RSD adjudicators as "objective data" (Good 2007, 2015) is anchored by a dynamic transnational tension fundamental to the contemporary refugee experience, a tension between domestic constraints on migration and the national obligations of the international system.

NOTES

1. Sakpata (Xapata) is an extremely powerful vodou and feared generally. His influence waned among vodou communities in the 1970s and 1980s with the eradication of smallpox, but more recently, with the emergence of HIV/AIDS, new strains of tuberculosis, and Ebola, he has regained prominence. See Verger (1995); Le Meur (2006).

2. Original testimony in possession of the author.

3. Ameh (1998); Dovlo and Adzoyi (1995); Erturk (2008); Rosenthal (1998).

4. National Voodoo Day (*la fête nationale du vaudou*) has been celebrated on January 10 since 1994. See BBC News, January 10, 2006, http://news.bbc.co.uk/2/hi/africa/4599392.stm.

5. Social Institutions and Gender Index (SIGI), https://www.genderindex.org/?s=Benin, citing a 2002 CEDAW report.

6. See US Agency for International Development, Annual Report on Good Practices, Lessons Learned, and Success Stories October 1, 2004 – September 30, 2005 [Women's Legal Rights Initiative under the Women in Development Iqc Contract No. Gew-i-00-02-00016-00, Task Order 01] June 2006, and interviews by Rotman (2004). Sources in French also indicate aspects of its prevalence [e.g., Christian Dieudonné Houegbe, "Le calvaire psychologique du lévirat," *Amazone, journal mensuel béninois*, no. 006 DE 08/99 (1999): 14.]

7. Loi N°2002-07 du 24 Août 2004 portant Code des Personnes et de la Famille (2004 Family Code), http://www.inpf.bj/IMG/pdf/code_des_personnes_et_de_la_famille.pdf.

8. An Immigration and Refugee Board of Canada report noted that forced marriage is still "practiced in certain rural areas." See, Canada: Immigration and Refugee Board of Canada, Benin: Forced marriages, in particular, marriages forced on men and protection offered by the state, 22 January 2007, BEN102408.FE: http://www.refworld.org/docid/469cd6cbc.html.

9. See Botchway (2008); Madison (2011).

REFERENCES

ACCORD (Austrian Centre for Country of Origin and Asylum Research and Documentation). 2013. *Researching Country of Origin Information: Training Manual, 2013 Edition.* http://www.coi-training.net/handbook/Researching-Country-of-Origin-Information-2013-edition-ACCORD-COI-Training-manual.pdf.

Afrique occidentale française, Gouvernement general, Colonie du Dahomey. 1933. *Coutumier du Dahomey: Circulaire A.P. 128 du 19 mars 1931.* Porto Novo: Imprimerie du Gouvernement.

Akeampong, Emmanuel Kwaku. 2001. *Between the Sea and the Lagoon: An Eco-Social History of the Anlo of Southeastern Ghana c. 1850 to Recent Times.* Athens: Ohio University Press.

Ameh, Robert K. 1998. "Trokosi (Child Slavery) in Ghana: A Policy Approach." *Ghana Studies* 1:35–62.

Appiah, Kwame Anthony. 2007. *Cosmopolitanism: Ethics in a World of Strangers.* New York: Norton.

ARC (Asylum Research Consultancy). 2013. "NGOs Working on Country of Origin Information in Europe: A Mapping Exercise."

Ashforth, Adam. 2005. *Witchcraft, Violence, and Democracy in South Africa.* Chicago: University of Chicago Press.

Barutciski, Michael. 2002. "A Critical View on UNHCR's Mandate Dilemmas." *International Journal of Refugee Law* 14 (2–3): 365–81.

Berger, Iris, Benjamin N. Lawrance, Meredith Terretta, Jo Tague, and Trish Hepner Redeker, eds. 2015. *African Asylum at a Crossroads: Activism, Expert Testimony, and Refugee Rights.* Athens: Ohio University Press.

Binet, Alfred. 1905. "La science du témoignage." *L'année psychologique* 11 (8): 128–36. (Reprinted in "Individus et politique," *Hermès*, nos. 5–6 [1989]: 125–31.)

Botchway, Aziza Naa-Kaa. 2008. "Abolished by Law—Maintained in Practice: The Trokosi as Practiced in Parts of the Republic of Ghana." *Florida International University Law Review* 3 (2): 369–93.

Brand, Roger. 2001. "Diversité ethnique et appropriation des cultes Vodoun dans une population de réfugiés au Sud Bénin." *Outre-Mers: Revue d'histoire* 330–31:269–97.

Brauman, Rony. 2010. *La médecine humanitaire.* Paris: Presses universitaires de France.

Bruynell, Melissa. 2012. "The Dangers of Modern Day Belief in the Supernatural: International Persecution of Witches and Albinos." *Suffolk Transnational Law Review* 35:393.

Byrne, Rosemary. 2005. "Credibility in Changing Contexts: International Justice and International Protection." In Noll, *Proof, Evidentiary Assessment and Credibility in Asylum Procedures*, 179–94.

Cheah, Pheng. 1998. *Cosmopolitics: Thinking and Feeling beyond the Nation.* Minneapolis: University of Minnesota Press.

———. 2006. "Cosmopolitanism." *Theory, Culture and Society* 23 (2–3): 486–96.

Claybaugh Amanda. 2010. "*How to Read the Victorian Novel* and *Why Victorian Literature Still Matters.*" Book reviews. *Victorian Studies* 52 (2): 342–44.

Cohen, Juliet. 2002. "Questions of Credibility: Omissions, Discrepancies and Errors of Recall in the Testimony of Asylum Seekers." *International Journal of Refugee Law* 13 (3): 293–309.

Comaroff, John L., and Jean Comaroff. 1993. *Modernity and Its Malcontents: Ritual and Power in Postcolonial Africa.* Chicago: University of Chicago Press.

CREDO. 2013. *Hungarian Helsinki Committee, Credibility Assessment in Asylum Procedures—A Multidisciplinary Training Manual, Volume 1.* Budapest: UNHCR.

De Genova, Nicholas, and Nathalie Peutz. 2010. *The Deportation Regime: Sovereignty, Space, and the Freedom of Movement.* Durham, NC: Duke University Press.

Delgado Alemán, Ana. 2010. "Activist Trust: The Diffusion of Green Expertise in a Brazilian Landscape." *Public Understanding of Science* 19 (5): 562–77.

Derrida, Jacques. 2001. *On Cosmopolitanism and Forgiveness.* New York: Routledge.

Doornbos, Nienke. 2005. "On Being Heard in Asylum Cases: Evidentiary Assessment through Asylum Interviews." In Noll, *Proof, Evidentiary Assessment and Credibility in Asylum Procedures*, 103–22.

Dovlo, Elom, and A. K. Adzoyi. 1995. *Report on the Trokosi Institution.* Legon, Ghana: Department of Religious Studies, University of Ghana,

ecoi.net (European Country of Origin Information Network). 2013. http://www.ecoi.net/8.f-a-q.htm.

Einhorn, Bruce, and S. Megan Berthold. 2015. "Reconstructing Babel: Bridging Cultural Dissonance between Asylum Seekers and Asylum Adjudicators." In Lawrance and Ruffer, *Adjudicating Asylum and Refugee Status*, 27–53.

Erturk, Yakin. 2008. "Report of the Special Rapporteur on Violence against Women, Mission to Ghana," Human Rights Council, Promotion and Protection of All Human Rights, Civil, Political, Economic, Social and Cultural, including the Rights to Development, Its Causes and Consequences, A/HRC/7/6/Add.3 (February 21).

Evans-Pritchard, E. E. 1976. *Witchcraft, Oracles, and Magic among the Azande.* Oxford: Clarendon Press.

Fassin, Didier. 2008. "The Humanitarian Politics of Testimony: Subjectification through Trauma in the Israeli-Palestinian Conflict." *Cultural Anthropology* 23 (3): 531–58.

Fassin, Didier, and Estelle D'Halluin. 2005. "The Truth from the Body: Medical Certificates as Ultimate Evidence for Asylum Seekers." *American Anthropologist* 107 (4): 597–608.

Gadamer, Hans-Georg. 1984. "The Hermeneutics of Suspicion." *In Hermeneutics: Questions and Prospects*, edited by Gary Shapiro and Alan Sica, 54–65. Amherst: University of Massachusetts Press.

Geschiere, Peter. 1997. *The Modernity of Witchcraft: Politics and the Occult in Postcolonial Africa.* Charlottesville: University of Virginia Press.

Gibney, Matthew. 2008 "Asylum and the Expansion of Deportation in the United Kingdom." *Government and Opposition* 43 (2): 146–67.

Good, Anthony. 2004a. "Expert Evidence in Asylum and Human Rights Appeals: An Expert's View." *International Journal of Refugee Law* 16:358–80.

———. 2004b. "Undoubtedly an Expert? Anthropologists in British Asylum Courts." *Journal of the Royal Anthropological Institute* 10 (1): 113–33.

———. 2007. *Anthropology and Expertise in the Asylum Courts.* London: Routledge.

———. 2008. "Cultural Evidence in Courts of Law." *Journal of the Royal Anthropological Institute Volume* 14 (s1): S47–S60.

———. 2015. "Anthropological Evidence and 'Country of Origin Information' in British Asylum Courts." In Lawrance and Ruffer, *Adjudicating Asylum and Refugee Status*, 122–46.

Good, Anthony, and Robert Gibb. 2013. "Do the Facts Speak for Themselves? Country of Origin Information in French and British Refugee Status Determination Procedures." *International Journal of Refugee Law* 25 (2): 291–322.

Goodwin-Gill, Guy S. 1999. "Refugee Identity and Protection's Fading Prospect." In *Refugee Rights and Realities: Evolving International Concepts and Regimes*, edited by Frances Nicholson and Patrick Twomey, 220–51. Cambridge: Cambridge University Press.

Graves, Maureen. 1989. "From Definition to Exploration: Social Groups and Political Asylum Eligibility." *San Diego Law Review* 26:739.

Gyulai, Gabor. 2011. *Country Information in Asylum Procedures: Quality as a Legal Requirement in the EU.* 2nd ed. Budapest: Hungarian Helsinki Committee.

Helton, Arthur C. 1983. Persecution on Account of Membership in a Social Group as a Basis for Refugee Status." *Columbia Human Rights Law Review* 15:39–52.

John, Mary E. 2014. "Feminist Vocabularies in Time and Space." In *Global Knowledge Production in the Social Sciences: Made in Circulation*, edited by Wiebke Keim, Ercüment Çelik, Christian Ersche, and Veronika Wöhner, 23–38. New York: Routledge.

Kagan, Michael. 2003. "Is Truth in the Eye of the Beholder? Objective Credibility Assessment in Refugee Status Determination." *Georgetown Immigration Law Journal* 17:367–415.

———. 2006. "The Beleaguered Gatekeeper: Protection Challenges Posed by U.N.H.C.R. Refugee Status Determination." *International Journal of Refugee Law* 18 (1): 1–29.

Kanstroom, Daniel. 2012. *Aftermath: Deportation Law and the New American Diaspora.* New York: Oxford University Press.

Kassindja, Fauziya and Layli Miller Bashir. 1998. *Do They Hear You When You Cry?* New York: Delacorte.

Keim, Wiebke, Ercüment Çelik, Christian Ersche, and Veronika Wöhner, eds. 2014. *Global Knowledge Production in the Social Sciences: Made in Circulation.* New York: Routledge.

Kessler, Amalia D. 2005. "Our Inquisitorial Tradition: Equity Procedure, Due Process, and the Search for an Alternative to the Adversarial." *Cornell Law Review* 90:1181–275.

Köhler, Bettina, and Markus Wissen. 2003. "Glocalizing Protest: Urban Conflicts and the Global Social Movements." *International Journal of Urban and Regional Research* 27 (4): 942–51.

Lawrance, Benjamin N. 2013. "Humanitarian Claims and Expert Testimonies: Contestation over Health Care for Ghanaian Migrants in the United Kingdom." *Ghana Studies* 15–16:251–86.

———. 2015. "'Health Tourism' or 'Atrocious Barbarism'? Contextualizing Migrant Agency, Expertise, and Humanitarian Medical Practice." In Lawrance and Ruffer, *Adjudicating Asylum and Refugee Status*, 221–44.

Lawrance, Benjamin N., and Charlotte Walker-Said. 2016. "Resisting Patriarchy, Contesting Homophobia: Expert Testimony and the Construction of African Forced Marriage Asylum Claims." In *Marriage by Force? Contestation over Consent and Coercion in Africa*, edited by Annie Bunting, Benjamin N. Lawrance, and Richard L. Roberts, 199–224. Athens: Ohio University Press.

Lawrance, Benjamin N., and Galya Ruffer, eds. 2015a. *Adjudicating Refugee and Asylum Status: The Role of Witness, Expertise, and Testimony.* Cambridge: Cambridge University Press.

———. 2015b. "Witness to the Persecution? Deciphering the Dialectic of Expert Testimony and Asylum Adjudication." In Lawrance and Ruffer, *Adjudicating Asylum and Refugee Status*, 1–25.

Lawrance, Benjamin N., Iris Berger, Meredith Terretta, Joanna Tague, and Tricia Redeker Hepner. 2015. "Law, Expertise, and Protean Ideas about African Migrants." In Berger et al., *African Asylum at a Crossroads*, 1–37.

Le Meur, P.-Y. 2006. "State Making and the Politics of the Frontier in Central Benin," *Development and Change* 37:871–900.

Livingston, Robert Eric. 2001. "Glocal Knowledges: Agency and Place in Literary Studies." *PMLA* 116 (1): 145–57.

Luongo, Katherine. 2011. *Witchcraft and Colonial Rule in Kenya.* Cambridge: Cambridge University Press.

———. 2015. "Allegations, Evidence, and Evaluation: Asylum Seeking in a World of Witchcraft." In Berger et al., *African Asylum at a Crossroads*, 182–202.

Lyotard, Jean-François. 1983. *Le différend.* Paris: Les Éditions de Minuit. (Translated as *The Differend: Phrases in Dispute.* Minneapolis. University of Minnesota Press, 1988.)

Madison, D. Soyini. 2011. *Acts of Activism: Human Rights as Radical Performance.* Cambridge: Cambridge University Press.

Mahajan, Manjari. 2008. "Designing Epidemics: Models, Policy-making, and Global Foreknowledge in India's AIDS Epidemic." *Science and Public Policy* 35 (8): 585–96.

Millbank, Jenni. 2009. "'The Ring of Truth': A Case Study of Credibility Assessment in Particular Social Group Refugee Determinations." *International Journal of Refugee Law* 21 (1): 1–30.

Musalo, Karen. 1998. "Ruminations on *In re Kasinga*: The Decision's Legacy." *USC Review of Law and Women's Studies* 7:35–37.

———. 2003. "Revisiting Social Group and Nexus in Gender Asylum Claims: A Unifying Rationale for Evolving Jurisprudence." *DePaul Law Review* 52:777–808.

Noll, Gregor, ed. *Proof, Evidentiary Assessment and Credibility in Asylum Procedures*. Leiden: Martinus Nijhoff.

Piot, Charles. 2007 "Representing Africa in the Kasinga Asylum Case." In *Transcultural Bodies: Female Genital Cutting in Global Context*, edited by Ylva Hernlund and Bettina Shell-Duncan, 157–66. New Brunswick, NJ: Rutgers University Press.

Radcliffe, Sarah. 2001 "Development, the State and Transnational Political Connections: State Formation and Networks in Latin America." *Global Networks* 1 (1): 19–36.

Ricœur, Paul. 1970. *Freud and Philosophy: An Essay on Interpretation*. Translated by Denis Savage. New Haven: Yale University Press.

Riles, Annelise. 2000. *The Network Inside Out*. Ann Arbor: University of Michigan Press.

Rosenthal, Judy. 1998. *Possession, Ecstasy, and Law in Ewe Voodoo*. Charlottesville: University of Virginia Press.

Rothstein, Fran. 2009. "Global Knowledge Flows: Participating in International Meetings." *Anthropology News* 50 (9): 20.

Rotmann, Anna. 2004. "Benin's Constitutional Court: An Institutional Model for Guaranteeing Human Rights." *Harvard Human Rights Journal* 17:281–315.

Rousseau, Cécile, François Crepeau, Patricia Foxen, and Francé Houle. 2002. "The Complexity of Determining Refugeehood: A Multidisciplinary Analysis of the Decision-Making Process of the Canadian Immigration and Refugee Board." *Journal of Refugee Studies* 15 (1): 43–70.

Schnoebelen, Jill. 2009. "Witchcraft Allegations, Refugee Protection and Human Rights: A Review of the Evidence." Research Paper No. 169. Geneva: Policy Development and Evaluation Service, UNHCR.

Smith, Hawthorne, Stuart L. Lustig, and David Gangsei. 2015. "Incredible until Proven Credible: Mental Health Expert Testimony and Systemic and Cultural Challenges for Asylum Applicants." In Lawrance and Ruffer, *Adjudicating Asylum and Refugee Status*, 180–201.

Squire, Vicki. 2009. *The Exclusionary Politics of Asylum*. Basingstoke, UK: Palgrave Macmillan.

Stevens, Jacqueline. 1999. *Reproducing the State*. Princeton, NJ: Princeton University Press.

Stewart, David. 1989. "The Hermeneutics of Suspicion." *Literature and Theology* 3 (3): 296–307.

Sweeney, James A. 2009. "Credibility, Proof and Refugee Law." *International Journal of Refugee Law* 21 (4): 700–726.

Swift, Nick. 2008. "Fact Finding Missions—Methodology and Guidance." 11th Meeting of the Advisory Panel on Country Information, 2008. Accessed January 14, 2012. http://apci.homeoffice.gov.uk/PDF/eleventh_meeting/APCI.11.6%20%20FFMs%20(methodology%20&%20guidance).pdf.

Thomas, Robert. 2006. "Assessing the Credibility of Asylum Claims: EU and UK Approaches Examined." *European Journal of Migration and Law* 8 (1): 79–96.

——— 2008. "Consistency in Asylum Adjudication: Country Guidance and the Asylum Process in the United Kingdom." *International Journal of Refugee Law* 20: 489–532.

UKBA (UK Border Agency). n.d. Accessed November 21, 2013. http://www.ukba.homeoffice.gov.uk/policyandlaw/guidance/coi/.

UNHCR (United Nations High Commissioner for Refugees). 2013. *Beyond Proof: Credibility Assessment in EU Asylum Systems*. Brussels: UNHCR.

Verger, Pierre Fátúmbí. 1995. *Dieux d'Afrique: Culte des orishas et vodouns à l'ancienne côte des esclaves en Afrique et à Bahia, la baie de tous les saints au Brésil*. Paris: Revue Noire.

Wallace, Rebecca M. M., and Karen Wylie. 2014. "The Reception of Expert Medical Evidence in Refugee Status Determination." *International Journal of Refugee Law* 25:749–67.

West, Harry. 2005. *Kupilikula: Governance and the Invisible Realm in Mozambique*. Chicago: University of Chicago Press.

———. 2007. *Ethnographic Sorcery*. Chicago: University of Chicago Press.

Weston, Amanda. 1998. "'A Witness of Truth': Credibility Findings in Asylum Appeals." *Immigration and Nationality Law and Practice* 12 (3): 87–89.

Chapter 6

The Digitalization of the Asylum Process (and the Digitizing of Evidence)

MARCO JACQUEMET

The contemporary sociolinguistic landscape is being transformed by digitalization—that is, the restructuring of social life around digital communication and media infrastructure. Focused, face-to-face interactions are now routinely layered with multifocal, multichanneled exchanges flowing through both local and distant nodes (Blommaert 2010; Jacquemet 2005). Digital communication technologies are much more than enablers of people's interactivity and mobility: they alter the very nature of this interactivity, transforming people's sense of place, belonging, and social relations. We are now witnessing the emergence of a telemediated cultural field, occupying a space in the everyday flow of experience that is distinct from yet integrated with physically close, face-to-face interactions. The integration of digital technologies in late modern communication transforms human experience in all its dimensions: from its social field (now globalized and deterritorialized) to the semiocapitalist marketplace (with its shifting methods of production, delivery, and consumption) to the production not only of new conveniences and excitements but also of new anxieties and pathologies (Duchêne and Heller 2012; Heller 2003; Tomlinson 2007). In this context, linguistic (and multilinguistic) skills have become valuable commodities in the global marketplace, and digital technologies have become the indispensable tools for its functioning. Moreover, because messages must become numbers before they can reach their recipient, digitalization has also placed translatability and reproducibility at the very core of these communicative exchanges and their sociolinguistic problems.

In judicial contexts, digitalization has produced an epochal transformation in the way interactions are managed and knowledge is accessed. In asylum proceedings, digital communication technologies are becoming the latest tool in the battle between, on one hand, immigration officers skeptical of asylum claims and, on the other, refugees and their advocates fighting for the right to asylum.

Until the late 1970s, agencies in charge of asylum determination placed high value on the asylum applicant's account. In the absence of written evidence, applicants were prompted to demonstrate their credibility through a detailed narration of their stories. Evidence provided directly by the asylum seeker was generally accepted at face value (Fassin and Rechtman 2009). Starting in the 1980s, however, we entered the current "age of suspicion" (Shuman and Haas, 2015): more restrictive policies were introduced in almost all Western nations (the final destination of most asylum seekers), and asylum agencies reduced their reliance on the credibility of the applicant's testimony. As a result, asylum depositions increasingly acquired the flavor of cross-examinations, with asylum officers systematically questioning applicants' narratives, seeking to disprove their accuracy, and at times curtailing their storytelling altogether (Haas and Shuman, this volume; Jacquemet 2010).

Since the turn of the twenty-first century, the digitalization of the asylum process has provided state agents and asylum seekers (and their advocates) with new power technologies. In this chapter, I will look in detail at three of these power technologies and their related communicative features: the storing of information on digital devices, the emergence of and reliance on digital translators, and the role of databases and search engines in the management of asylum cases.

MOBILE DIGITAL DEVICES: SEDENTARY VERSUS MOBILE POWER

The various agents involved in the asylum process—including government officials, refugee advocates, interpreters, and the asylum seekers themselves—can be understood as occupying a spectrum of positions generated by the structural tension between two opposing figures: the sedentary sovereign, represented by immigration officials, and the nomadic, deterritorialized subject, represented by asylum seekers (of which refugees are a subset). Intermediate players, such as court clerks, interpreters, lawyers, and other refugee advocates are scattered along this continuum.

The dichotomy between sedentary power and nomadic movement, first explored by Gilles Deleuze and Felix Guattari in their *Nomadology* (1987), provides a useful framework for examining the strategies used by asylum officers and asylum seekers. Government asylum agencies mostly operate in the striated space of the nation-state: gathering intelligence on refugees through the collection, coordination, and analysis of multiple databases; probing intra-Webs to gather additional evidence for assessing asylum claims; and relying on fixed digital infrastructures (such as networked office computers) during their interactions with claimants. On the other hand, asylum seekers occupy a smooth space, which they defend in the face of sedentary forces through their use of mobile digital devices. They use smartphones to organize and coordinate activities on the fly, orient themselves and navigate in smooth, unmarked territories, and maintain links with their social networks by storing valuable information (phone numbers, contact names, addresses, maps, and meeting points) in minimal space.

At the same time, we acknowledge that the structural opposition between sedentary and mobile power is a simplification of the complex phenomena of asylum, in which there is a continuum between sedentary and mobile uses of technology on the part of asylum seekers and authorities, who both employ hybrid strategies. Smartphones' advantages for asylum seekers (and for migrants overall) are clear, but they are not the only ones who use them. State and international agencies use a combination of fixed infrastructures (radars, observation posts, communication control-and-command centers) and mobile technologies (ships, high-speed inflatable boats, and surveillance camcopters, as well as smartphones and other communication technologies) to search, intercept, and at times rescue undocumented migrants and refugees crossing into state-controlled territory. On the other hand, asylum seekers sometimes adopt strategies of striated space, such as securing identity papers (real or fake), identifying secure departure and destination points, or tapping into the resources of land-based organizations (such as relief agencies).

The emergence of hybrid strategies of sedentary-mobile power does not, however, diminish the paramount importance of mobile technologies for deterritorialized subjects. To access and manage the asylum process, asylum seekers routinely rely on their cell phones to maintain contact with the lawyers and humanitarian organizations helping them, to communicate with asylum authorities, and to access valuable information about the asylum process. In addition, asylum seekers can use images and maps stored on smartphones during the asylum hearing itself.

Let me illustrate this point with a specific case I witnessed in May 2009 in Rome during the asylum deposition of a Kurdish Yazidi refugee from Syria who claimed that he fled his country because of religious persecution. The asylum court employed a young female Kurdish Muslim interpreter familiar with the Kurdish variety spoken by the claimant. When the asylum officer asked the claimant for information on his religion, the interpreter refused to translate the asylum seeker's full reply, at one point claiming, "Lui sta parlando del diavolo. . . . E io non posso più tradurre!" ("He speaks of the devil. . . . I cannot translate this!"). After a moment of stunned silence, the judge—who knew that the interpreter was Sunni and was familiar with previous asylum cases that exposed Sunni intolerance toward Yazidis' religion—asked the interpreter whether the claimant had any images on his cell phone linked to his faith. The interpreter was able to relay this question, and the asylum seeker, with a puzzled shrug, turned on his cell phone, searched through its images, and finally produced an image of Melek Taus, the "Peacock Angel."

Luckily for this asylum seeker, the judge knew that the Yazidis believe God placed the world under the care of seven holy beings or angels, most notably Melek Taus, who, as world ruler, causes both good and bad to befall individuals. The judge was also aware of the persecution Yazidis suffered at the hands of their Syrian Muslim neighbors. Because the asylum seeker was able to corroborate his claim to be Yazidi by producing the right religious image, he was deemed a credible refugee, and his claim was accepted.

In this case, the judge was able to tap into classic tools of sedentary power, such as sedimented knowledge encoded into court records, prior cases, and archived materials. Meanwhile, the mobile technology of digitizing images on cell phones (making them easily storable, transmissible, and portable) became an asset for the asylum seeker in his quest for credibility. These two power technologies, both geared toward storing information yet achieving their goal in opposite ways (sedentary/mobile), had a direct impact on the transidiomatic environment of the asylum hearing, allowing people to reach a mutual understanding without relying on a common language or forcing a recalcitrant interpreter into cooperating.

DIGITAL TRANSLATORS

The crucial role of interpreters in asylum-related interactions is well documented (Inghilleri 2005; Jacquemet 2011, 2013; Pollabauner 2009; Spotti 2015). For the past decade, asylum courts have coped with limitations on the availability and capabilities of human interpreters by relying on digital programs to solve some of the translation puzzles they routinely encounter. While the use of digital translators is still quite limited and their translations imprecise, these programs can still have value to a reader who can piece together meaning from less-than-well-formed texts.

Machine translation (MT), however, is nowhere near the dream of an automatic, smooth, and precise transfer of information from one language to another. MT was born in the late 1940s out of the cryptography and techniques for decoding German messages developed during World War II. Having demonstrated the ability of machines to use digital codes to decipher secret codes—such as the various cryptanalytical Bombes machines used to break the Enigma machine (see Churchhouse 2002), the intention of the first generation of computer programmers was to treat foreign languages (especially Russian) as codes to be unencrypted, forging a purely machinic link between source and target languages (Raley 2003; Weaver 1955).

However, by 1959, the dream of a perfect rule-governed MT was already over. Yehoshua Bar-Hillel, the first academic researcher in the United States to work full time on automatic translation (he was hired by the Massachusetts Institute of Technology in 1951), reached the conclusion that fully automatic, high-quality translation "was an unreachable goal, not only in the near future but altogether" (1959, 21). The inability to take context into consideration and to translate ambiguity, irregular syntax, and multiple meanings made MT the butt of the joke in many linguistics departments.[1]

Over the past two decades, however, MT has improved dramatically, propelled by cheap computing power, a spike in federal funding in the wake of 9/11, and, most important, a better idea for the design of MT programs. This idea dates from the late 1980s, when researchers at IBM stopped relying on grammar rules as the foundation for translation programs and began experimenting with comparisons of sets of original texts and their translations, known as parallel text. The most promising method to emerge from this work is called statistical MT. In statistical MT, algorithms analyze large collections of parallel texts (called parallel corpora), such as the proceedings of the European Parliament or newswire copy, to divine the statistical probability of words and phrases in one language ending up as particular words or phrases in another. A model is then built on those probabilities and used to evaluate and translate new text. A slew of researchers took up IBM's insights, and by the turn of the twenty-first century, the quality of statistical MT had drawn even with five decades of grammar-based MT.

The success of statistical systems, however, comes with a catch: such algorithms do well only when applied to the same type of text on which they have been "trained." Statistical MT software trained on English and Spanish parallel texts from the BBC World Service, for example, excels with other news articles but flops with software manuals. As a result, such systems require vast parallel corpora not only for every language pair they intend to translate—which may not be available for, say, Pashto—but also for different genres within those language pairs.

By 2016, MT had become reasonably accurate when input is basic and when both input and output are restricted in style, vocabulary, expression, and content. However, as was the case for C. K. Odgen and I. A. Richards's Basic English Project (also, by the way, developed to respond to military needs; see Koeneke 2003), MT language must be basic, common, and potentially neutral. In this way, MT has developed alongside economic globalization, highlighting the linguistic utilitarianism and functional pragmatics specific to intercultural exchanges in business trade.

The social consequences of these limitations are also becoming clear: MT in late-modern communication is shaped by the language of commerce and gives further priority to the principle of functionality and utilitarianism, since, as Jean-François Lyotard (1984) pointed out, "the technocratic values of efficiency, productivity, and performativity go hand in hand with the transmission of easily decodable messages" (5).

What is missing from the search for an accurate, precise MT is an awareness of the fuzzy, nonfunctional nature of most linguistic exchanges and of the way meanings are negotiated by social groups in the structuration, diffusion, and interpretation of language in context. As in face-to-face talk, where people manage to understand each other's fragmented sentences through continuous feedback and guesswork, human-computer interactions can also be facilitated by feedback mechanisms. In this logic, computer programmers have been developing digital translations that human users may check for intelligibility and, if needed, correct. Computer-assisted translation (CAT) incorporates a manual editing stage into the software, making translation an interactive process between human and computer. Some advanced CAT software provides a more complex set of tools available to the translator, which may include terminology management features and various other linguistic tools and utilities (Barrachina et al. 2009). Carefully customized user dictionaries based on correct terminology significantly improve the accuracy of MT and, as a result, aim at increasing the efficiency of the entire translation process.

MT in the legal sector may take advantage of the functional and utilitarian language used in most legal documents, but the situation becomes more complex when foreign nationals are asked to testify in a court of law. Human-computer synergies can be seen in the work of asylum agents (mainly interpreters but also judges and lawyers) who may utilize digital translation to produce comprehensible texts in the target language. Entire segments of the initial asylum application (especially the story accompanying the asylum request, which can be written in any number of languages) are routinely inserted into online translation services (such as Google Translate or GoFish) to get a glimpse of the main elements of a case. These inevitably imprecise and partial translations are then checked by professional translators with the support of digital databases from multiple languages to account for regional or nonstandard codes.

These interventions, however, tend to produce documents that highlight the denotational-heavy passages of the original text at the expenses of more metaphorical, but potentially ambiguous, narration, with the inevitable consequence of lessening the emotional impact of the original text (Jacquemet 2015).

The process of recontextualization proper of translation is here doubled. First a software program and then an asylum agent detach the speaking subject from the production of the judicial evidence. The "asylum speaker" (in the clever wordplay by UK-based hip-hop group Foreign Beggars), a term that itself had been recontextualized in academic writing by Katrijn Maryns (2005), is doubly distanced from their story, with potentially negative consequences for their credibility.

Moreover, in most judicial systems, MT and other digital tools (such as computer-generated transcriptions of voice mail) are not admissible evidence, being considered in the same class as hearsay—that is, out-of-court statements (Cornell 2011). These digital tools can however be used by trained professionals (such as court-certified translators) in their work (thus, including digital software), but these officers would have to certify personally that their digital tools are reliable and best practices.

This human-centered approach to the use of digital translation in contructing legal evidence can be further illustrate by turning to another techno-linguistic mechanism used in asylum proceedings: the online multilingual dictionary. Today many online dictionaries offer both word-to-word translation and text-to-speech capabilities (providing the standard pronunciation of any word). They contain millions of combined entries accessed via an array of user interfaces, from the very simple to the highly sophisticated.

Online dictionaries are quickly becoming the necessary tool for lexicographical translation, especially in institutional settings. The single most important impact that online dictionaries have on the translation process is in offering quick access to multiple solutions for the needed-to-be-translated term. In so doing, digital technology imposes, according to Anthony Pym (2011), a collapse of the paradigmatic axis over the syntagmatic one, disrupting linearity and flow. Just like in the case of the poetic function explored by Roman Jakobson (1960), MT, and more specifically online dictionaries, projects the principle of equivalence from the axis of selection (paradigmatic) into the axis of combination (syntagmatic) paradigmatic choices. The need to select, during the sequential development of a linguistic exchange among people not sharing the same language, the proper translated term from a paradigmatic list of equivalent ones causes inevitable breaks in the conversational flow, producing an interaction with distinct qualities, such as a syncopated rhythm, a start-and-stop cadence, and cutoff sentences.

When such digital intervention occurs during a judicial proceeding, we may wonder about its impact on the construction of evidence and on witness credibility. Let me illustrate this point with a case I uncovered during my fieldwork with an Italian humanitarian organization, Senza Confine, which provides logistical and legal support to asylum seekers in Rome. Senza Confine routinely relies on interpreters, but at times these interpreters are confronted with multilingual documents that test their linguistic competence.

Such was the case in summer 2009 during an interview between an Italian lawyer from Senza Confine and a Kurdish asylum seeker, assisted by a Kurdish interpreter. The asylum seeker had earlier managed to write in Turkish the story of his departure from Turkey and included it with his asylum application materials. While reviewing the materials during the interview, the lawyer asked the interpreter—who spoke some Turkish as well as Kurdish and Italian—for an oral translation of the story:

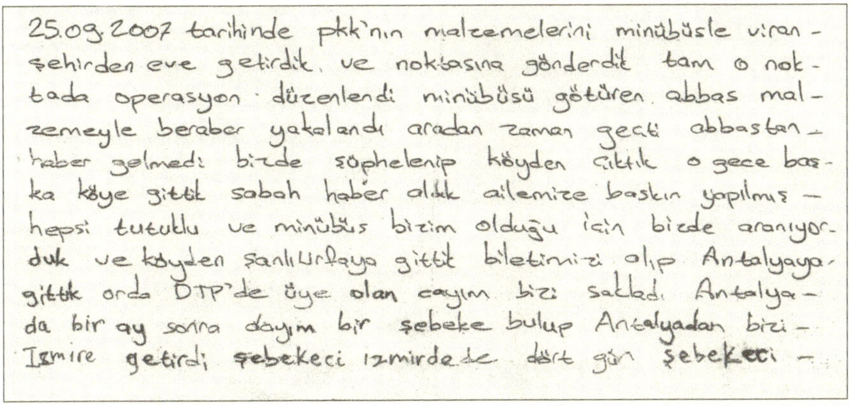
25.09.2007 tarihinde pkk'nın malzemelerini minübüsle viran-
şehirden eve getirdik. ve noktasına gönderdik tam o nok-
tada operasyon düzenlendi minübüsü götüren abbas mal-
zemeyle beraber yakalandı aradan zaman geçti abbastan-
haber gelmedi bizde şophelenip köyden çıktık o gece baş-
ka köye gittik sabah haber aldık ailemize baskın yapılmış -
hepsi tutuklu ve minübüs bizim olduğu için bizde aranıyor-
duk ve köyden Şanlıurfaya gittik biletimizi alıp Antalyaya-
gittik orda DTP'de üye olan dayım bizi sakladı Antalya-
da bir ay sonra dayım bir şebeke bulup Antalyadan bizi -
Izmire getirdi şebekeci izmirde de dört gün şebekeci -

Figure 6.1. Copy of the handwritten asylum claim, redacted by a Turkish speaker on behalf of the Kurdish asylum seeker (Asylum Processing Center, Crotone, Italy, November 2007).

When the Kurdish interpreter got to the Turkish word şebeke, he was unsure on how to render it for the lawyer. In the text above, şebeke is found in the next to the last line, which reads:

Antalyada bir ay sonra dayım bir şebeke bulup Antalyadan bizi İzmire getirdi
[Antalya-at one month after uncle-mine a şebeke finding Antalya-from us İzmir-to brought]
At Antalya my uncle found a şebeke after a month, and he brought us from Antalya to İzmir.

He decided to consult his smartphone. First he looked şebeke up in an online Turkish-Italian dictionary but was unsatisfied with the result: the words the dictionary offered—such as *alimentazione* (food) and *sulla griglia* (on the grill)—were completely unrelated to the topic. He then checked an online Turkish-English dictionary, which yielded "network, system, graticule, grid."

So he decided to render şebeke as "networker." This English word, however, did not satisfy the asylum lawyer, who asked the intepreter for a more precise explanation of "networker":

Transcript 1. Senza Confine, Roma, May 6, 2009

Law	Lawyer, young woman, Italian
Int	Intepreter, young man, Kurdish
AS	Asylum seeker, young man, Kurdish

Law	e chi e` questo networker?	Law	and who's this networker?
Int	volevo dire trafficanti	Int	I meant human traffickers
Law	ah, ok	Law	oh, ok
	e quanto li ha pagati?		how much did he pay them?
Int	te çiqas da şebekê?	Int	how much did you pay the trafficker?
AS	heft hezar euro	AS	7,000 euros
Int	settemila euro	Int	7,000 euros
Law	e vabbene	Law	oh, very well

As the transcript above shows, the interpreter realized that "networker" in this context could best be translated in Italian as *trafficanti* (traffickers or human smugglers), and the interview moved forward successfully.

Here we see a series of feedback mechanisms operating to translate the asylum seeker's story. The interpreter's interaction with an online dictionary, accessed through his smartphone, bridged the gap between the Turkish term and the interpreter's knowledge. Even though the interpreter's initial search was not fruitful and the second one turned up a word that was still quite ambiguous, the continuous interaction and feedback between digital and human agent achieved some form of shared knowledge.

If the lawyer had not questioned the word "networker" and instead allowed it to enter the legal deposition, the impreciseness and foreignness of this term could have had negative consequences for the asylum seeker. In the permanent culture of suspicion that characterizes asylum hearings (especially regarding the credibility of the asylum seekers; see Fassin and Rechtman 2009; Jacquemet 2011), a skeptical judge could have interpreted the use of such a nonstandard, "fuzzy" lexeme as sign that the asylum seeker had something to hide. It was only through the multiple reciprocal moves of all agents (interpreter, online dictionaries, lawyer) that the superdiverse, unclear nature of this story could be rendered in the acceptable, standard Italian of the asylum court.

If we want to translate literature by authors such as James Joyce (Eco 2000), we should stay clear of digital translation technologies for years to come and maybe forever. If, on the other hand, we are just looking for some pointers (a function, after all, crucial to all processes of indexicality) that can help us understand multilingual exchanges, then these technologies can be quite useful—especially when combined with human intelligence.

SEARCH ENGINES: DENOTATION IN A SUPERDIVERSE ENVIRONMENT

Most Western nations (as well as international organizations such as the United Nations High Commissioner for Refugees and the Jesuit Refugee Service) attempt to address the needs of asylum seekers by providing them with interpreters, access to websites containing information useful to their cases, and the services of lawyers, social workers, and cultural mediators.

Despite such efforts, the asylum process in Western countries remains a site where refugees' multilingual practices come into conflict with national language ideologies. State bureaucrats, in particular, impose norms and forms (shaped by national concerns and ethnocentric cultural assumptions) on immigrants barely able to understand the nation's local language, let alone the officials' procedures for conducting in-depth interviews, writing reports, and producing the records required in order for institutions to grant refugees access to local resources (Blommaert 2009; Eades and Arends 2004; Pollabauer 2004; Maryns and Blommaert 2001).

During the asylum process, state and international agencies operate within a regime of denotational-heavy registers. They focus mostly on the denotational axis (the link between description and the thing or event described) to determine the credibility of an asylum seeker's application. Applicants are asked at various steps in the procedure to provide denotational information (personal names, date and place of birth, names of relatives, place names, etc.), which is then probed by officers in order to assess the credibility of the applicants' claims. In this context, asylum seekers are responsible for the accuracy of their statements, while examiners and adjudicators use various technopolitical practices (questioning, producing a record, checking databases, and so on) to ensure that applicants' claims are verifiable in accordance with dominant understandings of the referential world. In such a multilingual environment, the officers' search for and the applicants' production of proper references are rendered problematic by intercultural breakdowns that can result from discrepant semiotics of the denotational world. Applicants must make sure that the information they supply is properly produced and interpreted. If it is not, the applicants alone face the charge of being not credible—which, as in the case discussed below, may lead to incarceration, deportation, torture, and death.

The ethnographic interviews I have conducted with asylum officers and my review of the existing literature reveal a particular linguistic register characterized by (over)reliance on proper names. The reasons for this are multiple. To start with, institutional agents (judges, police officers, bureaucrats, et al.) erroneously assume that proper names are stable signs that survive translation from one language to another in a fairly constant, recognizable form. They believe proper names carry denotation but not connotation (an idea that goes back to John Stuart Mill) and thus attribute to proper names high denotational value ("John F. Kennedy was assassinated on Friday, November 22, 1963, in Dallas, Texas" has higher denotational-referential value than "the president was killed in the sixties"). In other words, they think that proper names boost referential accuracy, making it possible to investigate the credibility of an asylum claim or the testimony the claimant subsequently gives before a judge.

Bureaucrats have routinely used proper names to examine and create dossiers since the formation of nation-states. In this sense, proper names have always functioned as specific communicative technologies for imposing disciplinary power (Foucault 1980; cf. also Battaglia's [1995] "representational economy" and Butler's [1997] "sovereign performatives"). Moreover, commonsense notions about the rigidity of proper names make them sought after—and heavily monitored—in asymmetrical multilingual environments where speakers do not have equal access to the various languages being spoken and must rely on interpreters or digital translation. Because proper names are believed to survive the linguistic mutations of the translation process, they are seen as the only linguistic resource equally available to all participants. In these situations, proper names are used by interactants in locating the interactional flow during turns in languages they do not comprehend. Proper names can thus be considered anaphoric cairns allowing listeners to follow, albeit approximately, the turns they do not understand in the staggered process of producing speech in language 1 (L1), translating it to L2 (and/or L3, L4, etc.), replying in L2 (and/or L3, L4), translating the reply back to L1, and so on.

This is particularly true within superdiverse settings where nonnative speakers (such as new immigrants, refugees, or asylum seekers) need to rely on interpreters (sometimes family members) to make sense of the interaction at hand (Davidson 2000; Orellana 2009; Reynolds and Orellana 2009). Consider for instance the following case from my fieldwork among asylum seekers in Rome. Here we see how an applicant—a young man from Afghanistan who could not comprehend a whole Italian sentence—was able to enter the conversation without the help of the interpreter:

Transcript 2. Senza Confine, Roma, May 20, 2009

AS Asylum seeker, young man, Pashtun
O Officer, young woman, Italian
I Interpreter, middle age woman, Farsi/Pashtun/Italian

O	[to I] l'udienza si terrà a Roma o a Ca=serta?=	O	[to I] the hearing will be held in Rome or Caserta?
AS	= Roma =	AS	Rome

The asylum seeker did not have to wait for the interpreter to relay the question and promptly overlapped the officer to provide an answer, eager to show his awareness of the exchange and his ability to answer based just on his knowledge of the context and recognition of proper names (in this case place names).

Personal names enter the asylum process at multiple points, from proving one's identity to the more involved step of providing external denotational references to corroborate an asylum claim. The difficulty of proving an asylum applicant's identity lies at the heart of the asylum process. In most cases, asylum seekers have had to compromise their identity: they may have destroyed their documents to conceal their identity from pursuers; their documents may have become irremediably damaged and unreadable along the way; they may have left them behind in their rush to escape; they may have had to forge identities; or they may never have had any identity papers to start with. This latter case is more complex than a case of missing documents. As Carol Bohmer and Amy Shuman (2007) state, "The applicants themselves find the whole idea of needing documents to prove identity incomprehensible. For them, identity is about much more than one's name on an unforged document" (88).

In the Italian situation, most asylum seekers arrive on small boats overloaded with people. They carry a minimal amount of baggage or none at all, and the majority lack identity papers. As a result, one of the first acts they are asked to perform in front of Italian immigration officers is to provide their names. This act, however, is far from unproblematic. Italian officers unfamiliar with foreign names, lacking proper interpreting support, and under pressure to process a boatful of people as expeditiously as possible routinely make mistakes in transcribing the names of asylum seekers. These failed "mini-entextualizations" can have serious consequences for the asylum seekers later on (Jacquemet 2009).

For instance, an Italian nongovernmental organization working on behalf of refugees reported the case of a Mr. Boukhari, a refugee from southern Morocco who made his way on a boat to the Italian island of Lampedusa. Mr. Boukhari did not understand Italian, but he could speak some French. The officer processing his case in the identification center in Lampedusa wrote down his name incorrectly in the transcription of the hearing. To compound the mistake, Mr. Boukhari, unfamiliar with the Roman alphabet, did not realize the spelling was wrong when he signed the report. He was admitted to the country on humanitarian grounds and was granted a one-year stay permit. Once settled, he applied for a permanent work visa. When the Immigration Office of the Italian Questura reviewed his application, they discovered the difference between the name recorded in his first interview in the identification center and the name he was using in his application for a work permit. He was accused of having entered the country under a false name, and his one-year stay permit was revoked (Rovelli 2006, 151).

In a similar case, a Mr. Adesida, a Nigerian refugee, was admitted to Italy in 2003 and given a one-year work permit. When the permit was about to expire, he went to the local Questura to renew it, where he was arrested on the grounds that he had filed his renewal form under a false name. It turned out that the immigration report of his initial interview had omitted one of his four personal names. Not only was his renewal denied, but he was arrested and confined in Milan's detention center for undocumented migrants, from which he was sent back to Nigeria (ICS 2005, 56).

With the digitalization of bureaucratic processes, proper names have become increasingly important. In fact, denotation is built into the technological affordances of digitalization: databases are structured so that personal names and numeric codes can be tracked and mined, Web search engines make it easy to find references to names, and social networks tag names (and link them to personal photographs) to establish their referentiality in the offline world.

Digitalization has allowed asylum courts to become "smart courtrooms," fully wired with access to the digital information infrastructure 24/7. In particular, digitalization has enabled the staff of asylum courts to conduct immediate online searches to verify proper names cited by applicants, even while the applicants are in process of giving their testimony. At the asylum hearings I observed in Italy, typically one member of the asylum commission would be assigned to conduct searches through both the public Internet and ministerial databases on foreign intelligence to try to verify (or discredit) the applicant's story.

The following example illustrates the obsession with proper names and the use of digital searches particular to asylum courts, including court interpreters, who often take it upon themselves to seek and produce clear denotational references. The asylum seeker in this case was a man from Turkish Kurdistan; the interpreter was a young woman fluent in the applicant's first language, Kurmanji, but unfamiliar with the political situation in his homeland. She mistakenly lexicalized and transformed a fragment from the applicant's story into a proper name, triggering a frantic search to verify the said proper name:

Transcript 3. Commissione Territoriale, Roma, May 26, 2009

AS Asylum seeker, young man, Kurdish
I Interpreter, young woman, Kurdish
O Officer, young woman, Italian
Law Lawyer, Italian woman

O	allora perche` i militari turchi ce l'avevano con lei?	O	so, why the Turkish army was after you?
I	cima leshkerè tirka tera neyarti? dikirin	I	why was the army after you?
AS	min arikari dida kurda u leshkerè kurda	AS	*because I helped the Kurds and the Kurd army*

I	aiutava i kurdi e l'armata kurda	I	he helped the Kurds and its army
O	come l'aiutavate?	O	how did you help it?
I	çawa te wanra arikari dikir?	I	*how did you help them?*
AS	min arikari dida wan kesè ciyada gerila bun	AS	*I helped the people waging a guerrilla war in the mountains*
I	aiutava i Guerrigli (...) sono dei soldati kurdi	I	he helped the Guerrigli they are Kurdish soldiers
O	I Guerrigli (..) questi non li ho mai sentiti (...) e chi sono?	O	The Guerrigli? these ones I never heard of... And who are they
-----[Fourteen minutes omitted]			
O	e che rapporti ci sono tra il PKK e questi Guerrigli	O	and what kind of relationship is there between the PKK and these Guerrigli
	che ho sentito qui per la prima volta		that I heard about here for the first time
	e che il collega non trova su internet?		and that my colleague cannot find on the internet
Law	guardi che c'è un errore di traduzione, lui ha detto che aiutava la guerriglia, cioè il PKK	Law	I believe there's a translation mistake he said he helped the guerrilla that is, the PKK
O	ah! voi aiutavate dei guerriglieri del PKK? [a I] chiedi un pò?	O	so, you helped the PKK guerrilla? [to I] can you ask him?
I	we arikari PKK è ra dikir?	I	*did you help the PKK*
AS	erè	AS	*yes*
I	si, aiutava il PKK	I	yes, he helped the PKK
O	oh, meno male!	O	well, finally!
(...)		(...)	
O	e come si chiamava una volta il PKK?	O	how was the PKK previously called?
I	PKK bi naveki dinè ra ji tè naskirinè?	I	*the PKK, is it know with another name?*
AS	KADEK	AS	KADEK
O	vabbene	O	very good.

This transcript begins with the asylum officer asking the applicant how he came to be persecuted by the Turkish army. The applicant replied in Kurmanji that he helped the "people waging a guerrilla war in the mountains." This description was mistranslated by the interpreter as "i Guerrigli" (which in English could be rendered as "the Warriors"). Faced with a proper noun she had not encountered in her five years of deposing Kurdish asylum seekers, the Italian officer expressed her skeptical curiosity and probed the applicant for more information. After listening for more than fifteen minutes to an interaction (not included in the transcript) between the asylum seeker and interpreter that turned increasingly nonsensical, the officer once again expressed her skepticism about the existence of such a guerrilla organization ("that I heard about here for the first time") and referred to her colleague, who was feverishly searching that supposed organization's name both on the Internet and the intranet of the Italian foreign office ("and that my colleague cannot find on internet"). At this point, the applicant's lawyer felt compelled to intervene and clarify that the "Guerrigli" were really the PKK, the Kurdistan Workers' Party (Partiya Karkerên Kurdistan). Once the officer ascertained that the applicant was indeed referring to the PKK when the interpreter translated his words as "Guerrigli," she quickly moved to establish an internal reference by asking the applicant whether the PKK had been known by a different name. When he provided the correct answer, "KADEK," the acronym for the Freedom and Democracy Congress of Kurdistan (Kongreya Azadî û Demokrasiya Kurdistanê), she was finally satisfied with his accuracy and expressed her satisfaction. Note that in the last turn, once the applicant produced the proper name KADEK, the officer did not wait for the interpreter because she immediately recognized the name. It took fifteen minutes, but they arrived at a successful decoding of the proper reference. The asylum seeker was subsequently granted the status of refugee and allowed to remain in Italy.

THE LEGAL IMPLICATIONS OF DIGITALIZATION

"Going digital" during asylum hearings has two somewhat contradictory consequences: it may speed up the entire process by facilitating translation and access to evidence (documents, recordings, etc.), but it can also result in proceedings that fail to disambiguate the complex heteroglossic nature of asylum seekers' depositions.

Asylum officials, including judges, identify the lack of time to properly process their cases as a major source of stress. A recent study published in the *New York Times* reveals that immigration judges in the United States alone handle more than seven hundred cases a year—twice as many as federal district court judges (Dickerson 2016). As a result, immigration judges must often decide the fate of asylum seekers in the time it takes to consume a fast-food lunch, leading to higher burnout rates among judges than among hospital workers and prison wardens (see Lusting et al. 2008).

In asylum courts, most testimony is filtered through interpreters, since judges are not usually fluent in the languages spoken by asylum seekers. Even simple questions that judges might ask of asylum applicants can increase the time required to process a case. As a result, judges seek to minimize their questioning—including questioning that could help establish an applicant's credibility. In the context of the ideology of suspicion described above (and in other chapters of this volume), this creates a situation in which judges make life-or-death decisions that are strongly influenced by their cultural biases and assumptions that asylum claims are often bogus.

As Gumperz suggested in his work on crosstalk (1979), the simplest and most effective way to combat intercultural bias is to avoid rushed decisions, slow down the entire process, and take the time to make sure questions are understood and answers are properly processed. But with more than five hundred thousand cases currently pending just in the United States, immigration judges do not have those options (TRAC 2017). This is where digital technologies may come in handy.

Digital technologies have ushered in an "age of immediacy" (Tomlinson 2007). Digitalization has not only allowed novel, faster methods of production, delivery, and consumption (the "just-in-time" economy), but they have also intensified and facilitated our connections with other people and/or institutions, making us increasingly available to others in our daily lives. In the asylum context, these technologies make it easier and faster to manage all aspects of the proceedings, from scheduling to translation. But even as they speed things up, some of these technologies interject new problems of their own.

MT and search engines seem to me the two technologies that carry the greatest risk of communicative breakdowns and bias against asylum seekers. As Rita Raley (2003) pointed out, MT transforms languages into basic, purely functional, and putatively neutral media for communicating information on a global scale—but it produces mixed results. On one hand,

MT can speed up the asylum process and facilitate understanding, but on the other hand, by introducing an extra layer of mediation that privileges basic and functional linguistic solutions and causes a syncopated, rushed, and disrupted conversational flow, MT may hurt witnesses' impression management and ultimately their credibility.

The ability to look up names through search engines can provide a speedy way to corroborate claimants' stories, dovetailing nicely with an institutional system already wired to privilege nominal identity and denotational accuracy. At the same time, search engines can further exacerbate the tendency of judges to focus on proper names, thus transforming the hearing into a quiz show where claimants need to come up with the correct words.

With both these technologies, we should remember that credibility is gained incrementally but is lost catastrophically. It can be lost not only when an asylum applicant uses a single erroneous—or seemingly erroneous—translated term but also when a nervous witness's halting narration is interpreted as evidence that there is something to hide (Jacquemet 2013).

In a recent paper, I argued that the process of determining asylum seekers' credibility calls for questioning methods that focus on the overall narrative rather than on the accuracy of single answers (Jacquemet 2015). This means allowing the applicants more leeway in using multiple turns to frame a particular statement, having more patience with looped or circular stories with scarce denotational load, and paying more attention to the stories themselves, their performative effect, and their overall rhetorical structure.

In this scenario, more than one turn of speaking may be needed before interactants have a sufficiently symmetric grasp of the referent. The recourse to digital mediations (including translation) seems to complicate the turn-taking organization of the asylum hearing, with as yet unknown consequences. What we can say with certainty is that the multiple de- and recontextualizations during these multiturn exchanges (both human and digital) will require more time, putting additional stress on a system already stretched to its breaking point.

NOTE

1. See for, instance, Eco 2000 for the hilarious consequences of subjecting a James Joyce piece to multiple MT passages (from language A to language B to language C and back to language A). This jocular animosity is shared and reciprocated by MT researchers

who have even their own jokes about linguists, dating from the period when their methods were heavily influenced by theoretical linguistics: "Every time we get rid of a linguist, our MT gets better" (quoted in Silberman 2004, 228).

REFERENCES

Bar-Hillel, Yehoshua. 1959. *Report on the State of Machine Translation in the United States and Great Britain.* Hebrew University for the United States Office of Naval Research Information Systems Branch.

Barrachina, Sergio, Oliver Bender, Francisco Casacuberta, and Jorge Civera. 2009. "Statistical Approaches to Computer Assisted Translation." *Computational Linguistics* 35 (1): 3–28.

Battaglia, Debbora. 1995. "Problematizing the Self." In *Rhetorics of Self-Making,* edited by Debbora Battaglia, 1–15. Berkeley: University of California Press.

Blommaert, Jan. 2001. "Investigating Narrative Inequality: African Asylum Seekers' Stories in Belgium." *Discourse and Society* 12 (4): 413–49.

———. 2009. "Language, Asylum, and the National Order." *Current Anthropology* 50 (4): 415–41.

———. 2010. *The Sociolinguistics of Globalization.* Cambridge: Cambridge University Press.

Bohmer, Carol, and Amy Shuman. 2007. *Rejecting Refugees: Political Asylum in the 21st Century.* London: Routledge.

Butler, Judith. 1997. *Excitable Speech: A Politics of the Performative.* New York: Routledge.

Churchhouse, Robert. 2002. *Codes and Ciphers: Julius Caesar, the Enigma and the Internet* Cambridge: Cambridge University Press.

Davidson, Brad. 2000. "The Interpreter as Institutional Gatekeeper: The Social-Linguistic Role of Interpreters in Spanish-English Medical Discourse." *Journal of Sociolinguistics* 4 (3): 379–405.

Deleuze, Gilles, and Felix Guattari. 1987. "Nomadology" in *A Thousand Plateaus: Capitalism and Schizophrenia.* 2nd ed. Minneapolis: University of Minnesota Press.

Dickerson, Caitlin. 2016. "How U.S. Immigration Judges Battle Their Own Prejudice." *New York Times,* September 5, 2016.

Duchêne, Alexandre, and Monica Heller. 2012. "Multilingualism and the New Economy." In *The Routledge Handbook of Multilingualism,* edited by Marilyn Martin-Jones, Adrian Blackledge, and Angela Creese, 369–85. London: Routledge.

Eades, Diana, and Jacques Arends, eds. 2004. *International Journal of Speech, Language and the Law* 11 (2). Special issue on language analysis in asylum hearings.

Eco, Umberto. 2000. *Experiences in Translation.* Toronto: University of Toronto Press.

Fassin, Didier, and Rechtman, Richard. 2009. *The Empire of Trauma: An Inquiry into the Condition of Victimhood.* Princeton, NJ: Princeton University Press.

Foucault, Michel. 1980. *Power/Knowledge: Selected Interviews and Other Writings 1972–1977.* New York: Pantheon.

Gumperz, J., et al. 1979. *Crosstalk: A Study of Crosscultural Communication.* London: National Center for Industrial Language Training (in association with the BBC Publications).

Heller, Monica. 2003. "Globalization, the New Economy, and the Commodification of Language and Identity." Special Issue: Sociolinguistics and Globalization. *Journal of Sociolinguistics* 7 (4): 473–92.

ICS (Consorzio Italiano Solidarietà). 2005. *La protezione negata.* Milan: Feltrinelli.

Inghilleri, Moira. 2005. "Mediating Zones of Uncertainty: Interpreter Agency, the Interpreting Habitus, and Political Asylum Adjudication." *Translator* 11 (1): 69–85.

Jacquemet, Marco. 2005. "Transidiomatic Practices: Language and Power in the Age of Globalization." *Language and Communication* 25:257–77.

———. 2009. Transcribing Refugees: The Entextualization of Asylum Seekers' Hearings in a Transidiomatic Environment. *Text and Talk* 29 (5): 525–46.

———. 2010. "The Registration Interview: Restricting Refugees' Narrative Performances." In *Critical Readings in Translation Studies,* edited by Mona Baker. London: Routledge.

———. 2011. "Crosstalk 2.0." *Text and Talk* 31 (4): 475–97.

———. 2013. "Language, Media, and Digital Landscapes." In *Language and Space: Applied Cases,* edited by Peter Auer and Anja Stuckenbrok. Berlin: De Gruyter Mouton.

———. 2015. "Asylum and Superdiversity." *Language and Communication* 44:72–81.

Jakobson, Roman. 1960. "Closing Statement: Linguistics and Poetics." In *Style in Language,* edited by Thomas Sebeok, 350–77. New York: Wiley.

Koeneke, Rodney. 2003. *Empires of the Mind: I. A. Richards and Basic English in China, 1929–1979.* Palo Alto, CA: Stanford University Press.

Lusting, Stuart, Kevin Delucchi, Lakshika Tennakoon, Brent Kaul, Dana Leigh Marks, and Denise Slavin. 2008. "Burnout and Stress among United States Immigration Judges." *Bender's Immigration Bulletin* 13:22–36.

Lyotard, Jean-François. 1984. *The Postmodern Condition: A Report on Knowledge.* Minneapolis: University of Minnesota Press.

Maryns, Katrijn. 2005. *The Asylum Speaker: Language in the Belgian Asylum Procedure.* Manchester, UK: St. Jerome Publishing.

Maryns, Katrijn, and Jan Blommaert. (2001). Stylistic and Thematic Shifting as a Narrative Resource: Assessing Asylum Seekers' Repertoires. *Multilingua* 20 (1): 61–84.

Orellana, Marjorie F. 2009. *Translating Childhoods: Immigrant Youth, Language, and Culture.* New Brunswick, NJ: Rutgers University Press.

Pollabauer, Sonja. 2004. "Interpreting in Asylum Hearings: Issues of Role, Responsibility and Power." *Interpreting* 6 (2): 143–80.

Pym, Anthony. 2011. "What Technology Does to Translating." *Translation and Interpreting* 3 (1): 1–9.

Raley, Rita. 2003. "Machine Translation and Global English." *Yale Journal of Criticism* 16 (2): 291–313.

Reynolds, Jennifer, and Majorie F. Orellana. 2009. "New Immigrant Youth Interpreting in White Public Space." *American Anthropologist* 111 (2): 211–23.

Rovelli, Marco. 2006. *Lager Italiani.* Milan: Biblioteca Universale Rizzoli.

Shuman, Amy, and Bridget M. Haas. 2015. "Introductory Remarks." Presentation at the conference Asylum and the Politics of Suspicion, Ohio State University, Columbus, OH, March 23, 2015.

Silberman, Steve. 2004. "Talking to Strangers." *Wired* 8.05.

Spotti, Massimiliano. 2015. "Sociolinguistic Shibboleths at the Institutional Gate: Language, Origin, and the Construction of Asylum Seekers' Identities." In *Language and Superdiversity*, edited by Karel Arnaut and Jan Blommaert, 261–78. New York: Routledge.

Tomlinson, John. 2007. *The Culture of Speed: The Coming of Immediacy*. London: Sage.

Transactional Records Access Clearinghouse (TRAC). 2017. http://trac.syr.edu/phptools/immigration/court_backlog/.

Weaver, W. (1955). "Translation." In *Machine Translation of Languages: Fourteen Essays*, edited by William N. Locke and A. Donald Booth, 15–23. Cambridge: MIT Press.

Part III

Enacting and Navigating Suspicion

Chapter 7

Mixed Migration and the Humanitarian Encounter

Sub-Saharan Asylum Seekers in Israel

ILIL BENJAMIN

In the asylum policy world, two types of migrants—forced migrants and economic migrants—are frequently presented as distinctly different in their motives and, consequentially, their eligibility for protection. While forced migrants are typically presumed to have fled persecution in order to save their lives, economic migrants are often presented by host countries as "merely" seeking to improve their life conditions, and their reasons are frequently presented as less pressing than those of individuals fleeing targeted violence (Van Hear 2011a, 2011b). As recent United Nations High Commissioner for Refugees (UNHCR) policy briefs make clear, the 1951 United Nations (UN) Convention Relating to the Status of Refugees was meant to serve so-called genuine refugees, not economic migrants (Feller 2011).

A 2003 UNHCR report to the UN General Assembly suggests that "asylum systems cannot function effectively without well-managed migration;

and migration management will not work without coherent systems and procedures for the international protection of refugees" (cited in Van Hear 2011b, 3). The presumption underlying this statement is that refugees should be treated as a privileged category, and that economic migrants will attempt to exploit the asylum system in their desperation to regularize their status in host countries, thereby diluting the refugee concept. Utilizing various techniques of deterrence, ranging from indefinite detention and family separation to visa restrictions and slow asylum adjudication processes, host countries have created a bureaucratic environment for migration that is punishing for forced and economic migrants alike. Such environments are presumed to discourage false asylum claims (Gibney 2004).

In practice, however, the 1951 refugee convention's signatory countries have found it increasingly difficult to distinguish forced migrants from economic ones (Castles 2003; Feller 2011; Van Hear 2011a, 2011b). Because economic turmoil tends to accompany ethnic violence, refugees and economic migrants often travel together, using the same migration paths and smugglers. Their motives for fleeing, moreover, are more difficult to differentiate than UNHCR policy briefs would suggest. Both groups may experience violence along the way, and both necessarily seek and pursue economic livelihoods in addition to physical safety. Stephen Castles (2003) characterizes forced migration and economic migration as "closely related (and indeed often indistinguishable) forms of expression of global inequalities" (17). He is one of numerous critical scholars who have suggested that the political subject imagined in refugee law is a deliberately narrow one. In the eyes of such critics, the convention is a fig leaf in a system designed to protect the Global North's borders by crafting highly restrictive criteria for asylum eligibility (Cabot 2013; Nathwani 2003; Ramji-Nogales 2014; Van Hear 2011a).

Employing terms such as "mixed migration" and the "migration-asylum nexus," UN actors have gradually acknowledged the overlap between economic and forced migration (Feller 2011; Van Hear 2011b). The presumption that one category clearly merits asylum whereas the other does not has increasingly been recognized as problematic (Gibney 2004). Judging from their policies, however, host countries often arguably appear more concerned by the threat to their borders that has been posed by the presumed contamination of the asylum category than they are by the possibility of deserving migrants being denied protection (Feller 2011; Terretta 2015; Van Hear 2011a, 2011b).

In this chapter, I draw upon ongoing debates regarding the distinction between economic and forced migrants in order to examine the humanitarian encounter between legal aid workers and sub-Saharan asylum seekers in Tel Aviv, Israel. These aid workers are part of a nongovernmental organization (NGO) that I call Assistance for African Refugees (AAR).[1] Based on semistructured interviews and ethnographic observations conducted in 2011 and 2012, I describe how AAR volunteers and paid workers worked to help sub-Saharan asylum seekers, primarily from Sudan and Eritrea, to demonstrate to Israeli asylum officers either that they merited temporary protection or that they qualified as 1951 convention refugees, and hence they deserved temporary or permanent asylum in Israel.

Founded in 2004, AAR is a small human rights NGO that has drawn international and local attention to the plight of asylum seekers in Israel while providing them with a variety of limited welfare services. In 2011–12, the activity that most set AAR apart from similar NGOs was its legal aid and refugee status determination (RSD) assistance. AAR staff helped prepare asylum seekers for asylum interviews at the Israeli Ministry of Interior (MOI), the institutional body that has adjudicated asylum requests in Israel since 2009. They served as first readers for both RSD and country of origin applications, advised asylum seekers on how to collect documentary evidence, and helped them to rewrite their narratives in linear terms emphasizing individual persecution, a transformation that involves the creation of what Susan S. Silbey (2005) has called a "legal consciousness."

As I show in this chapter, AAR aid workers habitually encountered asylum narratives that appeared embellished or fabricated, raising their doubts regarding whether these were "genuine" refugees. But a more difficult problem was that even if people did appear to have fled violence, their stories were often "messy" (Cabot 2013) and did not fit the criteria of the 1951 convention, or they lacked the evidence to prove it. The struggle for aid workers, then, was that sometimes it was not enough to find out who was lying and who was telling the truth, because even "honest" asylum seekers frequently lacked the documentary evidence necessary for a compelling asylum case.

I examine how AAR volunteers and workers understood their beneficiaries' stories and how they sometimes came to incorporate apparent fabrications or embellishments into a moral economy of deserving. I argue that with time, AAR volunteers came to realize that suffering manifested in many forms, whose severity did not necessarily correlate with the likelihood of being granted asylum. In doing so, I aim to explore how tensions between economic and forced migration were understood by legal aid workers.

My focus on aid workers, as opposed to merely on asylum seekers themselves, is deliberate. Even as aid workers and lawyers worldwide help asylum seekers reframe their narratives to fit the expectations of asylum officers (Haas 2012), their own insights and editorial remarks often remain private and uncodified (Cabot 2013; Farrell 2012). By describing how aid workers tried to help asylum seekers fit the 1951 convention, I also seek to stage a broader argument about the role of honesty and deception in the humanitarian sphere. I argue that applicants who were perceived to be lying about their pasts pose an ethical challenge for legal aid workers, whose commitment to helping them often presumed an honest beneficiary. Some aid volunteers, specifically, appeared to develop a cynical attitude about their beneficiaries' periodically embellished narratives, as well as about their own efforts to help them. At the same time, I suggest, volunteers were sometimes able to salvage their notion of a deserving aid beneficiary by shifting the target of their cynicism from the embellished asylum narratives to the asylum system itself.

SUB-SAHARAN ASYLUM SEEKERS IN ISRAEL

Since 2006, over fifty thousand sub-Saharan asylum seekers have arrived in Israel, a country of just over eight million, through the Sinai Desert, following a harrowing journey frequently involving smugglers exacting extortionist prices at best and, at worst, kidnapping, ransoming, and detainment along the way (Fezehai 2014; Harris 2013). Many of these asylum seekers are known to have fled ongoing ethnic violence in Sudan and indefinite conscription and extrajudicial executions in Eritrea (Human Rights Watch 2014). Although Israel is a signatory to the 1951 refugee convention, the Israeli MOI, in keeping with Israel's founding as a haven for Jews, has long been publicly opposed to granting asylum to non-Jews (Kritzman-Amir and Berman 2011). In August of 2011, the then minister of interior, Eli Yishai, characterized asylum seekers at large as "infiltrators" and as an "existential threat to the Jewish state," declaring that if he could not deport them, then he would "lock them up to make their lives miserable" (Human Rights Watch 2014, 21, 5).

Israeli MOI policies since then have largely reflected Yishai's view. The Israeli government, whose migration policies have long been limited almost exclusively to Jews, have scrambled since 2006 to administer, detain, and govern their new arrivals. In the late 2000s, the Israeli military often met asylum seekers at the Israel-Egypt border and briefly detained and registered them, providing them with temporary nondeportation documents known as conditional release visas. These documents permitted them to stay in Israel for a limited period of time but granted them no social or welfare rights. At this point, many were given one-way bus tickets to Beer-Sheva or Tel Aviv, where they joined up with their countrymen, often sleeping at first in public parks or, for those more fortunate, living in cramped conditions in tenement apartments in south Tel Aviv. Gradually, able-bodied asylum seekers began to fill Israel's high demand for under-the-table employment in construction, sanitary work, and agriculture. Several thousand more moved to the southern coastal city of Eilat in order to work in the hospitality industry, while governmental policies pertaining to their status and legality were still being established. In the early 2010s, the Israeli government's detention policies intensified, and the mobility of asylum seekers throughout Israel became accordingly much more intensely scrutinized and circumscribed.

In 2009, the MOI commenced RSD proceedings for sub-Saharan asylum seekers. Until late 2012, Sudanese and Eritrean asylum seekers, by far the largest groups, were not permitted to submit RSD applications (Human Rights Watch 2014, 8). Instead, Israel granted them a status widely known as "temporary protection," citing reports of lingering violence and oppression in those countries. Temporary protection, however, has typically meant little more than a right to temporarily remain in the country, and its grantees have still been subject to indefinite detention and lack healthcare and work rights.

As Israel's asylum seeker population grew, government policies pertaining to them have accordingly become more restrictive. To date, the MOI's RSD rejection rates for sub-Saharan asylum seekers at large have been higher than 99 percent. Israeli government statistics indicate that as of February 2015, of 3,165 Sudanese asylum applicants, none had been recognized as a refugee, and 2,200 cases were still undecided. Of 2,408 Eritrean asylum claims, only 4 were granted, over 1,000 have been denied, and 1,335 were still undecided (Lior 2015).

Israel, then, has been a reluctant 1951 convention signatory at best, waging a steady war of attrition against asylum seekers that has been meant to double as a deterrence against future asylum seekers (Kritzman-Amir 2012). The MOI has kept RSD applications in limbo for years, while also unpredictably revoking temporary protections and imprisoning thousands of asylum seekers sporadically and indefinitely in detention centers in the Negev Desert (Kershner 2013; Kestler-D'Amours 2013). Opaque and inconsistent policies have also been the norm regarding where asylum seekers were permitted to live in Israel, how and where they could renew their visas, and whether their employers would be fined for hiring them without a work permit (Guarnieri 2012).

In addition, in violation of the principle of nonrefoulement, which prohibits the deportation of asylum seekers from a signatory country to a place where they might face danger, the Israeli government has forcibly returned dozens of asylum seekers to the Egypt-controlled Sinai Peninsula within hours or days of their arrival (Kritzman-Amir and Spijkerboer 2013). Thousands of others, meanwhile, have been pressured to leave Israel "voluntarily" on threat of indefinite detention in the Negev Desert (Kestler-D'Amours 2014). Some, moreover, have been actively deported to third countries such as Rwanda and Uganda, where they faced the prospect of abduction, imprisonment, and deportation to their home countries (Human Rights Watch 2014; Omer-Man 2014).

These policies have elicited a public outcry on the Israeli political left as well as in the global human rights community. A number of NGOs in the Tel Aviv area, meanwhile, quickly sprang up or repurposed themselves to provide limited welfare and health-care services to asylum seekers, combined with heated advocacy campaigns for asylum policy reform. Outside the Israeli left, however, sympathy for asylum seekers has been decidedly limited, with dominant political voices in Israel characterizing asylum seekers at large as economic migrants masquerading as refugees who should be expelled from the country or, at most, permitted to stay with minimal services. "Anti-infiltrator" sentiments have run increasingly high throughout Israel over the past decade, mirroring a corresponding rightward shift in European politics (Couldrey and Herson 2015). In low-income urban areas populated by large numbers of asylum seekers, such sentiments have occasionally ignited into bursts of mob violence against asylum seekers. Meanwhile, Israeli right-of-center politicians have fanned the flames with alarmist rhetoric about Israel being imminently overrun by hundreds of millions of "infiltrators" from Africa.

A fence hastily built along the Israeli-Egyptian border in late 2012 effectively put an end to the flow of new asylum seekers from the Sinai, reducing the number of entries into Israel from over ten thousand in 2012 to just forty-three in 2013 (Omer-Man 2014). This abrupt change took NGO workers by surprise, many of whom had doubted that a mere fence could stop the flow of asylum seekers. Their main concerns then shifted from providing for a never-ending stream of new asylum seekers to providing for the tens of thousands already present and advocating for the release of several thousand of them from indefinite detention.

AAR was an exception in the Israeli NGO landscape. Unlike other NGOs, most of its paid staff and volunteers were not Israelis but rather young foreigners who came to Israel to spend several months at AAR as part of a volunteer program or to satisfy a study requirement back home. Most volunteers who helped with RSD and country of origin coaching, moreover, were not trained lawyers. A few were lawyers or law students, but others were trained and counseled by Israeli lawyers specializing in asylum. These lawyers also took on some of the more difficult, and occasionally the most promising, cases themselves.

THE ROLE OF PERCEIVED HONESTY IN ASYLUM ADJUDICATION

When asylum seekers first arrived at the AAR offices in south Tel Aviv, volunteers invited them to tell their stories. What had happened to them back home? Why did they leave? As volunteers put it, they generally sought to determine two things. First, was the asylum seeker's story of suffering credible? In other words, did it seem detailed and internally consistent? Did it cohere with what was known about the person's home country? Was it supported by documentary evidence, such as hospital reports or death certificates? And second, if it seemed credible, did it also fit the convention's criteria? In other words, was it a tale of individual persecution, as opposed to merely an escape from conflict or poverty?

As volunteers knew from experience, asylum judges expected documentary evidence of persecution and narratives that possess a clear chronology and causality, with the victims and perpetrators clearly identified (Shuman and Bohmer 2004). Narrative inconsistencies and absent documentary proof have routinely been invoked by asylum officers and judges to cast doubt on asylum applicants' credibility (Einhorn 2009; Millbank 2009; Shuman and Bohmer 2004).

In UN and academic circles, however, the equation of credibility with narrative consistency and with documentary evidence has increasingly been called into question. UNHCR handbooks and white papers increasingly advocate a more nuanced approach, reminding asylum officers and judges that asylum seekers fleeing persecution often have no time or ability to collect documentary evidence (Gorlick 2002; Lawrance and Ruffer 2014). Research on autobiographical memory, in addition, has shown the extent to which inconsistency and fragmentation are inherent characteristics of normal memory and do not necessarily reflect any deceptive intent (Conlan, Waters, and Berg 2012; Eyster 2012). Memories of trauma, in particular, are prone to fragmentation (Shuman and Bohmer 2004). As Benjamin Lawrance and Galya Ruffer (2014) point out, "What may appear to be 'inconsistencies' in a rape narrative may only be inconsistencies within a framework that expects linearity and fails to account for survival mechanisms like fragmented memory of a trauma" (13).

Assessments of plausibility are equally contested and culturally driven: behaviors and events that ring as plausible in one culture may not seem so in another (Millbank 2009, 11). For example, as Bruce Einhorn (2009), a former immigration judge, points out, an American immigration judge might find it implausible that in Cameroon someone might know someone else very well but only by the latter's first name. This is one reason why, Einhorn argues, credibility is so difficult to assess: asylum judges do not always think critically about the cultural variability of plausible evidence.

Catherine Farrell (2012) has similarly written of Scottish asylum judges who fail to reflect upon their own role in constructing the "truths" that they hear. On a day-to-day basis, she found, some judges labored under illusions of a universal truth, rarely pausing to consider how their own cultural backgrounds and biases might determine what rang as true in asylum proceedings (175). In turn, the difficulty of determining credibility results in "dramatic diversity in the decision-making process" among asylum judges, even among ones working in the same court (Einhorn 2009, 188). "Credibility," Einhorn (2009) writes, "is the single most inconsistently assessed variable in asylum adjudication" (189). The term "refugee roulette" has been used by refugee law scholars to capture the seeming arbitrariness of asylum adjudication and the disparities in asylum granting rates among adjudicators (Ramji-Nogales, Shoenholtz, and Schrag 2009).

Not only is how to assess credibility a contested matter, but the roles that credibility and honesty then go on to play in asylum adjudication are also under debate. It is widely acknowledged that the perceived honesty of asylum seekers can grant or refuse them asylum (Millbank 2009). Asylum seekers typically face a culture of disbelief in asylum adjudication, often pleading their case to courtrooms suffused with suspicion toward their testimonies (Malkki 1996; Shuman and Bohmer 2004; Souter 2011, 2016). As Malkki (1996) notes, refugees are regularly "regarded as unreliable informants prone to exaggeration" (384).

Yet expectations of absolute honesty, James Souter (2011, 2016) suggests, are unwarranted. Asylum seekers are often pressured, he points out, to exaggerate their tales of woe out of fear that their own stories would rank low in judges' personal hierarchies of suffering. Exaggerations, he claims, should not be taken to mean that applicants' true suffering or persecution histories are nonexistent. For instance, as Sam Dolnick (2011) and Suketu Mehta (2011) point out with respect to asylum seekers living in New York City, many are intimidated or misled by smugglers or self-styled asylum coaches into embellishing their stories of suffering, often to fit in with the latest news reports from their home countries. Asylum officers and judges regularly become aware of this, adopting a skeptical attitude toward the archetypal "Colombian rape story" or "Tibetan refugee story" (Mehta 2011).

The main issue judges should be assessing, argues Souter (2011), is not whether asylum seekers are lying but, rather, the risk they would face if returned to their home countries. The two, he argues, are not mutually exclusive. To an extent, UNHCR guidelines would appear to concur with this idea. "Untrue statements by themselves are not a reason for refusal of refugee status," one 2011 UNHCR handbook states. Rather, the evidence that asylum seekers provide "must be assessed as a whole. . . . The rejection of some, and in some cases even substantial, evidence on account of lack of credibility does not necessarily lead to rejection of the refugee claim" (Gorlick 2002, 6). In other words, some statements could still be true even if others were found to be false. Alternatively, an applicant may give an inaccurate account simply because she does not know exactly who her persecutors were—only that she was persecuted. Finally, danger to the applicant back home could still be demonstrated using outside sources even if the narrative itself were deemed partially or even primarily not credible.

UNHCR and other sources point out that RSD proceedings are not a matter of certainty but of likelihood (Conlan, Waters, and Berg 2012). These sources hold that applicants should only be required to demonstrate their well-founded fear of return "to a reasonable degree" and not necessarily beyond any doubt (Lawrance and Ruffer 2014, 2). Such statements would appear to reflect not a zero-tolerance policy toward apparent dishonesty but rather a more nuanced view. This view takes into account the difficulties of assessing credibility and acknowledges that asylum seekers may still be deserving of protection even if their testimonies contain dishonest or non-credible elements.

Yet asylum hearings seldom follow UNHCR directives and academic critiques. The UNHCR generally cannot impose its directives on asylum judges, who think not only of international refugee law but also of their own countries' domestic and foreign policy interests. Thus, judgments of honesty continue to play a central role in asylum adjudication. Moreover, as Lawrance and Ruffer (2014) point out, "An absence of documentation is increasingly invoked as grounds for doubting the credibility of an applicant's entire narrative" (8).

REFRAMING ASYLUM NARRATIVES

In her ethnography of asylum credibility determinations in the United States, Bridget M. Haas (2012) found that US asylum officers often instructed asylum seekers to "just be honest" (394). But as Haas shows, asylum seekers had to "just be honest" in very specific ways. Narratives had to be internally consistent but not too smooth. Officers sought documentary evidence of persecution, but having too *many* documents could also evoke suspicion. Additionally, vague narratives were considered suspect, and so narratives of one's persecution had to be detailed but could not sound rehearsed; the asylum seeker needed to show some emotion but could not be sobbing. Stories had to be told in clear, chronological order, but asylum seekers also needed to be able to reformulate their statements when asked to do so. Demeanor and expressions of emotion, in other words, mattered considerably in asylum hearings by lending particular inflections to the substance and rhythm of each narrative (see also Cabot 2013). Indeed, it would be impossible for demeanor *not* to matter, Jenni Millbank (2009) argues, even though it has not been shown to be a reliable marker of truthfulness.

In AAR in south Tel Aviv, volunteers were likewise aware of the need for asylum seekers to present consistent, detailed, logical narratives of their suffering. In Heath Cabot's (2013) ethnography of the asylum regime in Greece, legal aid workers found asylum seekers' stories to be "messy, vague

[and] scattered, demanding that lawyers actively re-narrate the accounts of claimants," yet lawyers found that "disciplining these life stories was difficult" (117). My informants in Tel Aviv encountered similar challenges. As they put it, their main aim was to help asylum seekers rewrite their statements in focused, factual terms that emphasized actions directed at individuals themselves, not the general political climate back home, as the 1951 convention was never about granting asylum en masse to entire populations. But many asylum applicants' narratives adumbrated broad strife lacking in clear targets, villains, and timelines.

As Amy Shuman and Carol Bohmer (2004) note, asylum seekers often struggle to grasp the chronology and causality requirements of asylum regimes, which rarely align with how events are actually experienced or remembered. They tell the story of Mustapha, an asylum seeker from Sierra Leone, who claimed his village had been destroyed amid widespread violence when he was thirteen and that he had been left behind in the chaos. Asked why he left Sierra Leone, he said only that "they were killing everyone," and he could not offer, perhaps because he did not know, a more specific account of who had persecuted him and why (400). Mustapha's story is highly reminiscent of many at AAR in Tel Aviv. Volunteers spoke to me often of their challenges in getting what they considered to be a "clear story" out of their beneficiaries.

In particular, some asylum seekers seemed to presume that the emotional weight of their stories was persuasive in its own right. As aid workers knew, emotional weight alone did not equal a credible narrative; indeed, extreme emotion and flowery prose were likely to trigger asylum officers' suspicion and were for that reason to be avoided (Haas 2012). In summer of 2011, for example, an asylum seeker from Nigeria arrived at the AAR offices with an autobiographical narrative he had written and addressed to the Israeli MOI. In the narrative, he begged for compassion from the "brethren of [his] savior Jesus Christ." When AAR volunteers attempted to politely persuade him that appealing to religious solidarity or mentioning Jesus might only alienate Jewish Israeli asylum officers, he rewrote his letter. The second draft no longer mentioned Jesus but still contained emotional pleas for salvation by a divine being.

Aghast, AAR volunteers attempted to communicate to him that any reference to religion could only hurt his case. He became despondent. For him, what was of primary importance was precisely those elements that would fail to move a dispassionate, evidence-seeking asylum officer: his sense of loss, his faith, and his hope that a people he saw as distant kin might demonstrate compassion and save him from harm. He had little idea of the dispassionate, restrictive manner in which asylum officers reviewed applications. Haas (2012) argues that translating narratives into a technical idiom alienates asylum seekers from their own understandings of suffering. Similarly, numerous asylum seekers in Tel Aviv expressed frustration with the fabricated subjectivities they had been advised to adopt.

In addition to adopting emotional registers that did not fit the "social aesthetics" of asylum interviews (Cabot 2013, 116), some asylum seekers, AAR volunteers said with frustration, seemed to go against their own best interests by unintentionally presenting themselves as economic migrants. Aid workers heard periodic reports, for instance, of Sudanese asylum seekers who, when asked by Israeli border officers, asylum officials, and civilians why they had come to Israel, responded, "I came to work." AAR volunteers were mortified to hear of this, especially since many Sudanese applicants had come from Darfur and often carried with them, for once, ample documentary evidence of persecution. As AAR volunteers knew well, moreover, any mention of economic motives would spell disaster for any asylum case.[2]

I asked one Darfuri asylum seeker in his twenties why some of his countrymen might say they had come to work. Did such a statement not present them as economic migrants, I asked, thereby undermining their asylum claims? "They do not know what refugee means!" He responded with a mixture of empathy and anger, adding, "They don't know to say 'my government would kill me because I am a black African, I had to flee'—no, they do not know to say this. And so they say they come to work. But it's not true! Because we were poor before! So why didn't we come twenty years ago?" As he indicated, poverty was not a new reality for his kin and fellow citizens. Yet Sudanese asylum seekers had largely begun arriving in Israel in the aftermath of the Darfur conflict in the mid-2000s, suggesting the economic motives, at least at that moment, were not central to their flight. More important, his comment illustrated that a particular narrative is often expected of asylum seekers who wish to make a convincing case. Namely, when asked, they need to clearly indicate who had persecuted them and why, and any reference to economic motives could only cast doubt on such a narrative (Shuman and Bohmer 2004). Yet as he put it, coming to work and fleeing death were not mutually exclusive. Seeking work to build a new life for oneself did not mean that one was not also fleeing violence and persecution. His words, indeed, captured well the concept of mixed-motive migration (Van Hear 2011a, 2011b).

For some of his Darfuri friends, he said, the word "refugee" also carried negative connotations of victimhood and helplessness. They wished to emphasize to their unwilling hosts their agency and their readiness to work and not to simply repeat, "I am a refugee," as NGOs constantly advised them to do. This was precisely, he implied, a performance that did not cohere with how they themselves understood their situation. It did not mean, however, that they would not qualify as refugees according to the 1951 convention. Yet the possibility that someone who sees herself as "coming to work" could still be a refugee generally fell on deaf ears in Israeli mainstream discourses about asylum seekers. Right-of-center politicians and civilians tended to cast the whole lot as economic migrants or "infiltrators," demanding their immediate expulsion from Israel. They delighted in such apparently incriminating statements as "I came to work."

Economic motives sprinkled throughout asylum seekers' narratives also added an important complication to aid workers' efforts to help them present a smooth front in asylum hearings. Even though life-threatening economic deprivation played an important role in many asylum seekers' life stories, AAR aid workers rushed to erase any semblance of it from their beneficiaries' narratives, lest their cases be dismissed out of hand for seeming to reflect voluntary rather than forced motives.

ASYLUM AID AND MUTUAL MISTRUST

When they first arrived at AAR, many volunteers assumed that asylum seekers were by and large honest about their pasts and that they had been doubly victimized: by their persecutors and by the MOI's overly restrictive and opaque asylum-adjudication process. Aid workers were determined to stem of tide of rejections in whatever manner they could, while offering asylum seekers their earnest solidarity and advocacy.

Not long after arriving, however, volunteers would typically encounter asylum stories that seemed implausible. "A lot of people make up outrageous things," Amanda, a volunteer, once stated matter-of-factly. She had spent nearly a year at AAR by that point and seemed no longer fazed by apparent fabrications. Writing of legal aid workers in Greece, Cabot (2013) notes that

"NGO workers sometimes described West African applicants as engaging storytellers who [were] also utterly untrustworthy" (118). These applicants' stories, Cabot writes, often reinforced "popular culture notions of a wild, strange, 'primitive' Africa," rife with themes of sacrifice and beheading (118). AAR aid workers in Tel Aviv encountered similar themes. As Amanda put it, some asylum seekers would

> play up the stereotypes we have of Africa. One person said he had been due to be king in his country, but he didn't want to be, so he fled and was persecuted. We asked him, "What king? That doesn't exist in your country. King of what?" Or they claim they are fleeing witchcraft, or that they're from Darfur because they know we know about Darfur, when in reality they're not from Darfur.

In some instances, claiming to come from an active war zone (whether or not it was true) could help asylum seekers in more specific ways than simply by creating a broad impression of urgency. Namely, Israel habitually declared a (very small) rotating list of countries to be danger zones, meaning that their nationals would temporarily not be deported from Israel. One day, a man came to the AAR offices claiming to be from the Democratic Republic of Congo (DRC), whose countrymen were at that point eligible for temporary protection in Israel. But he could not speak French or the local Bantu language he claimed to speak, Lingala. Sophie, an AAR coordinator, had found someone to speak Lingala with him, but he could not respond. "He was lying, clearly, saying he's from the DRC to get [protection]," she said. She had tried to offer him help, but he became angry and disappeared, she said, after she could not reassure him regarding his asylum prospects. "He was furious. He thought I was denying him asylum myself," she added. She did not fault him for lying, however. "I don't know what I would do in their situation," she said. "Probably I'd try anything. Also, we really don't know what they went through. I understand him trying to protect his life."

As legal scholar Itamar Mann (2012) points out, claiming to hail from a region officially designated by UNHCR as a zone of conflict has been a fairly common strategy among migrants desperate to avoid deportation, and such strategies have tended to be avidly shared and debated by asylum seekers together in cramped detention quarters. While visiting a detention center for asylum seekers in Greece, an important migration entry point to the European Union (Cabot 2013), Mann noted that asylum seekers incarcerated there had internalized such common wisdoms as "If you're black, say you're from Somalia. If you're from central Asia, say you're from Afghanistan. And if you're an Arab, you'd better be Palestinian."

When they first encountered similarly implausible stories, some AAR volunteers in Tel Aviv felt stunned, contemplating the absurdity of having come all this way to volunteer in difficult conditions not for the sake of refugees but for a more diverse population that might consist to a significant degree of economic migrants trying to game the system. Some wondered how they could advocate effectively for asylum seekers whom they did not trust. Did those who embellished their stories still deserve free legal aid? Moreover, could they be harming "real" refugees by muddying the pool?[3]

This sense of mistrust, in turn, undermined the fragile underpinnings of the humanitarian encounter between aid workers and asylum seekers. Aid organizations often profess an outspoken and unconditional concern for all of humankind (Barnett 2010, 112). Humanitarian assistance is deeply informed by ideals of humanity, which promises aid to anyone in need regardless of their country or origin, and of impartiality, which prohibits taking sides in armed conflict (Barnett and Weiss 2008). At the same time, aid workers are also concerned with questions of *conditional* worth and of who is most deserving of care (Barnett and Weiss 2008; Willen 2011). "Humanitarian practitioners," writes Čarna Brković (2014), even if they want to, "cannot treat lives as equal. Instead, they have to differentiate lives through intertwined influence of nationality, geopolitics, and compassion" (8).

At AAR, then, aid was nominally meant to establish a space of apolitical and unconditional support. At the same time, for many aid workers, their assistance hinged on the assumption of an honest asylum seeker in a state of acute and immediate need. Migrants who appeared to have embellished their narratives, especially if their primary motives for migration seemed economic, disrupted these foundational assumptions. Many volunteers had long been wedded, whether they realized it or not, to an emergency imaginary of humanitarian action: they had come to intervene in a specific, time-bound emergency, and need was often equated in their minds with images of violence, death, despair, and destruction (Calhoun 2010; Redfield 2010). Economic migrants, by comparison, presented decidedly more ambiguous needs, ones that were low-simmering and never-ending. They tested aid workers' professed responsibilities: what sorts of assistance could, and should, they offer to a Ghanaian migrant whose case was virtually guaranteed to be rejected and who, by her own admission, was simply trying to bide her time in Israel for as long as possible? In such instances, there was little of the comforting moral clarity that aid workers had come to rely on and crave as a form of guiding their actions and soothing their failures (Redfield 2010).

Craving clarity, NGO workers throughout Tel Aviv sometimes held on to sweeping, and problematic, assumptions regarding asylum seekers' countries of origin. Government actors and NGO actors alike associated particular countries, such as Sudan and Eritrea, with government oppression and violence and others, such as West African countries, with economic migration. At a medical NGO nor far from AAR, for example, Uri, a medical aid worker, once told me that a Ghanaian patient was not eligible to have his treatment covered by the NGO's asylum seeker fund. "Ghanaians are self-pay," he told me distractedly while rifling through medical files. Perplexed, I pointed out that this man had lodged an RSD application. "West Africans generally aren't [asylum seekers]—they're migrant workers." Uri responded matter-of-factly, disregarding my earlier statement. "We don't discuss it publicly, [but] 99 percent of them are here to buy time."[4] In Greece, Cabot (2013) similarly found that NGO workers were sometimes quick to reflexively declare South Asian asylum seekers ineligible for asylum, even though some of their asylum applications, upon closer examination, held merit.

This mistrust often became mutual. Just as volunteers habitually suspected their beneficiaries of deceptive intent, some asylum seekers in turn become convinced that AAR volunteers were themselves the ones denying them asylum or visas. More than once, I heard asylum seekers begging AAR volunteers to pull strings with the MOI in order to help them extend their stay in Israel somehow and reacting with disbelief or anger when told that AAR had no connections or power with the ministry. At the height of the refugee crisis in the late 2000s and early 2010s, the AAR offices were indeed rife with tensions and raised voices. Contrasting with the gratitude-suffused encounters that visitors might expect, instances of mutual anger and frustration were fairly common, and volunteers seemed habitually exhausted or embittered about their daily work.

Yet stories that might seem implausible in certain contexts, volunteers knew, did not necessarily mean that asylum seekers were lying or that they faced no risk back home. Although the man in the Lingala example above might really have been lying about being from the DRC, other country of origin cases were not so clear-cut. For example, since 2006, the Israeli government has routinely told Eritrean asylum seekers that they were really from Ethiopia as a pretext to deport them (Yaron 2013). Until the 1990s, Eritrea was a part of Ethiopia, and people in present-day Eritrea and Ethiopia share considerable ethnic, linguistic, and historic ties. These ties, then, have significantly complicated Eritrean asylum seekers' efforts to secure temporary nondeportation in Israel.

Another example is described in a report about contested ethnicity in the Israeli asylum regime (Yaron 2013). In 2006, a young male asylum seeker from southern Sudan arrived in Israel from Jakao, near the Ethiopian border. He spoke the Nuer tribal language. However, noting that he also spoke Amharic, MOI officers claimed that he was in reality an Ethiopian masquerading as Sudanese in order to qualify for protection. While they did not deport him, they refused to grant him a temporary nondeportation visa, keeping him in limbo for years. In 2011, when South Sudan was declared an independent country, with which Israel immediately established diplomatic ties, he was promptly deported.

As AAR volunteers gradually realized, plausibility was a complex matter to ascertain. Narratives that sounded implausible could have important kernels of truth to them or could belie suffering of a different, but no less extreme, kind. In her study of legal solicitors in Scotland, Farrell (2012) found that many of them routinely assumed that their beneficiaries were lying. One solicitor candidly said he believed himself to have handled only three or four "genuine" refugee cases in his entire career (171). But, as another solicitor put it, "appellants are so *desperate* to leave their own country for whatever reason that they will sometimes make up a claim and I think that is a reality" (172, emphasis added).

The word "desperate" serves here an important exculpatory role. While this solicitor did suspect deceit, he also suspected that what had happened to asylum seekers back home was likely bad enough to prompt enormous desperation to leave. The solicitor understood, moreover, that such desperation could prompt asylum seekers to amplify their narratives, even when their own stories might have been enough to grant them asylum. This recalls Souter's indictment of the asylum system itself as responsible for encouraging desperation-born deception (2011, 2016). Several solicitors in Farrell's (2012) study likewise noted the influence of smugglers on asylum seekers' stories, recalling Mehta (2011) and Dolnick's (2011) descriptions of asylum seekers in New York City being unwittingly coached to tell stereotypical narratives. As Haas (2012) and Cabot (2013) have shown, even "real" refugees must put a great deal of performative "work . . . into becoming recognizable as such" (Cabot 2013, 116).

Some AAR volunteers underwent a similar coming-of-age process. Even though they often questioned particular details in their beneficiaries' narratives, some developed an increasingly forgiving view of those they suspected of deception, guessing at the myriad pressures and past horrors that might prompt such deceit. This realization was gradual and did not happen to everyone. But when it did emerge, it often accompanied a second important realization that that myriad forms of suffering mattered, even if they did not always meet convention requirements. As Sophie, an AAR asylum assistance coordinator, recounted to me in 2012,

> In many cases, I've seen people whose reasons for fleeing wouldn't fit the [1951] convention but were horrific, and what do I do with these people? One man who lived in Ivory Coast till he was eight came to us. He had to flee because his parents were killed there during their civil war. Then the situation in the Ivory Coast changed, and he wasn't being persecuted any longer, but he still couldn't return: what awaited him back there? He had no one. And he's not just an economic migrant either.

DESERVING AND ECONOMIC MIGRATION

The phrase "he's not just an economic migrant either" is telling. While Sophie likely did not intend it that way, she, an aid worker, was implying that economic migrants' needs, unlike the boy's, were illegitimate. As her words indicated, it was easy to feel compassion for an eight-year-old boy whose parents had been killed in the Ivory Coast and who had no home to return to. It required a different degree of compassion, and a different process of self-reckoning, to develop sympathy for, and work tirelessly to save from deportation, tens of thousands of "run-of-the-mill" economic migrants, whose pasts were also rife with hardship but perhaps of a more prosaic kind.

Over time and especially after forming friendships with their beneficiaries, some AAR volunteers began to develop such a sympathy, decoupling their own personal calculus of deserving from that of the 1951 convention, which they had previously uncritically accepted as a legitimate means of differentiating deserving from undeserving migrants. Suffering and need, some of them came to realize, came in myriad forms, few of which would grant their bearers political asylum. In Israel, it was almost impossible, they knew, to win the "refugee roulette" no matter which form of suffering one had endured (Ramji-Nogales, Shoenholtz, and Schrag 2009).

Since 2006, aid workers and activists at AAR and other NGOs had campaigned throughout Israel for refugee rights, invoking the plight of twentieth-century European Jewish refugees and Holocaust victims in order to argue for similar compassion for sub-Saharan asylum seekers. However, in private, some aid workers admitted to me that people fleeing individual persecution likely constituted only a portion of their beneficiaries. Many, rather, particularly applicants from West Africa, seemed like economic migrants driven by less exotic forms of need.[5] Some of the volunteers I spoke with, however, appeared to have developed a habit of shifting their anger from their beneficiaries to the 1951 convention. They expressed a growing disillusionment with the convention as an instrument that seemed designed to keep people out, not let them in. Between forced and economic migration, they realized, lay not a chasm but an ambiguous landscape of ill-defined misery.

Yet there was arguably no good way for aid workers to voice such critiques in public venues or to argue for broader notions of deserving (Willen 2011). Many felt their roles constrained them to publicly repeat simple messages about everyone being a convention refugee because it was the only narrative that carried any or legitimacy or weight in the Israeli public sphere. Begging for compassion for economic migrants, many felt, would not be a wise in a political environment suffused with xenophobic sentiment.

Other aid workers questioned the wisdom of this approach. "We say they're all refugees, and the government says they're all economic migrants," one aid worker from the nearby medical NGO reflected ruefully. Neither side believes the other, she added, and meanwhile the MOI rejects everyone. She, like several of her AAR counterparts, privately thought that it would be wiser for NGOs to reverse their long-held "everyone's a refugee" position and to publicly admit that this was not the case. NGOs, she argued, should push for fairer RSD proceedings while acknowledging that some asylum seekers might not fit the 1951 convention and have to be deported or "shared" with other countries in the Global North. Such a move, she believed, would read as more palatable to the MOI and gradually help lower the 99 percent asylum rejection rate.

She had to be careful, however, with respect to how and where she expressed this opinion. In NGO settings, "economic migrant" was often a taboo term, a phrase that implied siding with the Israeli government's blanket descriptors of all asylum seekers as economic migrants. Some aid workers were afraid that publicly acknowledging the presence of economic migrants within their beneficiary pool might undermine NGOs' legitimacy and place all their beneficiaries in peril.

EVIDENCE OF PERSECUTION

As I have illustrated so far, while the formal challenge for AAR aid workers was to determine whether their beneficiaries' stories would persuade an asylum officer, a separate process of private self-reckoning also occurred, pertaining to the judgment of asylum seekers' "deserving" (irrespective of their formal eligibility for asylum). These two processes of adjudication, formerly seen as one and the same, increasingly diverged as aid workers became increasingly critical of the 1951 convention and as they encountered asylum seekers whom they felt were deserving of protection even though they would never meet the official requirements. Once in a while, however, these two separate processes of reckoning reconverged when certain asylum narratives simultaneously tested both aid workers' notions of evidence *and* of deserving.

An important example concerns an asylum seeker I will call Victor, whom I only knew to be an asylum seeker from a country in West Africa whose nationals did not qualify for group protection in Israel and thus had to undergo individual RSD proceedings. Amanda, an AAR volunteer, recalled Victor vividly. He had arrived at the AAR offices brandishing a Shell Oil Company worker identification card, she recalled, which showed his own photograph and his name alongside the yellow Shell logo. A militia group resentful of his Shell employment and privileged social standing back home, he told volunteers, had decided to take revenge on him and kill his sons. Startled, several AAR volunteers requested documentary evidence of their deaths. In response, Victor only repeated parts of his story tearfully and held out his Shell Oil ID.

"This Shell Oil ID only shows me you worked for Shell Oil," Amanda recalled having said to Victor. "It does not tell me your sons were killed. Do you have hospital reports, police reports, or death certificates?" In response, the man held out his Shell Oil ID again, with growing desperation. Amanda and her colleagues advised Victor to ask friends or family back home to send him the death certificates. In response, Victor vacillated between yes and no, finally claiming that he could not send back for the documents since his wife was illiterate. Amanda was taken aback, uncertain of how his wife's illiteracy related to her ability to collect documents. In recalling his story to me, she said incredulously, "He expected me to believe that he worked for Shell Oil yet his wife was illiterate?"

A few months later, Victor finally returned with death certificates that he had somehow acquired. But they seemed suspiciously new and contained dates that contradicted his narrative. The documents clearly seemed forged, Amanda recalled. She and her fellow volunteers inquired how Victor's sons could have been killed after he had already arrived in Israel, if their deaths were what had prompted him to escape. Victor broke down. Stopping short of admitting he had lied, he confessed that his government did not issue death certificates on demand, and then he begged for Amanda's help. Regretfully repeating AAR's most oft-heard mantra, she explained she had no power to decide his case. "But an asylum officer," she coolly remembered telling him, "would not find your story credible."

Confounding the volunteers, Victor did not give up. His Shell Oil ID itself became a central piece in a war of attrition—and mutual suspicion—between aid workers and asylum seekers. Every few weeks Victor would return to the AAR offices, waving his Shell Oil ID in tears and begging for help. Seeing aid workers had little new to offer him, he would storm out and then repeat this cycle a few weeks later, each time with mounting frustration. In recounting the story to me, Amanda was mystified that he thought his Shell Oil ID would be enough evidence to win him asylum.

Victor's story recalls that of Mustapha in Shuman and Bohmer's (2014) study, who, when asked to produce affidavits attesting to his persecution, instead presented a photograph of the docks from which he had escaped Sierra Leone as a stowaway on a ship to Brazil. Mustapha did not seem to realize that from the perspective of asylum officers, the photograph of the docks counted simply as another part of his narrative "rather than independent evidence to corroborate it" (408). Victor had used his Shell Oil ID in a similar way. Even if he did find the ID to be sufficient evidence of persecution, AAR aid workers did not see it as such, exemplifying the ways in which asylum seekers may disagree with both judges and their own legal advocates on what constitutes credible evidence (see Coffey 2003).

Cases like Victor's likewise further challenged AAR volunteers' reflexive distinctions between economic and forced migration and between problem zones and quiet zones. Amanda did not know why Victor's story was filled with inconsistencies. It was unclear, she said, if he was lying about his sons' deaths altogether, or whether they had indeed died in the manner he claimed and that he had fabricated their death certificates simply because he had no other way of obtaining them. Either way, she considered his case weak. As other AAR volunteers wondered, if Victor was indeed lying about parts of his narrative, was it was because he had been subject to a different form of persecution or violence that he did not care to disclose? Or was it because his motives were primarily economic? As Cabot (2013) has similarly found with respect to legal aid workers in Greece, significant "epistemic anxieties" and "guesswork" frequently accompany eligibility determinations (121). Whatever the answer in Victor's case was, over time Amanda began to suspect he had indeed undergone some kind of hardship back home that deserved recognition, regardless of whether it satisfied 1951 convention requirements. His emphatic, tangled narrative presented an important critique of the hierarchies of deserving that Amanda and her colleague had taken for granted. And even if he had been telling the truth, Amanda reflected ruefully, he might have genuinely been unable to acquire the documents to prove it.

WORKING THROUGH A 99 PERCENT REJECTION RATE

In her ethnography of asylum adjudications in the United States, Haas (2012) was able to interview asylum officers and gain insight into how they make their decisions. Yet I, and AAR volunteers, possessed little inside knowledge regarding the MOI's decision-making processes apart from what could be inferred from the rationales outlined in rejection letters. What AAR volunteers did know, however, was that they were almost guaranteed to fail. Mindful of the high RSD rejection rate, which has hovered above 99 percent since 2009, aid workers regularly contended with the possibility that they were constructing legalistic identities in vain, failing asylum seekers both morally (since they were thereby tacitly legitimizing a draconian asylum system) and practically (since doing so could not even help them win asylum).

In March of 2012, an Israeli lawyer and AAR volunteer whom I shall call Ya'el gave a lecture to a group of Tel Aviv NGOs about asylum eligibility determination in Israel. During the lecture, she related a particularly memorable story of an asylum seeker who was kidnapped by human traffickers in the Sinai Desert and who was then blindfolded and tortured by his captors before eventually being rescued. In his subsequent narrative, he estimated that based on the distinct voices he had heard, there were five or six different men torturing him. The MOI, Ya'el said, denied his asylum request. His rejection letter, she paraphrased, had stated, "In your first interview, you said you were tortured by five or six people, but in the second interview you said six or seven people. How do you explain this discrepancy?"

"As a lawyer," Yael said in her lecture, "such [cases] are difficult for me to tackle. Every minute detail change means to the officer that he's a liar. This is how they fail asylum seekers: they deliberately seek out every means to discredit them." Indeed, cases like that of the blindfolded man nurtured in aid workers a particular form of cynicism toward what Cabot (2013) has called the "'useless' shadowy bureaucracy" of asylum regimes (200). If the MOI denied a blindfolded man asylum for not knowing exactly how many men were beating him, they reckoned, then what was the point of trying to help anyone? Cases like these, aid workers felt, showed that the MOI was eager to reject all applicants and was not acting in good faith.

Another common ministry move was to decide by fiat that an asylum seeker, contrary to her own narrative, was in reality from a "safe" country that Israel could deport her to. Sophie, the asylum assistance coordinator, described how this was done: "A lot of north Sudanese too are now about to be deported because the MOI suddenly told them 'you're actually from South Sudan,' just so they could deport them. And the most frustrating part is that these people, because they are from Darfur, actually for once have everything they need to prove their identity: UN documents, birth certificates—more than usual, so much more." When asked how the MOI could deport card-carrying Darfuris without attracting international condemnation, Sophie speculated that it probably did not really care about appearances by this point, adding that "the MOI wants them to get fed up and leave. It's a war of attrition."

I often asked AAR volunteers how they could continue to do what they did every day while knowing that they were almost guaranteed to fail. Sophie surprised me with her response. "I don't think our job is to get them refugee status," she said. "It is their right to tell their full story if they want, and we should help them be heard." I was puzzled by her answer, which seemed out of step with her passionate devotion to her beneficiaries. Perhaps, I wondered, this was her way of persuading herself of the value of her work regardless of the outcome or of distancing herself at times from heart-wrenching questions of truth and deserving.

Meanwhile, Ya'el, who took on AAR's most complex cases pro bono, gave a different response. "As lawyers, it's tough to continue day after day when all our clients are rejected, or when one client succeeds in ten years," she said in her March 2012 lecture. "So my colleague says to me, 'No, no—don't look at it this way! Ask instead how many were deported? And if none so far, then okay—that's success!' So success depends on how you define it."

Yael's point highlights an important silver lining to aid work at AAR. Cases deemed weak were typically rejected by the MOI after a brief preliminary interview. But strong cases, as AAR staff put it, were left to linger in limbo for years before rejection. As they waited to hear back, these "stronger" applicants could stay in Israel, work, and send money back home. Some AAR volunteers took comfort in this fact, reckoning that even if asylum approval rates in Israel might be virtually nil, if they could still help their beneficiaries sound credible enough to not be dismissed out of hand, thereby allowing them some time to earn remittance money in Israel, then they had already done them an indisputable good.

Following anthropologist Natalia Roudakova (2013), who draws on German philosopher Peter Sloterdijk's (1987) work on cynical reason, I would like to suggest that some AAR aid workers cultivate a form of cynicism that Sloterdijk calls an "enlightened false consciousness." As Roudakova puts it, those suffering from *false* consciousness might misrecognize the grounds of their actions, thinking they are doing one thing while actually doing another. In contrast, *enlightened* false consciousness means that they do know what they are doing but continue to do it. In Slavoj Žižek's (1989) terms, "the cynical subject is quite aware of the distance between the ideological mask and the social reality, but he nonetheless still insists upon the mask" (29).

Some of the AAR volunteers I have described, I argue, behaved in ways that suggested an enlightened false consciousness. On the one hand, they worked tirelessly to help asylum seekers reframe their stories to suit the demands of an opaque asylum regime. On the other, they sometimes developed a deep, resentful skepticism—both of the asylum regime itself and of asylum seekers who might be embellishing parts of their narratives.

In other words, throughout their months or years at AAR, paid workers and volunteers parted with many illusions of honesty and good faith in the asylum system, wherein "deserving" applicants ultimately triumphed and won asylum. Dishonesty, instead, seemed rampant everywhere: by and large, the MOI did not appear to give a fair hearing to applicants, and the latter desperately tried to game the system.

For these aid workers, their cynicism itself became a tool of assigning blame and leveraging a political critique at the Israeli asylum system. As Roudakova (2013) puts it, this particular form of cynicism, which Sloterdijk (1987) has called the "cynicism of the oppressed" (143), "manifests itself in a variety of ways—from low-lying suspicion of the ideological pronouncements of those in power to active hostility towards the masters" (4). I argue that after their initial surprise at the prospect of fabricated narratives subsided, some AAR aid workers were able to shift their focus of cynicism from the seemingly dishonest asylum seeker to the theater of asylum itself. Then, to persevere in this thankless job despite a 99 percent rejection rate, some volunteers were additionally able to redefine success as nondeportation for the moment.

In this chapter, I have suggested that aid workers fluent in legalistic and nonlegalistic construals of suffering are a good place to examine the pitfalls of the asylum system and its categories of deserving. The immense difficulty of winning asylum in Israel, I have suggested, compelled AAR aid workers to reevaluate what they understood by "deserving" and to question the presumed gulf between economic and forced migration.

When I first arrived at AAR, I was fascinated by the cynicism I witnessed in the more seasoned aid workers. In contrast with the bright-eyed idealism of novices, many of the more experienced aid workers seemed to dispassionately roll with the punches of irate demands and implausible stories. I wondered how they were able to continue their daily work while maintaining such a high degree of cynicism. However, as this study shows, if aid workers could sometimes shift their target of cynicism from their beneficiaries to the asylum system itself, then they have effectively kept intact a key figure in the humanitarian repertoire—the deserving beneficiary.

NOTES

1. All names in this chapter are pseudonyms.
2. Heath Cabot's (2013) aid workers in Greece realized this as well.

3. Meredith Terretta (2015) describes asylum lawyers and aid workers who share such concerns regarding those who are presumed to be faking their narratives.

4. This aid volunteer was admittedly not from AAR but from a nearby medical NGO; he was not well versed in asylum technicalities. While I never heard AAR volunteers explicitly make such sweeping "99 percent of country X are economic migrants" statements, more toned-down versions of this assumption circulated at AAR as well. As Cabot (2013) shows with respect to asylum seekers in Greece, both NGO and government actors in Greece were prone to making broad generalizations about the asylum eligibility, or ineligibility, of applicants from particular countries of origin.

5. Such assumptions, however, Sophie was careful to explain to me, were not made about Sudanese and Eritreans.

REFERENCES

Barnett, Michael, and Thomas Weiss, eds. 2008. *Humanitarianism in Question: Politics, Power and Ethics.* Ithaca, NY: Cornell University Press.

Brković, Čarna. 2014. "Scaling Humanitarianism: Humanitarian Actions in a Bosnian Town." *Ethnos* 81 (1): 99–124.

Cabot, Heath. 2013. *On the Doorstep of Europe: Asylum and Citizenship in Greece.* Philadelphia: University of Pennsylvania Press.

Calhoun, Craig. 2010. "The Idea of Emergency: Humanitarian Action and Global (Dis)order. In Fassin and Pandolfi, *Contemporary States of Emergency,* 29–58.

Castles, Stephen. 2003. "Towards a Sociology of Forced Migration and Social Transformation." *Sociology* 37:13–34.

Coffey, Guy. 2003. "The Credibility of Credibility Evidence at the Refugee Review Tribunal." *International Journal of Review Law* 15:377–417.

Conlan, Sue, Sharon Waters, and Kajsa Berg. 2012. *Difficult to Believe: The Assessment of Asylum Claims in Ireland.* Dublin: Irish Refugee Council.

Couldry, Marion, and Maurice Herson, eds. 2015. "Destination: Europe." *Forced Migration Review* 51:4–97.

Dolnick, Sam. 2011. "Immigrants May Be Fed False Stories to Bolster Asylum Pleas." *New York Times,* July 11, 2011. http://www.nytimes.com/2011/07/12/nyregion/immigrants-may-be-fed-false-stories-to-bolster-asylum-pleas.html?_r=3&.

Einhorn, Bruce J. 2009. "Consistency, Credibility, and Culture." In *Refugee Roulette: Disparities in Asylum Adjudication and Proposals for Reform,* edited by Jaya Ramji-Nogales, Andrew Schoenholtz, and Philip Schrag, 187–201. New York: New York University Press.

Eyster, James P. 2012. "Searching for the Key in the Wrong Place: Why 'Common Sense' Credibility Rules Consistently Harm Refugees." *Boston University International Law Journal* 30:3–54.

Fassin, Didier, and Mariella Pandolfi. 2012. *Contemporary States of Emergency: The Politics of Military and Humanitarian Interventions.* New York: Zone Books.

Farrell, Catherine. 2012. "Asylum Narratives and Credibility Assessments: An Ethnographic Study of the Asylum Appeal Process in Scotland" (doctoral diss., University of Glasgow).

Feller, Erika. 2011. "The 1951 Convention at 60: Still Fit for Its Purpose?; Protection Tools for Protection Needs, Statement by Erika Feller, Assistant High Commissioner (Protection), UNHCR." http://www.refworld.org/docid/4ddb6e052.html.

Fezehai, Malin. 2014. "'A Kind of Purgatory': African Refugees in Israel." *Time*, July 7, 2014. http://time.com/3705591/african-refugees-in-israel/.

Gibney, Matthew J. 2004. *The Ethics and Politics of Asylum: Liberal Democracy and the Response to Refugees*. Cambridge: Cambridge University Press.

Gorlick, Brian. 2002. "Common Burdens and Standards: Legal Elements in Assessing Claims to Refugee Status." UNHCR New Issues in Refugee Research paper no. 68 (October): 1–19.

Guarnieri, Mya. 2012. "Forgotten Deportees: Israeli-Born Children of Migrant Workers." +972 *Magazine*, July 4, 2012. http://972mag.com/forgotten-deportees-israeli-born-children-of-migrant-workers/50077/.

Haas, Bridget M. 2012. "Suffering and the Struggle for Recognition: Lived Experiences of the U.S. Political Asylum Process." Doctoral diss., University of California, San Diego.

Harris, Emily. 2013. "African Migrants Find an Uneasy Asylum in Israel." National Public Radio, November 16, 2013. http://www.npr.org/sections/parallels/2013/11/16/244087004/african-migrants-find-an-uneasy-asylum-in-israel.

Human Rights Watch. 2014. "'Make Their Lives Miserable:' Israel's Coercion of Sudanese and Eritrean Asylum Seekers to Leave Israel." Human Rights Watch, September 9, 2014. https://www.hrw.org/report/2014/09/09/make-their-lives-miserable/israels-coercion-eritrean-and-sudanese-asylum-seekers.

Kershner, Isabel. 2013. "African Refugees Protest Detainment in Israel." *New York Times*, December 17, 2018. http://www.nytimes.com/2013/12/18/world/middleeast/african-refugees-protest-detainment-in-israel.html.

Kestler-D'Amours, Jillian. 2013. "Asylum Seekers Fear Worse to Come in Israel." Al Jazeera, November 23, 2018. http://www.aljazeera.com/indepth/features/2013/11/asylum-seekers-fear-worse-come-israel-20131120407115835.html.

———. 2014. "Israel 'Coercing African Migrants to Leave.'" Al Jazeera, September 9, 2014. http://www.aljazeera.com/news/middleeast/2014/09/israel-coerces-sudan-eritrea-migrants-deportation-201495130968214.html.

Kritzman-Amir, Tally. 2012. "Refugees and Asylum Seekers in the State of Israel." *Israel Journal of Foreign Affairs* 6 (3): 97–111.

Kritzman-Amir, Tally, and Thomas Spijkerboer. 2013. "On the Morality and Legality of Borders: Border Policies and Asylum Seekers." *Harvard Human Rights Journal* 26:1–38.

Kritzman-Amir, Tally, and Yonatan Berman. 2011. "Responsibility Sharing and the Rights of Refugees: The Case of Israel." *George Washington International Law Review* 41 (3): 619–49.

Lawrance, Benjamin N., and Galya Ruffer. 2014. "Introduction: Witness to the Persecution? Expertise, Testimony and Consistency in Asylum Adjudication." In *Adjudicating Asylum and Refugee Status: The Role of Witness, Expertise, and Testimony*, edited by Benjamin N. Lawrance and Galya Ruffer, 1–26. Cambridge: Cambridge University Press.

Lior, Ilan. 2015. "Israel Has Granted Refugee Status to Only Four Sudanese and Eritrean Asylum Seekers." *Haaretz*, February 19, 2015. http://www.haaretz.com/news/national/.premium-1.643134.

Malkki, Liisa H. 1996. "Speech Emissaries: Refugees, Humanitarianism, and Dehistoricization." *Cultural Anthropology* 11:377–404.

Mann, Itamar. 2012. "A Trip to Greece" [Hebrew]. Ha'oketz, June 5, 2012. http://www.haokets.org/2012/06/05/%D7%98%D7%99%D7%95%D7%9C-%D7%9C%D7%99%D7%95%D7%95%D7%9F/.

Mehta, Suketu. 2011. "The Asylum Seeker." *New Yorker*, August 1, 2011. http://www.newyorker.com/magazine/2011/08/01/the-asylum-seeker.

Millbank, Jenni. 2009. "'The Ring of Truth': A Case Study of Credibility Assessment in Particular Social Group Refugee Determinations." *International Journal of Refugee Law* 21:1–33.

Nathwani, Niraj. 2003. *Rethinking Refugee Law*. Boston: Martinus Nijhoff.

Omer-Man, Michael S. 2014. "The Origins and Politics of Israel's Refugee Debate." +972 *Magazine*, January 28, 2014. http://972mag.com/the-origins-and-politics-of-israels-refugee-debate/86180/.

Ramji-Nogales, Jaya. 2014. "Undocumented Migrations and the Failures of Universal Individualism." *Vanderbilt Journal of Transnational Law* 47 (699): 699–763.

Ramji-Nogales, Jaya, Andrew I. Shoenholtz, and Peter G. Schrag, eds. 2009. *Refugee Roulette: Disparities in Asylum Adjudication and Proposals for Reform*. New York: New York University Press.

Redfield, Peter. 2010. "The Verge of Crisis: Doctors Without Borders In Uganda." In Fassin and Pandolfi, *Contemporary States of Emergency*, 173–95.

Roudakova, Natalia. 2013. "Towards an Ethnographic Study of Cynicism." Paper presented at the American Anthropological Association Annual Meeting, Chicago, November 20–24, 2013.

Shuman, Amy, and Carol Bohmer. 2004. "Representing Trauma: Political Asylum Narrative." *Journal of American Folklore* 177:394–414.

Silbey, Susan S. 2005. "After Legal Consciousness." *Annual Review of Law and Social Science* 1:323–68.

Sloterdijk, Peter. 1987. *Critique of Cynical Reason*. Minneapolis: University of Minnesota Press.

Souter, James. 2011. "A Culture of Disbelief or Denial? Critiquing Refugee Status Determination in the United Kingdom." *Oxford Monitor of Forced Migration* 1 (1): 48–59.

———. 2016. "'Bogus' Asylum Seekers? The Ethics of Truth Telling in the Asylum System." 50.50: Gender, Sexuality, and Social Justice, October 26, 2016. https://www.opendemocracy.net/5050/james-souter/bogus-asylum-seekers-ethics-of-truth-telling-in-asylum-system.

Terretta, Meredith. 2015. "Fraudulent Asylum Seeking as Transnational Mobilization: The Case of Cameroon." In *African Asylum at a Crossroads: Activism, Expert Testimony, and Refugee Rights*, edited by Iris Berger, Benjamin N. Lawrance, Meredith Terretta, Jo Tague, and Trish Hepner Redeker, 58–74. Athens: Ohio University Press.

Van Hear, Nicholas. 2011a. "Forcing the Issue: Migration Crises and the Uneasy Dialogue between Refugee Research and Policy." *Journal of Refugee Studies* 25:2–24.

———. 2011b. *Mixed Migration: Policy Challenges*. Oxford: Migration Observatory, University of Oxford.

Willen, Sarah S. 2011. "How Is Health-Related 'Deservingness' Reckoned? Perspectives from Unauthorized Im/migrants in Tel Aviv." *Social Science & Medicine* 74:812–21.

Yaron, Hadas. 2013. "'You Are Ethiopian until Proven Otherwise': Contested Nationality, Ethnic Eritreans, and Stateless Persons in Israel." African Refugees Development Center and Hotline for Migrant Workers, Tel Aviv, Israel.

Žižek, Slavoj. 1989. *The Sublime Object of Ideology*. London: Verso.

Chapter 8

Transgendered Asylum and Gendered Fears in US Asylum Law and Politics

SARA L. MCKINNON

Individuals have been making gender- and sexuality-related asylum claims for almost as long as there have been asylum provisions in the United States, which started with the United States Refugee Act of 1980. These cases would fit into the "social group" category of the 1951 United Nations (UN) definition of a refugee as someone outside of their home country with a well-founded fear of persecution relating to their "race, religion, nationality, membership of a particular social group or political opinion" (UN 1951, 36). But, as many legal scholars have noted, the social group category is challenging because before you can make your argument for protection, you would first have to define your social group, which the immigration officials hearing your case could always state does not constitute a group or connect to the persecution you fear (Berg and Millbank 2013; Godfrey 1994; Musalo 2003; Southham 2011; Voss 2005). In 1994, the US attorney general, Janet Reno, articulated in US law that sexual orientation constituted a social group. No longer did gays and lesbians have to articulate the group they belonged to. Merely identifying as gay meant that they fit as refugees. This provision stated that "an individual who has been identified as homosexual and persecuted by his or her government for that reason alone may be eligible for relief under the refugee laws on the basis of persecution because of membership in a social group" (Reno 1994). Through this precedent, some transgender applicants were also able to gain refugee status, as "gay men with female sexual identities" (Hernandez-Montiel v. INS 2000).

Never has there been a similar recognition for gender to count as a social group in the United States. While feminist legal advocates suggested the amendment around the same time as the sexual orientation declaration, the courts and the attorney general remained silent on the question of gender's inclusion (Stevens 1993). Instead, the courts have consistently stated that gender is too broad to count as a social group because it applies to over 50 percent of any country's citizens.

While recognition of gender's inclusion has stalled, there has been much movement in the contemporary moment for understanding gender identity and expression as protected categories. In conjunction with energetic lesbian, gay, bisexual, and transgender (LGBT) immigration activism, in 2011 the United States released a framework that offered even more possibility in the ways transgender applicants might gain refugee status by adopting the language of gender identity and expression as constituting social groups. This chapter reads the incorporation of gender and sexuality in asylum law together to consider the politics undergirding who can be categorically received. In other work, I have discussed what the incorporation of particular subjects as asylum seekers does for a country of asylum (McKinnon 2011, 2016). Specifically, I show that the fact of being incorporable often means that a person or group is not seen as threatening in some way to the state and that the asylum grant can simultaneously be used to buttress or warrant state projects in the nation and around the world.

In this chapter, I am interested in this newest wave of incorporation—the incorporation of transgender asylum applicants—and what these incorporations reveal about US national and international aspirations and fears. In addition to trans applicants seeking asylum for reasons of their gender, cisgender women have also been seeking gendered protections since the beginning of the current US refugee and asylum system. If we recognize all of these instances as moments where individuals are using refugee protocol to protect their right to diverge in some way from the gendered social and cultural norms in their country of birth, then the question guiding this chapter is which kinds of gendered transgressions are incorporable and which are too suspicious, threatening and thus excluded? And finally, what politics undergird these incorporations and exclusions? I suggest that a fear of brown and black reproductivity, and the attendant threat that such reproductivity poses to the status of white America, is at the base of categorical inclusions and exceptions in US immigration and refugee law.

THEORY AND METHOD

Trans feminism is a useful theoretical frame to employ in engaging these questions because it evokes attention to the transgressions and crossings that come in disrupting gender norms and what those transgressions do. In articulating a trans feminist framework, Finn Enke (2012) points out that a part of the theoretical possibility of trans is that it is a prefix that means and functions "'to cross'" (5). This syncs with Susan Stryker's (2008) highlighting of the transgressive nature of the term as describing "*the movement across a socially imposed boundary way from an unchosen starting place*—rather than any particular destination or mode of transition" (1; emphasis in original). And as Gayle Salamon (2008) writes, "Genders beyond the binary of male and female are neither fictive or futural but are embodied and lived" (115). In taking these two points seriously, we must first of all recognize the range of socially imposed boundaries that may be crossed and what the "trans-ing" of those boundaries does. Boundary crossings have material implications for the trans-ing subject and society. A trans feminist framework allows us to consider the range of ways that people transgress this gender binary and the material impacts of boundary crossings and attempts to control them.

Another trans feminist framework—a transnational feminist approach—is also useful as it considers the material and lived conditions of such trans-ing and transgression. Specifically, this approach understands the trans in transnational to mean "the *trans*versal, the *trans*actional, the *trans*lational, and the *trans*gressive aspects of contemporary behavior" (Ong 1999, 4; emphasis in original). Such an approach not only examines what happens in trans-ing the nation but also what happens when people, ideas, or things trans nation-state borders and fall in the in-between or the "cracks and crevices, the silences and sutures of the global" (Shome 2006, 3). While some see trans and feminist perspectives as in tension, Gayle Salamon rightly notes that there is transformative potential in combining trans and feminist theorizing. Specifically, drawing trans and transnational feminist analyses together means paying attention to movement and the boundary transgressions that happen in that movement, while also maintaining focus on dynamics of power that play out in those movements and transgressions. Additionally, both approaches maintain focus on attempts at controlling such movement, which makes theories such as biopolitics and necropolitics especially useful to understand the conditions of trans incorporation and exclusion (Haritaworn, Kuntsman, and Posocco 2014). These analytics also place focus on understanding how boundary crossings and transgressions connect with limits, exclusions, and prohibitions. Where people transgress social norms, there are, quite often, subsequent forces that work to maintain and enforce the social order. And these power-enforcing actions also have ripple effects that are intended and unforeseen. I want to suggest here that while greater recognition for trans asylum seekers has meant an acknowledgment of the precariousness that comes with trans-ing gender boundaries and that necessarily also affords possibilities for certain trans and gender variant applicants to gain refuge, it does so at the expense of walling off the concepts of gender and gender-based violence from the concepts of gender identity and expression. Such recognitions articulate a figuring of other asylum seekers as suspicious.

A fear of brown and black reproductivity has been a constant in the history of white America (Collins 2004; Flavin 2009; Ordover 2003; Roberts 1997). Though brown and black masculine reproductivity is also feared, this latest iteration of US asylum law targets the female-assigned body, reproducing a dynamic where gendered protections seem to be expanding, all the while presumably heterosexual, cisgender women of color continue to have limited grounding in gaining gendered protections. This move to incorporate trans applicants enables the United States' global moral project of positioning itself as the authority on human rights issues, while containing the threat of expanding protections for women whose reproductive bodies are seen as threatening. This analysis demonstrates how the protection of some gender transgressions can also participate in or produce limits and foreclosures—transgressing others' possibilities for livability in the context of US transnational political aspirations and anxieties.

I take a rhetorical approach to the law to understand how particular gendered transgressions are incorporable while others are suspicious and fearful. A rhetorical approach to anything is particularly interested in the practical function of language or what language does in particular contexts. Within a legal context, this means that I analyze the claims, evidence, testimony, and message strategies that unfold in legal arguments and decisions but also the "extrajudicial" discourses and contexts that frame how cases are heard and evaluated (Hasian 2002). Because asylum law is an international form of law enacted in national contexts, I attend to both national and global public discourses that shape the success and failure of particular groups of asylum seekers, including transnational human rights advocacy, media reports, congressional records, and foreign policy debates.

HISTORICIZING TRANS ASYLUM

The US asylum system as we know it today began with the implementation of the United States Refugee Act of 1980, which harmonized US law with international law and created a system for evaluating asylum seekers' claims. By the mid-1990s, the courts had heard enough sexuality- and gender-related cases to realize that there were not only gaps in the protections offered through the application of the UN definition of "refugee" but also that it may be necessary to address those gaps.

Gender and gender-based claims to asylum were introduced early in the US system of managing refugees as a problem. The courts began consistently hearing these cases in the late 1980s, and by the early 1990s legal advocates were offering analyses that called for the courts to address the gap in protections around questions of gender (Godfrey 1994; Kelly 1993; Kim 1994; Love 1993). As these advocates pointed out, the contours of "social group" in the refugee definition posed significant challenges for women fleeing gender-based violence. Furthermore, the social imaginary of gender-based violence meant that many claimants were told that their experiences of violence were "personal," not "political," excluding them from protection under refugee provisions. In 1995, the Immigration and Naturalization Service offered gender-attentive guidance to immigration judges and officials who would be hearing such cases, but this document neither stated that gender was a recognizable social group, nor did it necessitate that officials follow the guidelines (INS 1995). As mere suggestion, the document did little to clarify and strengthen gender-based protections. Rather, as I show in other work, acknowledgment of cis women's gendered claims was incorporated through segregated case precedent. Through these cases, gender came to be recognized, almost exclusively, as something that cisgender, presumably heterosexual woman have, and gender-based asylum meant refuge for cis women who were fleeing violence easily intelligible as cultural, relational, or private (McKinnon 2016). The isolated and contingent nature of gender's incorporation meant that the social and cultural transgressions that most cis women experienced persecution for went largely unrecognized as forms of political violence, making them ineligible for refugee relief.

In contrast, Attorney General Reno moved on articulating sexual orientation (and because of the conflation of gender and sexuality, certain trans claimants as well) as a particular social group in 1994. This decision was based on the claim of Fidel Armando Toboso Alfonso, who sought asylum in 1986 on the basis of being persecuted in Cuba for being gay. Toboso Alfonso was originally denied asylum by the Board of Immigration Appeals in 1990 (Matter of Toboso Alfonso 1990). But in 1994, Reno reversed the case and used it to set precedent for gays and lesbians to be recognized in US asylum law as particular social groups (Reno 1994). As immigration advocates and journalists account, this ruling enabled thousands of gays and lesbians to win refugee relief in the United States (Millman 2014).

It would be another five years before Hernandez Montiel's case made it through the courts, setting a precedent for those who transgressed social and cultural norms through their gender identity and expression to gain relief. Specifically, the courts recognized these claimants as "gay men with female sexuality identities," a social group that made them eligible for asylum (Hernandez-Montiel v. INS 2000). This precedent certainly created space for some trans applicants to be recognized as refugees in accordance with international refugee and human rights protocol (Boer-Sedano v. Gonzales 2005; Comparan v. Gonzales 2005; Maldonado v. Attorney General 2006; Ornelas-Chavez v. Gonzales 2006; Reyes-Reyes v. Ashcroft 2004), but it left many other trans applicants, such as trans men, gender-variant, and gender-queer applicants, without good standing to be seen as refugees in accordance with the law, and the precedent did nothing for cis women also making claims related to their gender (Neilson 2004). The Hernandez Montiel precedent would continue to guide the way trans applicants navigated the immigration system for ten years. Yet, late in the first decade of the new millennium, the approach to trans asylum began to shift.

The shift in recognition for transgender applicants coincided with the mounting international and US "LGBT rights as human rights" agenda. This agenda first developed on the international stage. In 2007, the UN released the first set of guidelines for incorporating sexuality and gender-identity/expression principles into international law, a document that is now known as the Yogyakarta Principles (UN 2007). Since 2007, the international body and its member countries have released dozens of other reports, statements, and resolutions on the question of the place of sexual orientation and gender identity/expression in international human rights law. Additionally, the UN created a mass campaign to highlight the need for protecting the rights of LGBT persons. UN Free & Equal "raises awareness of homophobic and transphobic violence and discrimination, and promotes greater respect for the rights of LGBT people everywhere. . . . The campaign engages millions of people around the world in conversations to help promote the fair treatment of LGBT people and generate support for measures to protect their rights" (UN 2016). UN Free & Equal proudly proclaims that the campaign has been viewed by over a billion people and that it is circulating around the globe its message of "acceptance and respect" (UN 2016).

The mainstreaming of a sexual orientation and gender identity analysis at this international level has prompted similar mainstreaming at the nation-state level. In particular, in countries such as the United States and the United Kingdom, we see a rise in the use of the human rights concerns of special groups as warrants and justifications for foreign affairs and policy. This is especially true in the United States, where the end of the Cold War meant a shift in foreign affairs rhetoric from addressing communist states to human rights matters (Dietrich 2006). The United States has long positioned itself as the global pastoral power around issues of human rights (McKinnon 2016). Not having a significant sexual-orientation and gender-identity platform in national affairs, let alone in international affairs, the United States made significant steps to harmonize its LGBT agenda with the international platform. Mainstream LGBT organizations such as the Human Rights Campaign led the way in revising the national platform. Gays and lesbians can now serve openly in the military (after repeal of the "Don't Ask, Don't Tell" policy), can get married (after reversal of the Defense of Marriage Act), and are included in hate crimes legislation as protected groups (after signing of the Matthew Shepard and James Byrd Jr. Hate Crimes Prevention Act). Queer scholars and activists ardently critique the focus of gay rights mobilization for its focus on inclusionary politics. Not only does this modality have a very narrow focus on specific institutions, but these politics also normalize white, middle-class, professional status interests as the main concerns of the LGBT movement (Brandzel 2016; Puar 2013; Puar 2006). In particular, Jasbir Puar (2013) links political consolidation around this agenda to US capital accumulation through "the gay and lesbian human rights industry." This industry "continues to proliferate Euro-American constructs of identity (not to mention the notion of a sexual identity itself) that privilege identity politics, 'coming out,' public visibility, and legislative measures as the dominant barometers of social progress" (338). This agenda not only has impact at the national level but also increasingly is employed for globally oriented projects of US foreign policy.

Toward internationalizing the United States' use of this LGBT human rights framework, in 2009 President Barack Obama signed on to the UN's "Statement on Human Rights, Sexual Orientation and Gender Identity." In its press release, the Obama administration explained: "The United States is an outspoken defender of human rights and critic of human rights abuses around the world. As such, we join with the other supporters of this Statement and we will continue to remind countries of the importance of respecting the human rights of all people in all appropriate international fora" (US Department of State 2009). This globally oriented project is in line with earlier iterations of the "women's rights as human rights" platform that deployed protecting-women-and-girls rhetoric to justify US international defense, diplomacy, and development projects (Grewal 2005; Hesford and Kozol 2005). In fact, the 2011 speech by the then secretary of state Hillary Clinton popularly titled by the press her "Gay Rights as Human Rights" speech, eerily parallels her 1995 "Women's Rights as Human Rights" speech at the Beijing Conference. As she stated in the 2011 speech:

> It is violation of human rights when people are beaten or killed because of their sexual orientation, or because they do not conform to cultural norms about how men and women should look or behave. It is a violation of human rights when governments declare it illegal to be gay, or allow those who harm gay people to go unpunished. It is a violation of human rights when lesbian or transgendered women are subjected to so-called corrective

> rape, or forcibly subjected to hormone treatments, or when people are murdered after public calls for violence toward gays, or when they are forced to flee their nations and seek asylum in other lands to save their lives. . . . No matter what we look like, where we come from, or who we are, we are all equally entitled to our human rights and dignity. (Clinton 2011)

Because Clinton was a representative of the United States' international policy, her speech serves as a global orientation project. She begins by stating the problem—"It is a violation of human rights"—naming the abuses that follow as contrary, unjust, and incorrect. The strength of the statement serves as a soft-power warning to countries, calling them to orient correctly on the matter of LGBT rights. Specifically, the speech calls countries to orient their mode of enacting sovereignty so that they are not seen as countries that violate or condone violence against LGBT individuals. That this speech coincided with President Obama's executive memorandum to the heads of all US federal executive offices and agencies, instructing each office to implement an actionable plan centered on the LGBT human rights agenda, demonstrates the promise that supported the call to countries to correctly orient in matter of LGBT rights. Specifically, Obama directed departments to "ensure that U.S. diplomacy and foreign assistance promote and protect the human rights of LGBT persons." The order also initiated stronger refugee and asylum provisions for those fleeing LGBT persecution:

> In order to improve protection for LGBT refugees and asylum seekers at all stages of displacement, the Departments of State and Homeland Security shall enhance their ongoing efforts to ensure that LGBT refugees and asylum seekers have equal access to protection and assistance, particularly in countries of first asylum. In addition, the Departments of State, Justice, and Homeland Security shall ensure appropriate training is in place so that relevant Federal Government personnel and key partners can effectively address the protection of LGBT refugees and asylum seekers, including by providing to them adequate assistance and ensuring that the Federal Government has the ability to identify and expedite resettlement of highly vulnerable persons with urgent protection needs. (Obama 2011)

We can see in both this current LGBT rights platform and the earlier "women's rights as human rights" iteration, the organizing of US national and foreign policy agenda around what I have described in earlier work as an enactment of "pastoral power" in the name of particular special groups. This agenda then becomes actionable in geopolitical contexts to service the political-economic interests of the United States (McKinnon 2016).

The current version consolidates US aspirations for political power and control through trans rights rhetoric. In order to be prepared for the internationally oriented project of what the then US ambassador to the UN Susan Rice called in a speech "advancing US interests and values abroad," the United States must provide a symbol to the outside world that the country itself is recognizing trans rights (Rice 2013)

A symbolically powerful yet contained way to do this is through the adoption of legal language and protections for trans asylum seekers. As a national manifestation of international law, asylum law holds the symbolic power of duly representing a state's domestic and foreign orientation toward particular issues. In attempting to demonstrate the United States' defense of a person's right to transgress binarized gendered norms, the 2011 protocol and training began by historicizing LGBT asylum through mention of the precedent set with the Toboso Alfonso ruling in a document created by the United States Citizenship and Immigration Services (USCIS). Next, the document gestures to the international efforts to create LGBT protections, by citing the UN Resolution on Human Rights, Sexual Orientation, and Gender Identity, which states that "LGBT[I] persons are endowed with the same inalienable rights—and entitled to the same protections—as all human beings" (USCIS 2011, 11). It then moves to articulate terminology that asylum officers can use to distinguish the particularities of cases. This inclusion of terminology seemed particularly important given the previous conflation of sexual orientation and gender identity in the Hernandez Montiel case (Hernandez-Montiel v. INS 2000). The USCIS document explains:

> *Gender* is what society values as the roles and identities of being male or female. *Sex* is the assignment of one's maleness or femaleness on the basis of anatomy and reproductive organs. Gender and sex are assigned to every individual at birth. *Gender identity* is an individual's internal sense of being male, female, or something else. Since gender identity is internal, one's gender identity is not necessarily visible to others. Gender expression is how a person expresses one's gender

> identity to others, often through behavior, clothing, hairstyles, voice, or body characteristics. *Transgender* is a term used for people whose gender identity, expression, or behavior is different from those typically associated with their assigned sex at birth. . . . Transgender is a gender identity, not a sexual orientation. Thus, like any other man or woman, a transgender person may have a heterosexual, bisexual or homosexual sexual orientation. (USCIS 2011, 12–13)

The definition of gender offered here allows for cis women and men to be seen as having a gender, yet by linking gender identity and expression directly to trans-ness, the document forecloses the possibility that cis individuals might make legitimate claims on the basis of their gender identity and expression. There is one discussion in the manual of "gender-based mistreatment," but by only focusing on the struggles of cis gay women in this section, the document continues to reify the idea that cis women are those who have gender-based experiences (USCIS 2011, 23–24).

Since the implementation of this guidance for asylum officers, there has been further clarification of the protections for transgender asylum seekers. Specifically, the Ninth Circuit Court of Appeals approved three trans asylum cases from Mexico with the expressed social group connected to their memberships as transgender persons in Mexico. The Ninth Circuit used the case *Avendano-Hernandez v. Lynch* to articulate the precedent. While Edin Avendano Hernandez was prohibited from receiving asylum because of a prior conviction in the United States, she was granted immigration relief through the protections of the UN Convention Against Torture. This case does important work not only for future transgender applicants in providing legal precedent in which to ground their claims but also in separating out the previous conflation of sexuality with gender identity from the Hernandez Montiel precedent. Avendano Hernandez's legal counsel argued that a significant aspect of the two prior denials of the claimant's plea was the conflation of sexuality and gender identity, which necessarily meant that the claimant did not fit the standards of the previous precedent:

> The IJ [Immigration Judge] failed to recognize the difference between gender identity and sexual orientation, refusing to allow the use of female pronouns because she considered Avendano-Hernandez to be "still male," even though Avendano-Hernandez dresses as a woman, takes female hormones, and has identified as woman for over a decade.

> Although the BIA [Board of Immigration Appeals] correctly used female pronouns for Avendano-Hernandez, it wrongly adopted the IJ's analysis, which conflated transgender identity and sexual orientation. (Avendano-Hernandez v. Lynch 2015, 4)

In assessing the case, the Ninth Circuit judges agreed that the courts erroneously conflated the two. They also set language for distinguishing the categories:

> While the relationship between gender identity and sexual orientation is complex, and sometimes overlapping, the two identities are distinct. . . . Of course, transgender women and men may be subject to harassment precisely because of their association with homosexuality. . . . Yet significant evidence suggests that transgender persons are often especially visible, and vulnerable, to harassment and persecution due to their often public nonconformance with normative gender roles. (Avendano-Hernandez v. Lynch 2015, 16–17)

The training protocol and this recent precedent go far in shoring up the difference between sexuality and gender identity/expression in order to allow for greater recognition of transgender asylum claimants. Yet with this new recognition also comes the possibility to foreclose protections for other gendered groups.

Unintentionally or not, the development of trans protections in US asylum participates in the severing of gender as a concept that might refer to a whole spectrum of identities, expressions, and experiences that variously fit or transgress social and cultural norms. Gender, instead, is figured ontologically rather than something that is done and felt in a multitude of manners (Butler 2004; Salamon 2010). Instead, the protocol and latest precedent further entrench a division between gendered subjects as it solidifies distinct categories for gender and gender-based persecution (concepts associated with cis women) and gender identity and gender-identity persecution (concepts given to trans and gender-variant applicants). For example, Avendano Hernandez's case is evaluated solely on the basis of her persecution as a transgender woman. The beginning narrative of the case is framed as such:

> Avendano-Hernandez is a transgender woman who grew up in a rural town in Oaxaca, Mexico. Born biologically male, she knew from an early age that she was different. Her appearance and behavior were very

> feminine, and she liked to wear makeup, dress in her sister's clothes, and play with her sister and female cousins rather than boys her age. Because of her gender identity and perceived sexual orientation, as a child she suffered years of relentless abuse that included beatings, sexual assaults, and rape. The harassment and abuse continued into adulthood, and, eventually, she was raped and sexually assaulted by members of the Mexican police and military. (Avendano-Hernandez v. Lynch 2015, 3–4)

Avendano Hernandez is not figured here as seeking asylum on account of her gender alone. It is, instead, her gender identity and expression that serve as the basis of her claim. This seems like a small shift. Yet rhetorically the difference between gender and gender identity and expression, especially in a legal context, matters greatly. This articulation solidifies the courts' earlier equation that gender is something reserved for cis women, while gender identity and expression become new segregated legal categories reserved for trans applicants.

In my broader research I found that the segregation of gender-based persecution from sexuality-related persecution normalized a one-sex, one-gender system whereby male-assigned subjects are figured as the neutral subjects for which all categories (except gender) are available. By segregating gender from gender identity and expression, this latest incorporation of trans-inclusive protections also works within the logic of this one-sex system, naturalizing male-assigned applicants as more readily legible, and hence eligible, for all asylum claims. This normalization arguably allows for greater political protections for trans applicants (though time will tell). Yet in separating gender and gendered-forms of persecution into categories, it maintains the already uphill battle that cis women have in successfully proving that the gendered transgressions that they violated or were threatened for should enable their protection in accordance with international and US law. Instead, for cisgender women whose grounds for claiming asylum are connected to their gender, their options for claiming asylum remain, at best, contingent and segregated.

Cisgender women continue to struggle greatly in being seen as claimants with a legitimate basis for asylum. In the early years of asylum proceedings, it was easy to hear an immigration judge discredit a woman's gendered claim by saying that her social group didn't count because gender is too broad to count as a social group. Upon sharing experiences of violent sexual assault at the hands of military officials, women were also told that their experiences attest more to "personal mistreatment" than "persecution." Unfortunately, such approaches to evaluate cisgender women's claims are still quite common. This was the case for Reina Izabel Garcia Martinez in 2004. Garcia Martinez's experiences with political violence began at age nine when a guerrilla group moved into her small community in Guatemala. The group began forcibly recruiting villagers to participate, including her family. Her brother was murdered in resistance. Soon thereafter, the Guatemalan military also came to Garcia Martinez' community to "protect" the village from the guerrillas. Instead of protection, the military began to physically and sexually violate the community members. As reported in the court's detail of this case,

> "Over the course of the next several years, someone in the village was raped by soldiers about every 8 to 15 days." According to Garcia, the military targeted the village, and retaliated against its residents based on the mistaken belief that the villagers had voluntarily joined, and were thus attempting to aid, the guerillas. (Garcia-Martinez v. Ashcroft 2004, 1070)

The judge who evaluated the case believed that Garcia-Martinez "had 'testified sincerely and genuinely without hesitation' about her experiences" but ultimately denied her claim, stating:

> "The evidence in the record simply does not substantiate a finding that [Garcia] had been a victim of past persecution. Particularly, [Garcia] has failed to show . . . that her attack had anything to do with . . . her political opinion, her race, religion, her political affiliation or membership in a particular social group." Garcia's rape was simply "a criminal act that was committed against her by a soldier[,]" and there was no evidence that the rape was "condoned by the government." (Garcia-Martinez v. Ashcroft 2004, 1071–72)

Sonia Maribel Lopez Juarez experienced similar challenges to gain asylum relief. Despite testifying to years of brutal rape by a man from her hometown who had a lot more power and money than she did, the judge consistently doubted her testimony, at one point asking,

> How do I know that you're not making up this story? That you're coming here as an economic refugee and you have no legal right to be

> here and you're making up a story so you can claim asylum? And there's reasons [*sic*] for you to misstate the facts, because you want to stay here and there's no other way that you can stay here unless you make up a story. Now, how do I know, do I have anything other than your statement that you claim that you were raped by this young man in Guatemala? (Juarez-Lopez v. Gonzales 2007, 2)

The Seventh Circuit would ultimately vacate the previous denials by the immigration judge and the Board of Immigration Appeals, but it was not before significant doubt had been raised about Lopez Juarez's claim for gendered refuge reliefs. Across the range of gender-based asylum claims made by cisgender women, claimants are consistently not believed, told that their experiences are not political, or are discredited as having experiences that do not rise to the level of persecution. The severing of gender from gender identity and expression makes the discounting of cis women's claims that much easier to contain as segregated from the broader political question of how particular groups are recognized and received as worthy of asylum.

I argue that this legal segregation of gender from gender identity and expression, rather than being an accidental and incidental happening, serves to create boundaries around a particularly suspicious and fearful figure in US law and politics—the figure of the reproductive brown cis woman. The separation of gender from gender identity guards the state from the threat of the nonwhite reproductive woman's body. As I have demonstrated in previous work, one of the primary logics that shapes who is incorporable as an immigrant subject is national anxiety around protecting white America from the reproductive threat that nonwhite women, by the nature of how their bodies are rhetorically perceived, bring with them (McKinnon 2010). While some migrant subjects are valued for their entrepreneurial possibilities, others are racialized through "schemes that serve to blacken and stigmatize" the way they are imagined as subjects with potential for belonging to the nation-state (Ong 2003, 13). Eithne Luibhéid (2013) demonstrates that a particularly fear-producing subject in contemporary Western national contexts is the nonwhite immigrant woman who is "pregnant on arrival." The actual or possible reproductivity of an immigrant woman is, across many Western national contexts, central to the discursive boundaries created between who is a desirable immigrant subject and who is not, who is "legal" and who is "illegal," as well as who might be tolerable enough for incorporation and who must be excluded. This happens in the United States because, as Carrie Crenshaw demonstrates, the definitional difference in US law between men and women is based on cis women's reproductivity and the differences that are presumed to be associated with that characteristic (Crenshaw 1996). In the immigration context of asylum where we are speaking mostly about nonwhite women's possible reproductivity, this difference is deployed as a means of exclusion to protect the primacy of white America from the risk of nonwhite reproductivity. In an age of the neoliberal US state, all immigrant subjects are also weighed as variously desirable or undesirable alongside their ability to reduce the image that they will be a burden to the state. This happens through having access to capital, having a degree in a sought-after academic field, having family connections, or having sponsorship through an employer. Since there is almost no way to reduce the way the cis women's bodies are read as reproductive, cis women making gender-based claims are figured overwhelmingly as undesirable and threatening. In accepting such gendered subjects as widely as might happen for trans applicants through the new legal language, the US state would be transgressing boundaries around state investments in power that have been present, and continue remake themselves, since the beginning of the white-settler colonial nation-state.

In conclusion, in walling off gender from gender identity and expression, the United States can receive trans applicants as gendered claimants because their gendered claims do not also come with the threat of the reproductive body that challenges the white capitalist structure of the state. As a side benefit, this incorporation then allows the state to deploy rhetoric about itself as a leader in human rights for groups such as women and LGBT individuals in order to promote its global project of "advancing democracy" abroad. Meanwhile, the threat to the primacy of white America remains limited. Segregated and contained in a contingent and conditional category, cis women and their presumed-to-be reproductive bodies are buffered from impacting the transnational aspirations that mobilize the US nation-state.

REFERENCES

Arc International. "SOGI Statements." http://arc-international.net/global-advocacy/sogi-statements/.

Avendano-Hernandez v. Lynch, No. 13–73744 (9th Cir. 2015).

Berg, Laurie, and Jenni Millbank. 2013. "Developing a Jurisprudence of Transgender Particular Social Group." In *Fleeing Homophobia: Sexual Orientation, Gender Identity and Asylum*, edited by Thomas Spijkerboer, 121–53. New York: Routledge.

Boer-Sedano v. Gonzales, 418 F.3d 1082 (9th Cir. 2005).

Brandzel, Amy L. 2016. *Against Citizenship: The Violence of the Normative*. Urbana: University of Illinois Press.

Butler, Judith. 2004. *Undoing Gender*. New York: Routledge.

Clinton, Hillary R. 2011. "Remarks in Recognition of International Human Rights Day." Geneva. https://2009-2017.state.gov/secretary/20092013clinton/rm/2011/12/178368.htm.

Collins, Patricia Hill. 2004. *Black Sexual Politics: African Americans, Gender, and the New Racism*. New York: Routledge.

Comparan v. Gonzales, 144 Fed. Appx. 673 (9th Cir. 2005).

Crenshaw, Carrie. 1996. "The Normality of Man and Female Otherness: (Re)Producing Patriarchal Lines of Argument in the Law and the News." *Argumentation and Advocacy* 32 (4): 170–85.

Dietrich, John W. 2006. "U.S. Human Rights Policy in the Post-Cold War Era." *Political Science Quarterly* 121 (2): 269–94.

Enke, Finn, ed. 2012. *Transfeminist Perspectives in and beyond Transgender and Gender Studies*. Philadelphia: Temple University Press.

Flavin, Jeanne. 2009. *Our Bodies, Our Crimes: The Policing of Women's Reproduction in America*. New York: New York University Press.

Garcia-Martinez v. Ashcroft, 371 F.3 1066 (US Court of Appeals for the 9th Cir. 2004).

Godfrey, Peter C. 1994. "Defining the Social Group in Asylum Proceedings: The Expansion of the Social Group to Include a Broader Class of Refugees." *Journal of Law and Policy* 3:257–88.

Grewal, Inderpal. 2005. *Transnational America: Feminisms, Diasporas, Neoliberalisms*. Durham, NC: Duke University Press.

Haritaworn, Jin, Adi Kuntsman, and Silvia Posocco, eds. 2014. *Queer Necropolitics*. New York: Routledge.

Hasian, Marouf. 2002. *Colonial Legacies in Postcolonial Contexts: A Critical Rhetorical Examination of Legal Histories*. New York: Peter Lang.

Hernandez-Montiel v. INS, 225 F. 3d 1084 (9th Cir. 2000).

Hesford, Wendy S., and Wendy Kozol, eds. 2005. *Just Advocacy? Women's Human Rights, Transnational Feminisms, and the Politics of Representation*. Piscataway, NJ: Rutgers University Press.

INS (Immigration and Naturalization Service). 1995. "Considerations for Asylum Officers Adjudicating Asylum Claims from Women." Office of International Affairs, May 26, 1995. http://www.refworld.org/docid/3ae6b31e7.html.

Juarez-Lopez v. Gonzales, 235 Fed. Appx. 361, 2 (7th Cir. 2007).

Kelly, Nancy. 1993. "Gender-Related Persecution: Assessing the Asylum Claims of Women." *Cornell International Law Journal* 26:625–75.

Kim, Sunny. 1994. "Gender-Related Persecution: A Legal Analysis of Gender Bias in Asylum Law." *American University Journal of Gender and Law* 107:108–37.

Love, Emily. 1993. "Recent Developments: Equality in Political Asylum Law; For a Legislative Recognition of Gender-Based Persecution." *Harvard Women's Law Journal* 17:133–56.

Luibhéid, Eithne. 2013. *Pregnant on Arrival: Making the Illegal Immigrant.* Minneapolis: University of Minnesota Press.

Maldonado v. Attorney General, 188 Fed. Appx. 101 (3rd Cir. 2006).

Matter of Toboso Alfonso, Board of Immigration Appeals (1990). https://www.justice.gov/sites/default/files/eoir/legacy/2012/08/14/3222.pdf.

McKinnon, Sara L. 2010. "(In)hospitable Publics: Theorizing Modalities of Access to U.S. Publics." In *Public Modalities: Rhetoric, Culture, Media, and the Shape of Public Life*, edited by Daniel C. Brouwer and Robert Asen, 131–53. Tuscaloosa: University of Alabama Press.

———. 2011. "Positioned in/by the State: Incorporation, Exclusion, and Appropriation of Women's Gender-Based Claims to Political Asylum in the United States." *Quarterly Journal of Speech* 97 (2): 178–200.

———. 2016. *Gendered Asylum: Race and Violence in US Law and Politics.* Urbana: University of Illinois Press.

Millman, Joel. 2014. "The Battle for Gay Asylum: Why Sexual Minorities Have an Inside Track to a US Green Card." *Wall Street Journal*, June 13, 2014. http://www.wsj.com/articles/why-sexual-minorities-have-an-inside-track-to-a-u-s-green-card-1402676258.

Musalo, Karen. 2003. "Revisiting Social Group and Nexus in Gender Asylum Claims: A Unifying Rationale for Evolving Jurisprudence." *DePaul Law Review* 52:777–808.

Neilson, Victoria. 2004. "Uncharted Territory: Choosing an Effective Approach in Transgender-Based Asylum Claims." *Fordham Urban Law Journal* 32 (2): 101–24.

Obama, Barack. 2011. "Presidential Memorandum: International Initiatives to Advance the Human Rights of Lesbian, Gay, Bisexual, and Transgender Persons." White House, Office of the Press Secretary. https://www.whitehouse.gov/the-press-office/2011/12/06/presidential-memorandum-international-initiatives-advance-human-rights-l.

Ong, Aihwa. 1999. *Flexible Citizenship: The Cultural Logics of Transnationality.* Durham, NC: Duke University Press.

———. 2003. *Buddha Is Hiding: Refugees, Citizenship, The New America.* Berkeley: University of California Press.

Ordover, Nancy. 2003. *American Eugenics: Race, Queer Anatomy and the Science of Nationalism.* Minneapolis: University of Minnesota Press.

Ornelas-Chavez v. Gonzales, 458 F.3d 1052 (9th Cir. 2006).

Puar, Jasbir. 2013. "Rethinking Homonationalism." *International Journal of Middle East Studies* 45:336–39.

Puar, Jasbir K. 2006. "Mapping US Homonormativities." *Gender, Place and Culture: A Journal of Feminist Geography* 13 (1): 67–88.

Reno, Janet. 1994. "Attorney General Order Designating Board of Immigration Appeals Case as Precedent." Office of the Attorney General, Washington, DC, June 16, 1994.

Reyes-Reyes v. Ashcroft, 384 F.3d 782 (9th Cir. 2004).

Rice, Susan E. 2013. "Human Rights: Advancing American Interests and Values." White House, Office of the Press Secretary. https://www.whitehouse.gov/the-press

-office/2013/12/04/remarks-national-security-advisor-susan-e-rice-human-rights-advancing-am.

Roberts, Dorthy E. 1997. *Killing the Black Body: Race, Reproduction, and the Meaning of Liberty.* New York: Random House.

Salamon, Gayle. 2008. "Transfeminism and the Future of Gender." In *Women's Studies on the Edge*, edited by Joan W. Scott, 115–36. Durham, NC: Duke University Press.

———. 2010. *Assuming a Body: Transgender and Rhetorics of Materiality*. New York: Columbia University Press.

Shome, Raka. 2006. "Transnational Feminism and Communication Studies." *Communication Review* 9 (4): 255–67.

Southham, Keith. 2011. "Who Am I and Who Do You Want Me to Be? Effectively Defining a Lesbian, Gay, Bisexual, and Transgender Social Group in Asylum Applications." *Chicago-Kent Law Review* 86:1363–87.

Stevens, Mattie L. 1993. "Recognizing Gender-Specific Persecution: A Proposal to Add Gender as a Sixth Refugee Category." *Cornell Journal of Law and Public Policy* 3:179–219.

Stryker, Susan. 2008. *Transgender History*. Berkeley, CA: Seal Press.

UN (United Nations). 1951. Convention Relating to the Status of Refugees. https://cms.emergency.unhcr.org/documents/11982/55726/Convention+relating+to+the+Status+of+Refugees+%28signed+28+July+1951%2C+entered+into+force+22+April+1954%29+189+UNTS+150+and+Protocol+relating+to+the+Status+of+Refugees+%28signed+31+January+1967%2C+entered+into+force+4+October+1967%29+606+UNTS+267/0bf3248a-cfa8-4a60-864d-65cdfece1d47.

———. 2007. *Yogyakarta Principles on the Application of International Human Rights Law in Relation to Sexual Orientation and Gender Identity*. https://yogyakartaprinciples.org/.

———. 2016. "About UN Free & Equal." https://www.unfe.org/en/about.

USCIS (United States Citizenship and Immigration Services). 2011. *Refugee, Asylum, and International Operations Directorate—Officer Training: Guidance for Adjudicating Lesbian, Gay, Bisexual, Transgender, and Intersex (LGBTI) Refugee and Asylum Claims.*

US Department of State. 2009. "UN Statement on 'Human Rights, Sexual Orientation, and Gender Identity.'" Press statement, Bureau of Public Affairs, March 18, 2009. https://2009-2017.state.gov/r/pa/prs/ps/2009/03/120509.htm.

Voss, M. A. (2005). "Young and Marked for Death: Expanding the Definition of 'Particular Social Group' in Asylum Law to Include Youth Victims of Gang Persecution." *Rutgers Law Journal* 37:263–74.

Chapter 9

"And Suddenly I Became a Lesbian!"

Performing Lesbian Identity in the Political Asylum Process

RACHEL A. LEWIS

They say that they don't believe that I am a genuine lesbian. What does that mean? I don't understand. How should I prove it?

—*Lesbian asylum seeker, United Kingdom*

In April, 2015, a Nigerian lesbian, Aderonke Apata, was denied political asylum in the United Kingdom on the grounds that she could not provide "proof" of her homosexuality. Despite presenting evidence that her girlfriend, brother, and three-year-old son had been killed in vigilante violence related to her lesbian, gay, bisexual, and transgender (LGBT) activism in Nigeria, the UK Home Office refused to recognize Apata's claim for political asylum. In *Apata, R. v Secretary of State for the Home Department* (2015), the judge in charge of Apata's case argued that because she had been in a previous relationship with a man, she "cannot be a lesbian." In an attempt to prove her sexual orientation, Apata and her fiancée, Happiness Agboro, whom Apata met while in the Yarl's Wood Immigration Removal Centre, submitted photographs and visual material documenting their sexual relationship as evidence in Apata's case. However, the judge nonetheless proceeded to argue that while Apata had "indulged in same-sex activity," she was not "part of the social group known as lesbians." As he put it, "*Lesbian is not a sexual choice.* . . . You can't be a heterosexual one day and a lesbian the next day. Just as you can't change your race." He even went so far as to suggest that Apata had "*deliberately altered her appearance . . . to a lesbian stereotype*" (my emphasis).

The rejection of Apata's asylum claim on the grounds that she had "deliberately altered her appearance . . . to a lesbian stereotype" attracted a significant amount of critical attention in the British tabloid media. For example, the *Daily Mirror* ran a satirical news quiz designed to educate its readers about the absurdity of Britain's treatment of lesbian and gay asylum seekers titled "Does the Home Office think you're gay?" (Leach 2015). Questions in the quiz range from detailed inquiries about applicants' attendance at gay bars, their sexual and/or marital history, and their religious belief systems, to whether or not they have children and/or have campaigned on behalf of gay rights. At the end of the quiz, the *Daily Mirror* informs its readers that unless they answer every question "correctly," they are "not gay enough for the Home Office" (Leach 2015). In the context of the quiz, answering every question "correctly" means conforming to heteronormative stereotypes that all lesbians are butch, politically outspoken, and childless and that they like to hang out in lesbian bars.

The increasingly absurd lengths to which lesbian and gay asylum seekers in the United Kingdom are having to go to "prove" their sexual orientation may help to account for the growing perception among queer asylum applicants that the only way in which they can establish a credible claim for political asylum is by filming themselves having sex. Indeed, many lesbian asylum seekers, such as Apata, feel that immigration officials will not believe that they are lesbians unless they film themselves having sex with another woman. As Jennifer, a lesbian woman from Jamaica, remarked:

> I wanted my case to be on the merit of what happened to me, not that I had to go and give you pictures of me and my girlfriend in bed to say "I am lesbian," which is what it basically came down to, they had pictures of

> me and my girlfriend and various partners actually, over time, not having sex but in pretty compromising positions to prove that I'm lesbian. (cited in Held 2016, 140–41)

In an interview with the BBC's "Today" program, a lesbian asylum seeker from Uganda similarly stated that she was pressured by immigration officials to produce sexually explicit material as evidence in her asylum case:

> I had my asylum appeals rejected twice. At one time I thought of committing suicide. Basically, they said I wasn't gay. I had met my current partner in the detention center. We presented the gifts we were exchanging—birthday cards, Valentine's cards and everything was in the pictures we took. And even when we were in court my partner was very much cross-examined about our relationship, and the questions we were asked, they were embarrassing. To bring home a point that we are really in a relationship this is what we do in bed. You can't imagine how humiliating that is. (cited in Lewis 2014)

Not only does the use of pornographic material as evidence of sexual orientation violate these women's right to privacy, but it has also produced a catch-22 situation for lesbian asylum applicants in which they are potentially damned if they fail to provide the tapes as proof of sexuality and damned if they do (the evidence can easily be dismissed as "fake," as in the case of Apata). Within such a scenario, the political asylum system is actually responsible for creating the very system of fraud that it is attempting to eradicate. As a result, decision-makers still have no idea what claimants need to do to prove their sexual orientation, the bureaucracy has taken on a life of its own, and proving sexuality in order to establish credibility for the purposes of political asylum has become, quite literally, an impossible task (Lewis 2014).

The United Kingdom's treatment of lesbian and gay asylum seekers is, in many ways, symptomatic of the Kafkaesque world of contemporary immigration controls in which asylum seekers are either trapped in a bureaucratic situation in which they cannot prove who they say they are or are detained in prisons operated by private security companies unconstrained by the rule of law. The absurd treatment of lesbian asylum applicants, in particular, derives from the fact that what we are witnessing in lesbian asylum cases is the point at which multiple systems of negation—including state-sanctioned forms of racism and compulsory heterosexuality—converge. If, as asylum advocates and scholars have argued, the general assumption on the part of immigration officials is that all asylum seekers are "bogus" until proven otherwise (Bohmer and Shuman 2008), then the lesbian asylum seeker is, in many ways, an ideal asylum applicant because her claims to authenticity within heteronormative, patriarchal culture can always be denied. As Judith Butler (1991) reminds us, lesbian oppression frequently takes place through relegating the lesbian to a position of "unthinkability" within the dominant order. Within the kind of binary sex/gender system where gender is always already constituted by compulsory heterosexuality, lesbian sexuality either imitates heterosexuality, functions for the benefit of the male spectator, or is, quite simply, inconceivable. What feminist and lesbian theorists have helped us to recognize is that within compulsory heterosexuality lesbians are frequently represented in terms of their *unrepresentability*—that the lesbian possibility, in other words, is denied (Lewis 2010). Thus, while gay male asylum claims are often disputed on the grounds that the applicant is perceived to be "faking it," the reality of male homosexuality is rarely denied. For lesbian asylum seekers, however, the very possibility of female same-sex desire is repeatedly subject to erasure within the political asylum process. Marking the limits of asylum law, lesbian refugees embody an institutionally and culturally assigned erotic precarity.[1]

Given the disproportionately negative impact of UK asylum policies on lesbian migrants, it is perhaps not surprising that a growing body of cultural activism has emerged to challenge the ways in which the political asylum system deprives lesbian asylum seekers of the opportunity to make credible asylum claims. Media and cultural productions about lesbian migration and asylum range from narrative and experimental films, documentaries, visual and sound art, poetry, theater, and performance art to online social media campaigns. During the past five years, there has been a particular growth in feminist theater and performance art devoted to documenting the challenges faced by lesbian refugees and asylum seekers in the United Kingdom.[2] Recent plays and performance art focusing on lesbian asylum include Oreet Ashery's *Staying: Dream, Bin, Soft Stud and Other Stories* (2010) and *The World Is Flooding* (2014), Cheril Clarke's *Asylum* (2012), Chris MacDonald's *Eye of a Needle* (2014), Clare Summerskill's *Rights of Passage* (2015), and Carol Campbell's *The Lesbian Wannabe* (2016). What interests me here are feminist and queer performances of asylum that grapple with the absurdity of having to prove one's sexuality in the context of the political asylum process. To this end, I will discuss two plays—MacDonald's *Eye of a Needle* and Campbell's *The Lesbian Wannabe*—both of which represent the UK asylum system as a Kafkaesque nightmare for lesbian asylum seekers. As these plays reveal through their critique of the asylum system's reliance on identity categories that only make sense from an administrative perspective, the UK asylum regime utilizes narratives of bureaucratic absurdity as a way of concealing state-sanctioned forms of racism and xenophobia.

LESBIAN ASYLUM AND THE RACIALIZED LENS OF SUSPICION IN *EYE OF A NEEDLE*

Chris MacDonald's play *Eye of a Needle* was first performed at Southwark Playhouse in London on August 27, 2014. Sponsored by the UK Lesbian and Gay Immigration Group, the leading organization devoted to representing LGBT asylum seekers in the United Kingdom, *Eye of a Needle* revolves around the story of a Ugandan lesbian refugee, Natale Bamadi, who is trapped in an absurd series of exchanges with two male immigration officials in which she cannot prove her sexual orientation. Set entirely within the context of an immigration detention center, the action moves back and forth between the interview room and the men's room where the two male immigration officials are seen masturbating after interrogating lesbian asylum applicants about their sexual relationships with women.

Eye of a Needle was originally inspired by the real-life asylum case of Ugandan lesbian Brenda Namigadde, who was denied political asylum in the United Kingdom on the grounds that she could not provide proof of her homosexuality. Upon the rejection of her asylum appeal, Namigadde was placed in detention, from where she was due to be deported to Uganda on January 28, 2011. Two days before Namigadde's scheduled deportation, however, Ugandan gay rights activist David Kato was brutally murdered after he successfully took out a legal injunction against the Ugandan magazine *Rolling Stone* for its role in inciting homophobic hate crimes. In response to Kato's murder, journalist Melanie Nathan of the US-based website LezGetReal: A Gay Girl's View on the World launched a massive global Internet campaign in which she demanded that Namigadde be granted a stay of deportation. LezGetReal's online campaign subsequently attracted the attention of David Bahati, the author of Uganda's proposed antihomosexuality legislation, who, after reading one of Nathan's articles, called her directly and asked her to give Namigadde a "message." Bahati informed Nathan that Namigadde would be welcomed back to Uganda on one condition: that she "abandon" her homosexual behavior (Lewis 2013). If she did not do so, he told her, Namigadde would be imprisoned upon her return. On the morning of Namigadde's scheduled deportation, her story appeared on the front cover of *Metro*, a magazine distributed for free in most British cities, with a readership of approximately 3.5 million people. As a result of the intense media coverage surrounding her case, Namigadde was eventually granted a stay of deportation in the United Kingdom just minutes before her plane was scheduled to depart, despite the fact that the UK Border and Immigration Agency continued to maintain that she was not a lesbian (Lewis 2013).

The rejection of Namigadde's asylum case is connected to the United Kingdom's 2010 Supreme Court decision to overturn the "discretion" requirement—or the notion that lesbian, gay, bisexual, transsexual, and intersexed (LGBTI) asylum applicants can return to their country of origin and be "discreet" about their sexual orientation or gender identity—which has led to the denial of lesbian and gay asylum claims on the grounds that the applicant's claimed sexual orientation is disbelieved (UKLGIG 2010 and 2013). In the 2010 Supreme Court decision *HJ (Iran) and HT (Cameroon)*, the chief judge, Lord Rodger, concluded that only those individuals who are "practicing homosexuals," or who choose to "live openly," constitute a particular social group for the purposes of the refugee convention. Those who adopt what he refers to as a "voluntary choice of discretion" do not qualify as convention refugees.[3] By assuming a scenario of "natural discretion" and "voluntary concealment," Lord Rodger makes a distinction between those who are "openly gay" and those who choose to remain "discreet" about their sexual orientation. The result of the Supreme Court's decision is that gay and lesbian applicants who cannot prove that they lived openly in their countries of origin must convince decision-makers that the primary reason they concealed their sexual orientation was because of a fear of persecution, rather than as a result of so-called voluntary discretion. By encouraging immigration officials to focus their attention on the expected future behavior of the applicant, the language of discretion that underwrites the Supreme Court decision gives adjudicators increased power to interrogate asylum applicants about their sexual orientation in a way that lends itself to negative credibility assessments (Lewis 2014).

The presumption that gay and lesbian asylum applicants are "voluntarily discreet" until proven otherwise is central to the challenges that Natale faces in attempting to prove her sexual orientation in *Eye of a Needle*. Despite the facts that Natale was a friend of David Kato and her photograph had been printed in a popular Kampala newspaper as well as on the Internet, the male immigration official in charge of her case nonetheless proceeds to question her as to why she cannot be "discreet" about her sexual orientation in Uganda. Not satisfied with Natale's account of her persecution in Uganda, he chooses instead to focus on her sexual history. In act 1, scene 4, he repeatedly interrogates Natale about how many women she has slept with in Uganda:

> Laurence: So . . . how have you, er, expressed your sexuality previously?
>
> Natale: I have done all the things a woman can do with another woman.
>
> Laurence: Can you give me any examples?
>
> Natale: I have made love with women. I have kissed ladies, I have had sex with them. I have done it all.
>
> Laurence: And do you have any evidence of any of these sexual relations or of your sexuality?

As is evident in the above scene, the discretion logic that underwrites queer asylum policies in the United Kingdom has not only produced the expectation of visibility and an identity in the public sphere but, perhaps more disturbingly, has also resulted in an excessive focus on the sexuality of individual claimants. The distinction made by the Supreme Court between those who are "openly gay" and those who are "voluntarily discreet" means that immigration officials are increasingly relying on an individual's participation in specific sexual acts as the basis for proving sexual orientation. Indeed, a recent report produced by the UK Lesbian and Gay Immigration Group has documented that immigration officials frequently engage in sexually explicit questioning of political asylum applicants, making decisions on the basis of claimants' sexual practice and behavior (UKLGIG 2013). For many asylum applicants like Natale, however, living openly and freely in their country of origin would have been virtually impossible. Consequently they are subjected to an increased burden of proof to establish that they are living as "openly gay" in the country in which they are seeking asylum.

Later in act 1 of *Eye of a Needle,* a second male immigration official enters the interview with Natale and Laurence and similarly demands to see visual material documenting Natale's sexuality:

> Natale: I have videos of marches, of protests, there are photos of me at a bar we go to in Kampala. It allows gay people. There is a manifesto from my time in Cape Town and—
>
> Ted: Any sex tapes?
>
> Laurence: Um, we were talking about the documents that Miss Bamadi was going to submit.
>
> Ted: I was listening. I was wondering if there was any video evidence of you having lesbian sex? Miss Bamadi?
>
> Natale: I don't have anything like that.
>
> Ted: Any pornographic photographs of you performing sex acts with other women?
>
> Natale: No.
>
> Ted: Well, in these "documents" you talk about then, do you ever mention any lesbianic sex acts? What about photos from the gay bar, are you kissing women in them? Dancing with them?
>
> Natale: Of course I am dancing with them, they are my friends.
>
> Ted: I mean, dancing with them, sexually, you know? Grinding, twerking, kissing?

Despite the fact that Natale possesses substantial media coverage documenting her career as an LGBT activist in Uganda, the male immigration officials in *Eye of a Needle* still rely on the sex tapes as primary proof of sexuality. In this way, MacDonald cleverly exposes the extent to which the political asylum system simultaneously treats lesbian sexuality as invisible and in a manner verging on the pornographic. As *Eye of a Needle* demonstrates, what drives the contradictory production of lesbian invisibility and hypersexualization in the political asylum process is the heteronormative assumption that it is possible for women to be "voluntarily discreet" about their sexual orientation—or the tired patriarchal notion that female sexuality is somehow "less active" than male sexuality. Because it is difficult for many women to be openly gay in their countries of origin, a high burden of proof is placed on them to convince officials that their acts of discretion are involuntary. Transferring the burden of credibility to lesbian asylum applicants in this way opens up a loophole for negative lesbian asylum decisions because it permits immigration officials to interrogate applicants about specific sexual acts under the pretext that this will help them to establish whether or not the women before them desire to be "openly gay." The result is that heteronormative stereotypes about lesbian sexuality based on the assumption that lesbians are naturally more "discreet" about their sexual orientation than gay men become the basis for excluding queer female migrants from accessing refugee protection (Lewis 2014).

In *Eye of a Needle*, Natale's failure to conform to heteronormative stereotypes of lesbian identity based on visibility, hypersexualization, and frequent attendance at lesbian bars means that her asylum claim is denied and she is deported to Uganda. At the end of the play, we learn that, as a result of her deportation, Natale was stoned to death outside her apartment in Kampala. The play thus concludes with a disillusioned Laurence quitting his job and a pro bono lawyer named Caroline informing Ted that Natale has been murdered. Ted's final response to the news of Natale's murder is "We can't run the place like this. . . . We cannot do this properly. We aren't coping. We can't cope." In this way, the play ends in a fittingly dystopian manner with the poignant image of a failing, dysfunctional bureaucratic system. The fact that the scene concludes in the men's restroom only heightens the sense of absurdity and abjection. As Chris Macdonald has commented regarding the Kafkaesque nature of his play, "The impression that we get of the detention center is that it is in chaos. The chaos of the system is unfathomable from the outside" (MacDonald 2014).

By showing the absurdity—and ultimate impossibility—of successfully performing lesbian sexuality in the context of the political asylum process, MacDonald's play illustrates how gendered and racialized notions of credibility have a disproportionately negative impact on the treatment of queer female migrants of color. In doing so, *Eye of a Needle* unveils how gendered, racialized, and heteronormative discourses of suspicion in the political asylum system work to produce lesbian migrants as precarious populations through differentially exposing them to deportation and, in the case of MacDonald's protagonist, premature death.

SEXUAL CITIZENSHIP, ASYLUM, AND HOMONORMATIVITY IN *THE LESBIAN WANNABE*

It is the racialized, classed, and gendered stereotypes of lesbian identity at work in the political asylum process that are similarly rendered absurd in Carol Campbell's new play, *The Lesbian Wannabe* (2016). Moving back and forth between the immigration office and a local lesbian bar, *The Lesbian Wannabe* exposes the racist and heteronormative policing of black lesbian migrant and femme identities across multiple institutional and cultural sites—queer and nonqueer alike. The play centers upon the story of Jacqui Kabumba, a Ugandan lesbian seeking asylum in the United Kingdom. Jacqui's claim for asylum is initially denied on the basis that she cannot prove her homosexuality. After being put in touch with a visibly "out" lesbian pro bono asylum lawyer, Jacqui is encouraged to make a film of herself having sex with another woman, which ultimately leads to her being granted asylum in the United Kingdom.

The Lesbian Wannabe opens with a scene between an unnamed male immigration official and Jacqui, who cannot prove her sexual orientation. In act 1, scene 1, the dialogue revolves around the absurdity of how lesbian asylum cases such as Jacqui's are evaluated, including the imperative that lesbian asylum seekers read lesbian magazines, watch lesbian shows, use sex toys, and listen to lesbian musicians:

> Immigration Officer: What sex toys do you use?
>
> Jacqui: What sex toys do I use? What kind of question is that?
>
> Immigration Officer: Okay, you are definitely becoming overwrought. These are straight-forward questions to help streamline the process of naturalization. Answer yes or no, do you read Oscar Wilde?
>
> Jacqui: No.
>
> Immigration Officer: Do you attend pride marches?
>
> Jacqui: No.
>
> Immigration Officer: Do you listen to Melissa Etheridge?
>
> Jacqui: Yes.
>
> Immigration Officer: When did you first think you were a lesbian?

Jacqui: When I was a little girl . . .

Immigration Officer: You must tell me about every sexual relationship you've ever had with a woman, every feeling or thought about any woman you've ever liked.

Remarkably, much of the dialogue in this opening scene is taken from actual interviews with lesbian asylum seekers, as reported by the UK Lesbian and Gay Immigration Group, the charity Stonewall, and official legal transcripts. Indeed, as Human Rights Watch has observed, immigration officials' questioning about specific sexual acts can be especially common in lesbian asylum cases (Human Rights Watch 2010). As recently as 2013, questions posed by UK judges to lesbian asylum applicants under the pretext of establishing claimants' sexual orientation included "Was it loving sex or rough?," "How many sexual encounters have you had with your partner?," and "You have never had a relationship with a man. How do you know you are a lesbian?" (UKLGIG 2013, 20). Lesbian asylum seekers in the United Kingdom have also been interrogated about whether or not they "use sex toys," which sexual positions they like to adopt in bed, the novels of Oscar Wilde, and which (lesbian) shows they watch (Bennett 2013). Additionally, judges have told women that they do not "look like" lesbians, that lesbians "don't have children," and that all lesbians "enjoy the gay scene" and like to attend gay pride marches (Bennett 2013). Indeed, the final line in act 1, scene 1 of *The Lesbian Wannabe*—"A homosexual lesbian can avoid the risk of harm by being discreet in her conduct"—is extracted from a lesbian asylum case discussed by Alice Miller, one she refers to as that of the "Discreet Chinese Lesbian Wannabe," who was denied political asylum in Australia on the grounds that she was not a "practicing lesbian" (Miller 2005).

During the reading of this opening scene from *The Lesbian Wannabe* at the symposium Crisis, Migration and Performance at the National University of Ireland in Galway in 2016, audience reactions ranged from mild discomfort and muted laughter to complete shock when Carol Campbell revealed that a good portion of the scene's dialogue was taken from actual lesbian asylum cases. Arguably, much of the comic absurdity in the initial scene of *The Lesbian Wannabe* derives from the imperative that queer asylum applicants be "openly gay" in order to be granted refugee protection. As discussed earlier, while the claim to refugee protection is based on sexual orientation, the imperative to be openly gay—to be a sexual citizen—is the product of neoliberal ideologies of sexual citizenship that are racialized, classed, and gendered. In her ethnographic study of lesbian asylum seekers navigating the UK asylum process and lesbian bar spaces in Manchester, Nina Held examines how the 2010 Supreme Court decision reproduces racialized, classed, and gendered norms of lesbian identity. As she rightly notes,

> By dividing the group of gay and lesbian asylum seekers into two categories, those who live their sexuality openly and those who do not, it draws on a Western model of sexuality that requires public expression of sexual behavior. . . . Part of this is to produce evidence of a (white) gay lifestyle. In the asylum system, proof of "belonging to a particular social group" is based on normative and racialized notions of the genuine lesbian. (Held 2016, 145)

A crucial part of how asylum applicants produce evidence of the "white gay lifestyle" to which Held refers is by attending gay bars. And yet the kinds of racialized and classed sexual citizenship norms that get codified in the immigration process also emerge in lesbian and queer bar spaces, many of which similarly reproduce racialized standards of lesbian identity and behavior (Held 2016). Not only have immigration officials been known to telephone gay bars to inquire about the presence of queer asylum applicants, but the lesbian bar spaces themselves often generate the same kinds of normative racial and gender stereotypes of lesbian identity that are oppressive to queer female refugees when they seek political asylum. In this way, lesbian migrants frequently find themselves caught between heteronormative narratives of lesbian identity in the political asylum process and homonormative forms of gate-keeping in lesbian bar spaces, all of which prevent queer women of color from exercising the kind of "consumer citizenship" needed to support their claim to be "openly gay."

In act 1, scene 2 of *The Lesbian Wannabe,* Campbell offers a stinging critique of the catch-22 situation facing queer women of color as they attempt to prove their sexual orientation in the political asylum process. In this scene, we are introduced to butch-femme lesbian couple, Diesel Sheila (DD) and Felicia, whose relationship conforms to heteronormative stereotypes of lesbian sexuality and behavior. In a lesbian bar, Babe's, the butch lesbian DD, like the male immigration official before her, is similarly critical of Jacqui's claim to be a "real lesbian":

DD: You don't look like a gay girl.

Jacqui: No?

DD: Have you ever slept with a guy?

Felicia: DD!

DD: Have you ever kissed a guy?

Jacqui: Not willingly.

DD: You do know this is a lesbian bar, don't you?

Felicia: DD, stop it. (*To Jacqui*) Sorry, my girlfriend gets a little concerned for my welfare. (*To DD*) Back off. Jacqueline here was just telling me that she's about to leave the country because she applied for asylum for being queer and they denied her claim.

DD: That's because you don't look lesbian enough.

Jacqui: Why am I continually having this conversation?

DD: Doesn't matter. You could appeal it.

Jacqui: Really?

DD: They didn't tell you that?

Jacqui: No.

DD: Of course not. Where are you from?

Jacqui: Uganda.

DD: Yeah, they're still pretty ruthless to gays over there.

Jacqui: You could say that.

DD: Parading gays naked out in the street. It's barbaric.

Jacqui: I prefer not to use the term *barbaric*. But it is certainly an abusive practice. And my girlfriend was killed two years ago.

DD: Yeah, you should totally fight this. You just need some pointers on how to dress more butch.

Jacqui: That's not who I am. It just plays into stereotypes.

DD: If you're a femme lesbian, everybody knows it's just a matter of time before you're tempted by a guy.

In this scene, the femmephobia and racialized exoticism directed by DD toward Jacqui mimics the kinds of heteronormative and colonialist narratives of lesbian identity that are typically reproduced in the political asylum process. As with women's asylum narratives more generally, lesbian identity is frequently constituted through the invocation of a colonialist narrative of oppression, according to which the victimized "third world lesbian" escapes from a "barbaric" Africa (in this case, Uganda) to find sexual maturity and self-knowledge in a supposedly enlightened and liberal West (i.e., the United Kingdom). Indeed, queer refugee law as it is interpreted in the vast majority of asylum cases is little more than a continuation of the Western colonizing project, whereby the West constructs the body of the Other in its own image, which in the case of the lesbian asylum seeker means passing as visibly and stereotypically lesbian as possible (Lewis 2010).

Through the critique of racism and xenophobia in lesbian bar spaces, *The Lesbian Wannabe* directs our attention to the kinds of racist stereotypes about the sexuality of African women that contribute to the erasure of queer women of color in the political asylum process. As Tracy Reynolds observes in her work on the sexuality of black female migrants in the United Kingdom, colonialist myths of black women as either hypersexual heterosexuals or asexual mammies foreclose the possibility of a nonnormative or queer black female sexuality (Reynolds 2016, 101). In *The Lesbian Wannabe*, the dialogue between DD and Jacqui similarly encourages us to see how race is implicated in the sexual citizenship norms to which black lesbian migrants in the United Kingdom are subjected. As LGBT rights and the concept of sexual democracy in Europe have acquired increasingly nationalist and racist undertones (El-Tayeb 2011), black queer migrants have become impossible subjects. In the ideology of racelessness that frequently underwrites mainstream LGBT human rights advocacy, "the African" is marked as black through his or her lack of gay rights, as a homonormative notion of "gay rights" emerges "as a single-issue and race-free mode of difference" (Agathangelou 2013, 454). The result of this redacting of race in LGBT human rights and sexual citizenship discourses is the creation of a politics of black queer impossibility, whereby one cannot be both queer and black. As Agatha Agathangelou argues, "In the narrative wherein an imperial global structure of white supremacy protects 'the gays' from 'the blacks', . . . the displacement of racialized gays and lesbians becomes visible" (Agathangelou 2013, 472).

In *The Lesbian Wannabe*, Carol Campbell parodies the kinds of racialized and homonormative stereotypes of queer identity and sexual citizenship that render black lesbian identity invisible. In act 1, scene 4, Jacqui meets with a butch immigration lawyer, Germaine Finch, who, we learn, is a "Jane Lynch type lawyer." While Germaine acknowledges the problems with the immigration system's treatment of gay and lesbian asylum claims, she nonetheless encourages her client to reproduce these norms anyway, handing her a brochure titled "How to Be a Lesbian." The brochure contains questions such as "Do I feel nervous or out of place with friends who are girls?" and "Do I read lesbian magazines?" By encouraging Jacqui to perform lesbian stereotypes in order to prove her sexual orientation, this scene mocks the extent to which the political asylum process urges applicants to become reflexive and responsible "entrepreneurs of the self" or the kinds of individuals who are encouraged to represent themselves in their own immigration hearings (Conlon and Gill 2013, 245).[4]

In *The Lesbian Wannabe*, the absurdity of the kind of personal responsibility that Jacqui must exercise in order to prove her sexual orientation is illustrated in the filming of the sex scene between Jacqui and Felicia for the benefit of the male immigration official. Parodying the tired sexual predilections of the male heteropornographic imaginary, Germaine humorously opines regarding the rationale for having another femme lesbian "act" in the film alongside Jacqui that "a butch-femme portrayal only reproduces heteronormative stereotypes, or in this case homonormative ones. And it'll turn the guy off. No, we need a more delicate representation." In this way, *The Lesbian Wannabe* offers an astute parody of the extent to which lesbian sexuality is repeatedly treated in a manner verging on the pornographic in the political asylum process. The character of Germaine knowingly mocks such heteronormative stereotypes, insisting, "Your last rehearsal didn't cut it for the level of passion I'm asking for. It was *not* loving enough." As she comments to Felicia, who plays Jacqui's lover, "You looked like a call girl," and, to Jacqui, "You were acting like some sort of blind dental hygienist."

The absurdity of Germaine's running commentary on Felicia and Jacqui's sexual performance is not as far removed as one might think from the ways in which gay and lesbian asylum cases are evaluated. Immigration officials often "view" sex tapes and evaluate applicants' performance(s) therein as to establish whether or not they demonstrate a "credible" gay identity. In her work on sexuality and asylum law, Jenni Millbank (2009) discusses two asylum cases in Canada and Australia in which courts viewed sex tapes produced by gay male asylum applicants but ultimately rejected the tapes as evidence of sexual orientation. While in the Australian case the tape was discredited on the basis that the oral evidence "lacked important detail" about "the nature and type of sexual activity in the video" (22), in the Canadian case the tape was rejected because the court held that it did not involve the applicant's claimed partner. As the judge argued, "The sex acts appear so mechanical it looks more like an encounter between a 'John and a male prostitute, rather than two men very much in love with each other" (Millbank 2009, 22).

From the bizarre scenes in the immigration office to the racism in Babe's to the play's ultimate conclusion with the sleazy male official lurching for the sex tape as Jacqui is granted refugee status, *The Lesbian Wannabe* offers a powerful comic critique of the absurdity of having to prove one's sexual orientation in the context of the political asylum process. As *The Lesbian Wannabe* illustrates through its strategies of parody and disidentification, practices of credibility assessment in the political asylum process produce racialized forms of sexual citizenship and belonging that constitute queer migrants as unfit for citizenship and thus subject to deportation. Such sexual citizenship ideologies, according to which rights are defined primarily in relation to consumption (Duggan 2004), create an impossible burden of proof and a narrative that so few queer female refugees are able to reproduce due to lack of access to legal representation, detention, and extreme poverty. Thus, as *The Lesbian Wannabe* suggests, while gay and lesbian claims for asylum are not explicitly prohibited in countries such as the United Kingdom, black lesbian migrants are frequently excluded from accessing such rights through their failure to achieve the status of "consumer citizen" (Lewis 2014).

By showing how the burden of proof is discharged within the political asylum process in a way that renders black lesbian migrants deportable subjects, both *Eye of a Needle* and *The Lesbian Wannabe* call attention to how the political asylum system operates as a site of legalized violence by which queer female migrants of color are differentially deprived of the resources needed to make credible asylum claims. Successfully demonstrating how the political asylum system seeks to make racism and its effects invisible, these plays reveal the urgency of tackling practices of credibility determination in the political asylum process from feminist, queer, and antiracist perspectives. Indeed, both plays point toward the need for greater coalitions between feminist, queer, immigrant, and antiracist activists in advocacy for LGBT refugees and asylum seekers. In doing so, they illustrate how feminist and queer performances can become part of the solution to the problems of black lesbian invisibility and representation in the asylum process that they portray.

In response to the dominant role played by assessments of credibility in LGBT asylum claims, asylum advocates have suggested that immigration adjudicators need to be sensitive to the difficulties of proving sexual orientation and gender identity and to focus instead on narratives that help individuals articulate their sexual histories. Such an approach to LGBT asylum cases on the part of officials would require open-ended questions about sexuality that would enable applicants to carefully narrate their sexual histories rather than solely respond to intrusive questions about specific sexual practices. In the case of lesbian asylum claims, there is a need for greater self-awareness on the part of asylum adjudicators about the obstacles to establishing credibility. To more accurately assess lesbian applications, asylum officials need to acknowledge the intersectional challenges to narrativizing lesbian visibility. Recognizing the challenges to narrativizing visibility in lesbian asylum claims will require immigration officials to address the ways that previous experiences of passing or of concealment of sexual identity can produce a credibility gap for lesbian asylum applicants. As I have argued elsewhere, ensuring that asylum adjudicators are able to adequately engage with the gender-specific dimensions of women's asylum narratives is also crucial if the United Nations refugee convention is to be appropriately applied to lesbian asylum claims (Lewis 2013).

What is clear from the feminist and queer performances of asylum examined here is the importance of media and cultural advocacy for conceptualizing the relationship between sexuality and political asylum narratives. In the context of LGBT asylum cases, the challenges of representation and (in)visibility that are specific to lesbian asylum claims suggest that media and cultural production will continue to function as a powerful site of activism and resistance for lesbian migrants for some time to come. As I have argued here, feminist and queer performances of asylum not only offer a fascinating and unique perspective on the intersections between bureaucratic performance and theatrical performance—they also show how theater and performance can become part of the solution to the social problems that it portrays.

NOTES

1. For a more detailed discussion of lesbian invisibility and erasure in the political asylum process, see Lewis 2010, 2013, and 2014.

2. Since the early 1990s, there has been a significant growth in arts and cultural activities in the United Kingdom devoted to addressing the challenges faced by refugee populations more generally in navigating the political asylum bureaucracy. For a discussion of theater forms by, for, and about refugees and asylum seekers, see the special issue of *Research in Drama Education*, Gilbert and Nield 2008; Balfour 2013; and Jeffers 2012.

3. Lord Rodger uses "a trivial example" from "the Western context" to illustrate his rationale behind the need for refugee protection for those who are "openly gay": "Just as straight men are free to enjoy themselves playing rugby, drinking beer and talking about girls with their mates, so male homosexuals are to be free to enjoy themselves going to Kylie concerts, drinking exotically colored cocktails and talking about boys with their straight female mates" (cited in Keenan 2011, 35).

4. In their work on political asylum in the United Kingdom, Deirdre Conlon and Nick Gill discuss how asylum seekers placed in detention are provided with an educational program that encourages them to become familiar with self-representation notebooks that can serve as a legal-orientation tool in the asylum process. These notebooks are designed, first and foremost, to allow asylum seekers to represent themselves at their immigration hearings. What the notebooks aim to do is to teach asylum seekers about appropriate forms of demeanor and self-expression in the political asylum process so that they may become reflexive and responsible "entrepreneurs of the self" (Conlon and Gill 2013, 245). In this context, as I have discussed elsewhere, proving sexual orientation or credibility as a member of a particular social group becomes, quite literally, the personal responsibility of the applicant (Lewis 2014).

REFERENCES

Apata R. v. Secretary of State for the Home Department. 2015. http://www.bailii.org/ew/cases/EWHC/Admin/2015/888.html.

Balfour, Michael, ed. 2013. *Refugee Performance: Practical Encounters*. Bristol, UK: Intellect.

Bennett, Claire. 2013. "Claiming Asylum on the Basis of Your Sexuality: The Views of Lesbians in the UK." *Women's Asylum News* 115 (January/February): 1–4.

———. 2014. "Sexuality and the Asylum Process: The Perspectives of Lesbians Seeking Asylum in the UK." Unpublished doctoral thesis, University of Sussex. http://sro.sussex.ac.uk/51595/.

Bohmer, Carol, and Amy Shuman. 2007. "Producing Epistemologies of Ignorance in the Political Asylum Application Process." *Identities: Global Studies in Culture and Power* 14 (5): 603–29.

———. 2008. *Rejecting Refugees: Political Asylum in the Twenty-First Century.* New York: Routledge.

Butler, Judith. 1991. "Imitation and Gender Insubordination." In *Inside/Out: Lesbian Theories, Gay Theories,* edited by Diana Fuss, 13–31. New York: Routledge.

Campbell, Carol. 2016. *The Lesbian Wannabe.* Unpublished script.

Conlon, Deirdre, and Nick Gill. 2013. "Gagging Orders: Asylum Seekers and Paradoxes of Freedom and Protest in Liberal Society." *Citizenship Studies* 17 (2): 241–59.

Dauvergne, Catherine, and Jenni Millbank. 2003. "Burdened by Proof: How the Australian Refugee Review Tribunal Has Failed Lesbian and Gay Asylum-Seekers. *Federal Law Review* 300 (31): 299–342.

Duggan, Lisa. 2004. *The Twilight of Equality? Neoliberalism, Cultural Politics, and the Attack on Democracy.* Boston: Beacon Press.

El-Tayeb, Fatima. 2011. *European Others: Queering Race and Ethnicity in Postnational Europe.* Minneapolis: University of Minnesota Press.

Gilbert, Helen, and Sophie Nield, eds. 2008. "Performance and Asylum: Embodiment, Ethics." *Research in Drama Education: The Journal of Applied Theatre and Performance* 13 (2): 133–269.

Held, Nina. 2016. "What Does a Genuine Lesbian Look Like? Intersections of Sexuality and Race in Manchester's Gay Village and in the UK Asylum System." In Stella et al., *Sexuality, Citizenship and Belonging,* 131–48.

Human Rights Watch. 2010. *Fast-Tracked Unfairness: Detention and Denial of Women Asylum Seekers in the UK.* http://www.hrw.org/sites/default/files/reports/uk0210webwcover.pdf.

Jeffers, Alison. 2012. *Refugees, Theatre and Crisis: Performing Global Identities.* London: Palgrave Macmillan.

Keenan, Sarah. 2011. "Safe Spaces for Dykes in Danger? Refugee Law's Production of Vulnerable Lesbians." In *Regulating the International Movement of Women: From Protection to Control,* edited by Sharron FitzGerald, 29–47. New York: Routledge.

Leach, Anna. 2015. "Does the Home Office Think You're Gay?" *Daily Mirror,* March 6, 2015. http://www.mirror.co.uk/news/ampp3d/home-office-think-youre-gay-5280895.

Lewis, Rachel. 2010. "The Cultural Politics of Lesbian Asylum: Angelina Maccarone's *Unveiled* (2005) and the Case of the Lesbian Asylum-Seeker." *International Feminist Journal of Politics* 12 (3–4): 424–43.

———. 2013. "Deportable Subjects: Lesbians and Political Asylum." *Feminist Formations* 25 (2): 174–94.

———. 2014. "'Gay? Prove It': The Politics of Queer Anti-Deportation Activism." *Sexualities* 17 (8): 958–75.

MacDonald, Chris. 2014. *Eye of a Needle.* London: Oberon Books.

Miles, Nathaniel. 2010. "No Going Back: Lesbian and Gay People and the Asylum System. Report." Stonewall. http://www.stonewall.org.uk/what_we_do/research_and_policy/2874.

Millbank, Jenni. 2002. "Imagining Otherness: Refugee Claims on the Basis of Sexuality in Canada and Australia." *Melbourne University Law Review* 26 (1): 1–33.

———. 2009. "'The Ring of Truth': A Case Study of Credibility Assessment in Particular Social Group Refugee Determinations." *International Journal of Refugee Law* 21 (1): 1–33.

Miller, Alice. 2005. "Gay Enough: Some Tensions in Seeking the Grant of Asylum and Protecting Global Sexual Diversity." In *Passing Lines: Sexuality and Immigration,* edited by Brad Epps, Keja Valens, and Bill Johnson González, 137–88. Cambridge, MA: Harvard University Press.

Reynolds, Tracy. 2016. "Black Mammy and Company: Exploring Constructions of Black Womanhood in Britain." In Stella et al., *Sexuality, Citizenship and Belonging,* 95–111.

Stella, Francesca, Yvette Taylor, Tracey Reynolds, and Antoine Rogers, eds. 2016. *Sexuality, Citizenship and Belonging: Trans-National and Intersectional Perspectives.* London: Routledge.

UKLGIG (UK Lesbian and Gay Immigration Group). 2010. "Failing the Grade: Home Office Initial Decisions on Lesbian and Gay Claims for Asylum." https://uklgig.org.uk/wp-content/uploads/2014/04/Failing-the-Grade.pdf.

———. 2013. "Missing the Mark: Decision Making on Lesbian, Gay (Bisexual, Trans and Intersex) Asylum Claims." http://www.uklgig.org.uk/docs/publications/Missing_the_Mark.pdf.

UK Supreme Court. 2010. HJ (Iran) and HT (Cameroon) v. Secretary of State for the Home Department. http://www.supremecourt.gov.uk/decided-cases/docs/UKSC_2009_0054_Judgment.pdf.

Chapter 10

Political Asylum Narratives and the Construction of Suspicious Subjects

AMY SHUMAN AND CAROL BOHMER

Political asylum hearings are both interrogations and narrative performances. Lacking any other documentation of the atrocities they suffered or any proof of their identity, asylum applicants rely on their narratives of their experiences. The immigration officials scrutinize those narratives for inconsistencies and missing details. Interrogation and trauma narrative are incompatible in themselves, but cultural expectations exacerbate these incompatibilities. Some of the experiences reported by the asylum applicants are unfathomable; others are overly familiar. The immigration officials often regard what they perceive as unfathomable to be not credible, and often they view commonly heard reports as fraudulent. In our work, we have described some of the narrative failures in the asylum process. Using examples from cases in the United States and United Kingdom, we observe how interrogations and narrations conflict. We pay particular attention to the problem that asylum seekers' experiences are saturated with contradictions. Of necessity, they often have occupied multiple and contradictory subject positions to survive, and they must create a coherent narrative to persuade the asylum officials of their credibility. The goal of our work is both scholarly and applied; in addition to research, we instruct asylum applicants in the intricacies of the system and help them to understand the complexities of the narrative performances required of them.

Many scholars have observed the significance of narrative in the political asylum process—for example, by attending to the complexities of tellability and detail, especially misinterpretations on the part of the asylum officials (Bloomaert 2001; Bohmer and Shuman 2007b; Jackson 2002; Jacquemet 2009, 2011; Malkki 2007; Ranger, 2005; Shuman and Bohmer 2004). Like other narratives produced in courtroom settings, the political asylum narratives are a coproduction that is primarily controlled by the immigration officials. Some asylum applicants or their advocates attempt to wrest control from the officials and to reclaim ownership, but the applicants often have a tenuous hold on their stories either because they did not know the details of who was harming them and why or because they cannot bring themselves to retell the atrocities they experienced (Jackson 2002; Jacquemet 2009, 2011; Shuman and Bohmer 2004).

Considerations of credibility have always been a cornerstone of the political asylum process. Applicants are interrogated throughout the hearing process to determine whether they are who they say they are and to assess whether their narratives are accurate accounts of what they say they endured. Until recently, those considered not credible were most often suspected of being economic migrants. In recent years, the discourses of credibility in the asylum process have shifted to include the question of whether an asylum applicant might be a terrorist.

Differentiating between economic migrants and legitimate asylum seekers is never simple, especially since violent conflict produces economic migrants: people who cannot sustain a livelihood because their homes have been destroyed, because warfare has destroyed crops, or because ordinary life is no longer safe. For the asylum official, the question of this differentiation is a matter of first determining whether the person's narrative is credible and, second, assessing whether the atrocities experienced fall within one of the five categories of political asylum. Differentiating between asylum seekers and terrorists raises different questions, not only about the credibility of the narrative but also about the categories of victim and perpetrator. The political asylum process has always sought to determine whether an asylum applicant was engaged in armed conflict, but in the current climate of suspicion about terrorism, *every* asylum applicant is potentially under suspicion. This represents a paradigm shift in the discourses of political asylum and intensifies the conflicting discourses of protecting people who fear to return to their home countries and maintaining safety and security in the receiving country.

Although the categories of perpetrator and victim are sometimes clearly defined, they easily blur, especially in conflicts arising between neighbors or closely associated groups. Further, in addition to perpetrator and victim, individuals can occupy many other categories, including bystanders who do not engage, providers of refuge, providers of assistance, people who look the other way, informers, betrayers, and protectors, among others.[1] Each of these positions requires complex narrative discourses that position individuals in relation to each other, often in complex compromised relationships in which people sometimes explain limited choices between equally impossible situations.

In a particularly dramatic example of impossible choices that position individuals in contradictory categories, survivors of the Holocaust describe the role of the designated survivor, a member of a community or family appointed to do anything necessary to survive to be able to tell the story of what happened. Letty Cottin Pogrebin (1991) describes her Uncle Isaac:

> I remember especially my mother's cousin Isaac, who came to New York immediately after the war and lived with us for several months. Isaac is my connection to dozens of other family members who were murdered in the concentration camps. Because he was blond and blue-eyed, he had been chosen as the "designated survivor" of his town; that is, the Jewish councils had instructed him to do anything to stay alive and tell the story. For Isaac, "anything" turned out to mean this: the Germans suspected his forged Aryan papers and decided he would have to prove by his actions that he was not a Jew. They put him on a transport train with the Jews of his town and then gave him the task of herding into the gas chambers everyone in his trainload. After he fulfilled that assignment with patriotic Germanic efficiency, the Nazis accepted the authenticity of his identity papers and let him go.
>
> Among those whom Isaac packed into the gas chamber that day, dispassionately, as if shoving a few more items into an overstuffed closet, were his wife and two children.

> The "designated survivor" arrived in America at about age forty, with prematurely white hair and a dead gaze within the sky-blue eyes that had helped save his life. As promised, he told his story to dozens of Jewish agencies and community leaders, and to groups of family and friends. . . . For months he talked, speaking the unspeakable, describing a horror that American Jews had suspected but could not conceive, a monstrous tale that dwarfed the demonology of legend and gave me the nightmare I still dream to this day. And as he talked, Isaac seemed to grow older and older until one night a few months later, when he finished telling everything he knew, he died. (304–5)

Pogrebin's Uncle Isaac committed many atrocities to disprove the suspicions about his forged papers. Today, if he faced an asylum hearing, the category of "designated survivor" might not be credible and, having admitted to being a forger and a perpetrator, he might see his case discredited.

After the Holocaust, Jews did not need to prove their credibility, a situation that also permitted perpetrators such as John Demjanjuk to resettle in the United States and other countries. After moving to Cleveland, Ohio, and living "quietly," for decades, Demjanjuk was convicted at the age of ninety-one of having been a concentration camp guard. A *New York Times* article asks, "Had he been, as he and his family claimed, a Ukrainian prisoner of war in Germany and Poland who made his way to America and became a victim of mistaken identity? Or had he been, as prosecutors charged, a collaborating guard who willingly participated in the killing of Jews at the Treblinka, Majdanek and Sobibor death camps?" (McFadden 2012).

The discovery and prosecution of Nazi perpetrators who masqueraded as refugees was undertaken not by governmental offices, which have not had the funds for such detective work, but by individual associations. The pursuit of Demjanjuk was funded by the Simon Wiesenthal Center, established in part to "bring Nazi War Criminals to justice."[2]

The categories of victim and perpetrator initially are blurred by violence that turns neighbors into enemies and that forces people who do not trust each other to rely upon each other, sometimes briefly and sometimes over extended periods of time, whether linked by bribery or temporary alliances against a third, worse group. Further, these blurred alliances, forged for some mutual benefit between individuals who otherwise either distrust each other, create the possibility of available narratives, in which people can cross enemy lines and position themselves as allies of the victims, rather than perpetrators, in asylum applications.

The Rwandan genocide provides one example of these blurred categories and the available narratives produced in the aftermath. The genocide itself was the result of decades of tension, most likely fostered by the Belgian colonizers who had initiated the idea of identity cards differentiating the Tutsi, Hutu, and Twa ethnic groups and who replaced the Tutsi leadership with Hutu rulers, who were more amenable. Even during these years of tension, various forms of alliance, including intermarriage, were not uncommon between Tutsis and Hutus. When the genocide erupted, many Tutsis relied on these alliances when seeking protection from Hutus. In the aftermath of the genocide, offering protection became one available narrative for Hutus seeking to resettle in asylee-receiving countries.

Edouard Kayihura and Kerry Zukus (2014) documented the complexity of these alliances in their book *Inside Hotel Rwanda*, written from the perspective of survivor Kayihura and as a response to what they argue were misleading and false representations in the film *Hotel Rwanda*. Kayihura relied on a Hutu friend to help him cross militia barriers and checkpoints as he fled to get to the Hôtel des Milles Collines (called Hotel Rwanda in the film), where Tutsis were seeking refuge. The film, the book, discussions of the controversies the book addresses, and conversations with Kayihura (who is a colleague of Amy Shuman), provide a rich opportunity to explore the complex available positions produced in violent conflict. We discuss these at length before returning to how they are considered in a political asylum hearing.

Paul Rusesabagina was the protagonist of the film *Hotel Rwanda*, produced in 2004, a decade after the Rwandan genocide. According to one description, "the 2004 film Hotel Rwanda told the story of how Mr Rusesabagina, a middle-class Hutu married to a Tutsi, used his influence—and bribes—to convince military officials to secure a safe escape for the estimated 1,200 people who sought shelter at the Mille Collines Hotel in Kigali" (BBC 2011).

Many newspaper articles, blogs, and books have criticized the veracity of the film, with a few articles defending it. Kayihura and Zukus's book both tells Kayihura's own story and denounces Rusesabinga's claims to heroism. In response to the film's claim to portray "the quiet heroism of one man, Paul Rusesabagina, during the Rwandan Genocide," they write that all of the people who stayed at the hotel during the genocide would describe

Rusesabagina as "the *furthest* from a hero any of us could imagine. Rusesabagina had been a war profiteer, a friend to the architects of the genocide, a man willing to starve those without money while hoarding piles of food, drink, and riches for himself and his friends" (Kayihura and Zukus 2014, 11).

The stories of heroic protectors are one kind of available narrative, a category that in Rusesabagina's case (and the stories of many others) existed prior his occupying that position in the chronicles of the genocide. Terry George, the filmmaker, describes having done extensive research to find people who had experienced the horrors of the genocide. One person led to another, and another to Rusesabagina, who was at that point driving a cab in Brussels. George defends his efforts to substantiate the accuracy of Rusesabagina's story, but such substantiation would not have been necessary if people had not made such efforts to discredit the account. Roger Ebert's 2004 review of the film, before the controversy took hold, provides as good a justification as any for George's choice:

> I have known a few hotel managers fairly well, and I think if I were hiring diplomats, they would make excellent candidates. They speak several languages. They are discreet. They know how to function appropriately in different cultures. They know when a bottle of scotch will repay itself six times over. They know how to handle complaints. And they know everything that happens under their roof, from the millionaire in the penthouse to the bellboy who can get you a girl.
>
> Paul is such a hotel manager. He is a Hutu, married to a Tutsi named Tatiana (Sophie Okonedo). He has been trained in Belgium and runs the four-star Hotel Des Milles Collines in the capital city of Kigali. He does his job very well. He understands that when a general's briefcase is taken for safekeeping, it contains bottles of good scotch when it is returned. He understands that to get the imported beer he needs, a bribe must take place. He understands that his guests are accustomed to luxury, which must be supplied even here in a tiny central African nation wedged against Tanzania, Uganda and the Congo. Do these understandings make him a bad man? Just the opposite. They make him an expert on situational ethics. The result of all the things he knows is that the hotel runs well and everyone is happy. (Ebert 2004)

Here Ebert articulates a dominant narrative of hotel managers, good ones, who are experts on situational ethics. Rusesabagina does seem to have been such a manager. The problem is that although these skills, as portrayed in the film, support the idea that, as hotel manager, Rusesabagina was also in a position to maintain the safety of the refugees, and the skills he deployed are also the skills of the opportunist, the label given by many of the people who repudiate Rusesabagina's heroism. Situational ethics is one thing, and opportunism is another. The repudiators focus on the disparities and contradictions between heroes and opportunist and then charge Rusesabagina as a false hero.

Kayihura, Zukus, and others complain that Rusesabagina has been compared to Oskar Schindler, but Schindler, too, was an opportunist. How the skills of the manager are described, whether as skillful diplomat or as opportunist, make a big difference narratively. Positioning Rusesabagina as an opportunist during the genocide is important for those who wish to deprive him of a credible platform for how he portrays himself afterward. As George (2015) points out, in the end most, if not all, of his detractors are motivated not as much by the question of his role as opportunist or hero during the genocide but by the ways he took advantage of his celebrity as the hero depicted in the film to later mount a political platform in opposition to the current government.

Paul Rusesabagina has been acclaimed as a hero, receiving the Wallenberg Medal from the University of Michigan and the Presidential Medal of Freedom from President George W. Bush, among other accolades. According to Kayihura and Zukus,

> in speech after speech before audiences around the world, Rusesabagina has used his influence to champion "Hutu Power" politics (an ethnic hatemongering against the Tutsi), raising money for causes that have less to do with peace than with revenge against current Rwandan President Paul Kagame. Most flagrant of the words Rusesabagina speaks are his attempts to paint the murderous actions of the Hutu Power extremists during what we came to call The 100 Days as a natural byproduct of civil war and *not* genocide. Rusesabagina even testifies at trials on behalf of those who took up machetes against the unarmed, all the while blaming the victims and claiming they were the true murderers. As one of the most famous men in Rwanda today, Rusesabagina is the smiling public face of the murderous opposition groups who were driven out of Rwanda to end the genocide (Kayihura and Zukus 2014, 15).

What is at stake here is an ongoing disputed cultural memory that invokes events before the genocide and is central to contemporary claims to justice and power. The Hutu narrative—and Rusesabagina is a Hutu—is that the Tutsis were not native to the area but came four hundred years before. What is at stake are questions of the legitimacy of rulers and the history of subjugation. Thus, for Rusesabagina, the genocide was part of a larger historical struggle. Many survival narratives recount the moment when the Hutu Rwandan president's plane was shot down as the moment when the violence began, and in ongoing discussions (published and online), scholars, activists, and survivors debate whether or not the Tutsi rebels were responsible for the plane crash.

In the film, Rusesabagina is positioned as the person responsible for preventing the Hutu soldiers from killing the refugees seeking haven in the hotel. He is portrayed as clever and manipulative, as someone who is playing both sides at the same time. In one scene, he complains to the United Nations (UN) commander that he is being overwhelmed by refugees and that the hotel "is not a refugee camp; can you not take them with you to your facilities?" The UN commander explains that he cannot, saying, "When we stabilize the situation; then I'll take them." In almost the next scene, Rusesabagina calls the hotel owner in Belgium and persuades him to keep the hotel open. Paul lies, saying, "The hotel is an oasis of calm for all our loyal customers. . . . I assure you the United Nation has everything under control." Rusesabagina is portrayed as genuinely caring for the refugees in his charge. When told that the UN will evacuate only the Westerners, leaving the Rwandans almost unprotected, he confesses to his wife that he has been taken for a fool, made to believe he would be protected along with the Westerners. His wife responds, "You are no fool. I know who you are" (George 2004).

In the film, Rusesabagina is positioned as strategically managing different interests. In the film, he is a credible, coherent player who says different things to the UN commander and the hotel owners not as a lie but as a strategy. His self-portrayal as a fool makes him even more sympathetic and more credible; his wife, someone who knows him well, serves as a witness.

The central criticism of Rusesabagina that most seriously undermines his credibility as a heroic protector of refugees is the report that he demanded money from the refugees and threatened to force them to leave if they did not pay. Narratively, this is the moment at which his heroism is questionable, in which he is depicted as a profiteer. In the film, he asks the refugees to pay as a strategy to persuade the Hutu militia personnel that they are guests of the hotel, not refugees. In the film, it is all part of his effort to protect them. Rusesabagina's strategy is consistent with his role as hotel manager, especially the skills of the diplomat described by Roger Ebert. The exchange of money is the gray area of heroism that separates the hero from the profiteer, the term the critics use for Rusesabagina.

Edouard Kayihura and others particularly condemn Rusesabagina's demands for money from the refugees. Filmmaker Terry George (2015) reports, "On Oct. 28 a reporter for the Rwandan daily newspaper the *New Times* ran a long story on the 'true nature' of Rusesabagina, which quoted a former receptionist at the hotel as saying that he had saved only his few friends, and that he had charged people to stay in the rooms (a fact we had highlighted and explained in the film)."

The exchange of money occurs several times in the film, primarily in instances in which Rusesabagina greases the palm of someone in power. At one point, when the journalists and other white people are evacuated, leaving the African refugees behind, one of the journalists gives Rusesabagina money to take care of his African woman friend. Rusesabagina refuses the money and says, "That's not necessary." Rusesabagina explains, "This cannot be a refugee camp. The Interahamwe [a Hutu militia] believe that the Mille Collines is a four-star hotel. That is the only thing that is keeping us alive."

Rusesabagina defends his request for money by positioning himself as holding up the façade of the four-star hotel against the militia's suspicions that it had become a refugee camp. It is here that his heroism is most contested.

One of the primary complaints against him is that he required the Tutsis seeking refuge and his employees to pay for their stay and for their food (including food he received free from the Red Cross) and that the employees were no longer being paid for their work. From Kayihura and Zukus's (2014) book:

> He [Rusesabagina] told everyone working in the restaurant to start making all the people pay. We told him that we couldn't. That makes no sense, making people pay. They are in the hotel to save their lives. Nobody really thought about bringing any money. . . . For the next few meals over the next few days, those who had money—and there were

> indeed some who still did—shared graciously with those of us who did not. I [Kayihura] got to see the greatest demonstrations of man's humanity toward his fellow man. I thought about Christophe's story of how he had begged a French journalist for assistance to protect a two-year-old child from slaughter and was turned down. Here in the hotel, everyone—Westerners, Hutu, Tutsi, refugees, guests, employees, UN soldiers—faced each new struggle together, living communally, living with love. I will never forget it so long as I live. Our fear, though, was over how long this situation would last. What would happen when *everyone's* money ran out? What would the hotel manager do then? And who could we appeal to positioned above him? (82–84)

Kayihura and Zukus's narrative of desperation counters the portrayal of Rusesabagina as protector. Instead, in their portrayal, Rusesabagina is an opportunist whose demand that people pay for food and shelter contradicts his beneficence as someone interested in saving lives. Kayihura and Zukus (2014) write:

> As for the food from the Red Cross, Paul insisted the hotel kitchen staff cook that. And because the hotel staff cooked it, Paul charged the refugees for it. He turned it into a profit center. If you could not afford to pay, you did not get cooked corn and beans that the Red Cross had given to the hotel for free. (89)

In response to these criticisms, Rusesabagina says that he killed no one and that if he had wanted to kill someone, he would have. This is the heart of the contested narrative. Was Rusesabagina the expert diplomat, canny, always one step ahead of his aggressors, successfully warding off the killers, or was he protecting only himself, profiting from his position? He is true to no one, not even his wife, who only discovers at the last moment that he was not leaving with her and the children on a UN truck for the airport. Rusesabagina and his wife say that this was changed for the film; in fact, they had agreed that she would leave without him. As portrayed in the film, however, it makes Rusesabagina duplicitous with everyone. And yet the film audience does not discredit him. Instead, he is quite credible as the masterful hotel manager with a good heart. In contrast, the critics say, he was closely allied with the Hutus, during and after the genocide, and he currently is a "genocide denier."[3]

Like many people involved in violent conflict, Rusesabagina is a strategic actor who plays one side against the other. He is part of a complex moral geography that brings the rescued and rescuer together and often exposes the fault lines of their temporary interdependence (Modan 2008, 90). The Tutsi survivors' testimonies describe a moral geography of havens (especially homes) that become unsafe and of marginal spaces that become spaces for hiding.[4] Within the shifting moral geographies of conflict and survival, the positions of conspirator, spy, persecutor, and victim are understandably contradictory. Rusesabagina is, at best, a stand-in for these contradictions: he is vulnerable to conflicts larger than his own story.

Rusesabagina is accused of being an opportunist when he has claimed to be a protector; he is not accused of being a genocidal murderer. We have discussed his case at length in part because the gray area separating the victim of persecution, deserving of asylum, and the fraudulent applicant often involves opportunism, whether in the case of economic migrants or in recent cases of migrants who claim to have been forced to pilot dinghies across the Mediterranean.

Narratives create, rather than merely refer to, the events they describe. What is at stake in the competing narratives about the Rwandan genocide, told retrospectively, is not only the accuracy of reports of what happened in the past but also the consequences of those narrators for present and future relationships among the participants. For example, in truth and reconciliation events, some narrators describe positive interactions between Tutsis and Hutus before and during the violence as signs pointing to the possibility of a peaceful future.[5]

Political asylum hearings, designed to determine the legitimacy of an applicant's narrative, place more emphasis on the consistency of the facts represented than on the way that narrators position themselves in relation to others. This positioning is crucial to differentiating between victims and persecutors, categories that, as we have discussed in the cases of both Holocaust designated survivors and the Rwandan genocide, can be blurred. In the remainder of this essay, we discuss three dimensions of narrative, orientation, positioning, and narrative logics that, we argue, are more precise tools than comparisons of consistency in the determination of the credibility of an applicant's narrative.[6]

Narrative scholars use the term "orientation" to refer to information about places, the people relevant to the story, the activities described, or the larger situation or cultural context.[7] Unlike conversational narrative exchanges, in legal proceedings lawyers or other officials ask questions to elicit orienting details. In asylum hearings the official is then able to control what counts as relevant details; in doing so, the hearing officer also can propose alternative narrative logics that contradict the applicant's narrative. These narrative logics can establish or discredit the narrator's authority and credibility. We doubt that the hearing officers are aware of these narrative strategies or of the ways that interrogations and interviews place control of orientation, positioning, and narrative logics in the hands of the interrogator.

To demonstrate how these narrative strategies work, we now turn to a close reading of one hearing, observed by Carol Bohmer in the United Kingdom in 2014. The applicant, an eighteen-year-old Albanian man who arrived in 2012, claimed to be a potential victim of a blood feud over water rights in which the applicant's father or uncle (this is unclear) killed his neighbor, named Murati. According the Kanuni i Lekë Dukagjinit, a set of traditional Albanian laws often referred to more simply as Kanun law, revenge can be extracted from males over sixteen. The applicant says that the family was threatened and in particular that the Murati family said they would kill the applicant. The issue at stake in the hearing was whether or not the applicant had actually been targeted for revenge and whether his fear warranted asylum. The following exchange, establishing some of the orienting details, provides a typical example of how a hearing officer probes the details of background information in search of inconsistencies or inaccuracies. "HO" indicates the Home Office representative (in this case, a lawyer hired to take the case), "J" indicates the judge, "R" indicates the applicant's representative, and "AP" indicates the applicant:

HO: The Murati family lived in the same village as yours?

AP: Yes, the same village

HO: How close to home did they live?

AP: Near. It is a small village.

J: When you came this morning, did you see the Tesco's shop? Are we talking the same distance?

AP: About the same, maybe a bit further.

HO: Were there other houses in between?

AP: No. It is our house and then Murati's house in front of ours.

HO: Were they one of your neighbours?

AP: Yes.

In narrative studies, orientation has been regarded as a relatively neutral part of the narrative—it sets the stage and provides background. Interrogators, then, often appear to motivated by a desire to create an accurate record rather than to manipulate the narrative. In this narrative, the interrogator poses seemingly neutral questions by focusing orientation questions on the distance between the applicant's house and the house of the person who, he says, will kill him as an act of revenge.

However, questions about location become important for establishing credibility when the Home Office lawyer asks, "If Akrim's brother lives in another country and your father was around 60 years old, who exactly was threatening to kill you and/or your father?" The applicant responds, "So it is usually Akrim's family and they've got cousins so their own people." This seemingly neutral question, requesting information about geography and age, becomes crucial in the judge's skepticism about the case. The problem could be seen as a matter of cultural misunderstandings regarding the application of Kanun law: the hearing officer does not know that relatives will cross geographic distances to seek revenge. However, as Marco Jacquemet (2011) argues, "We need to consider asylum hearings through a paradigm that goes beyond the dominance/difference divide. In the power-saturated environments of these hearings, we are not dealing with intercultural interactions between equal partners holding 'different cultural assumptions,' etc. (as we can find in an international business meeting), but with clearly asymmetrical encounters, in which one side seeks help and provides personal information and the other listens and adjudicates" (493).

Significantly, the Home Office lawyer has not asked about Kanun law but about the location of Akrim's brother and the age of the applicant's father. These questions reposition the applicant's narrative within the Home Office lawyer's narrative logic; within that logic, the lawyer mobilizes suspicion of the applicant's account of his fear of revenge.

The issue at stake is whether the applicant is a legitimate asylum seeker who fears return to his own country where he would be the victim of vengeance or is an economic migrant masquerading as an asylum seeker. These positions are constructed narratively (De Fina, Schiffrin, and Bamberg 2006). People seeking political asylum often have to negotiate complex and seemingly contradictory positions as victims of persecution who, for example, may have bribed or made bargains with their enemies to escape (Bohmer and Shuman 2010). Further, an individual case is often evaluated within the context of more general assumptions about people from a particular country. At the time this case was heard, increasing numbers of Albanians were seeking asylum, and many were suspected of being economic migrants. In a political asylum hearing, positioning is not only, or even primarily, about the construction of identity. Applicants do need to prove that they are who they claim to be, but beyond that they need to satisfy the requirement of a well-founded fear of return. Narratively, they have to establish not only that past events occurred but also that future protection is warranted. Many asylum cases have failed because the hearing officers determined that the future fear was too nebulous.[8]

In the Albanian case, the credibility of the applicant's position as a victim depends on his assertion that the Murati family will seek revenge according to Kanun law. The interrogator asks about the fact that the applicant was under the age permitted as a target for such revenge. Interestingly, here, in response to an orientation question, the applicant offers a narrative and further orientation information:

> AP: I was 15 years old at the time, and if they wanted to kill me they would incur a huge pain among my family.
>
> J: Do you know why they were going outside ordinary principles and targeting you even though you were not 16?
>
> AP: They were very sad and grieving and wanted to take revenge as soon as possible and sometimes they don't look at the Kanun law.

The Home Office lawyer seems somewhat satisfied by the possibility that the applicant might be the victim of revenge, but his credibility is nonetheless suspect.

Later in the interrogation, following detailed discussion of the fact that when the applicant arrived in the United Kingdom he stayed with a friend of his uncle, he says that he cannot provide the friend's name and did not have a contact number for him. This line of questioning, seemingly peripheral to the question of the applicant's fear of being killed, is typical of asylum hearings. Perplexed by the applicant's lack of information about names and phone numbers, the judge offers his own narrative: "I'm trying to put myself in the position you must have been in. You're going to leave everything you know, going to somewhere far away and very different, you could have had a number and you're refusing to take it." The judge refers to the applicant's position hypothetically. The judge positions the applicant as someone who refuses to take a phone number he could have had. Following this hearing, Carol Bohmer spoke to the judge who, she says, was quite open about assuming someone of a different culture would behave as he himself would. Note that the "you" in the judge's hypothetical narrative is a generalized "you," implying something that *anyone* would have done. The judge has created an alternative narrative logic based on his own cultural assumptions. This logic supersedes that of the applicant, and it is in this sense that identifying cultural misunderstanding is insufficient to understanding the obstacles applicants face in political asylum hearings.

Narrative logics, or morphologies, refer to the cultural scripts imposed on narratives. We are not suggesting that these scripts exist prior to the narrative exchange.[9] To the contrary, they are produced as part of the interrogation. Like other political asylum scholars, we have been interested in the problems asylum applicants face in telling their stories at all (Shuman and Bohmer 2004; Jackson 2002), and we are not disputing that here. In addition to the paramount problems of tellability, we are suggesting that these narrative dimensions also play a significant role in the political asylum interrogations by asserting an alternative, hypothetical narrative that casts doubt on the applicant's narrative.[10]

The Albanian applicant must prove that he would be targeted for harm if he were to return home. He acknowledged that the law would be loosely interpreted to permit a fifteen-year-old to be killed, and the interrogator asks whether that assertion is based on information or conjecture: "You've been asked about something in someone's mind to which you say I don't know what was in their mind. . . . I'm trying to understand if this was a guess or if you had positive information." This move on the part of the interrogator is crucial for establishing an alternative narrative logic. From the interrogator's perspective, the idea of revenge is hypothetical, a conjecture, not based on facts. For the Albanian applicant, revenge is not only a fact but also a law in which a killing may be avenged by another killing.[11]

The applicant's claim rests on the narrative logic in which he is in danger of being killed as an act of revenge against his family. The judge questions both the logic of the revenge killing and the applicant's narrative about his arrival in the United Kingdom. For the judge, the credibility of these two narratives is linked.

Later in the interrogation, the judge asks, "None of that answers the question I asked. Why when you were saying goodbye to your uncle, and you haven't got your mother and father's number, you don't ask him, when you're going to a strange place?"

The judge offers a hypothetical narrative, familiar to him, in which people ask for phone numbers when they go to strange places. Responding also to the hypothetical narrative, the applicant says, "If I contacted my family, something would come out and people would learn I am in England." Additionally, the applicant explains, "In Albania, if you change places from one to another, you need to get registered. The Murati family for a bit of money, giving bribes, they could find me."

The case hinges on the narrative logic of the applicant's failure to get the phone number and to contact his family. It is possible that the applicant did not think to ask for the phone number. It is possible that as he says, contacting his family would put him in jeopardy. It is also surprising that the judge did not consider these possibilities. At the same time, it is also possible that the whole story is a ruse and that the applicant is an economic migrant.

The judge persists in his skepticism that the applicant would be discovered by the Murati family. He asks, "How could they know you were there?" The applicant replies, "With a bit of money." The judge then offers another narrative logic and reframes the applicant's statement and says, "Are you saying that since you left the Murati family have been throwing their money away finding where you are?"

This reframing of the narrative "throwing money away" is based on the judge's idea that such an act would be a waste of money. It might be "throwing money away" according to the narrative logic of the United Kingdom. The interrogation pits one narrative logic against another, but these logics are naturalized by both sides. The idea that the Murati family would spend money to find the applicant is unfathomable to the judge, who, as we noted earlier, acknowledged his ethnocentrism.

People fleeing atrocities in their home countries have experienced unfathomable losses and violence, and often they cannot find the words to narrate their experiences. The Albanian applicant anticipates being murdered according to a cultural system of revenge, but even though he provides a potentially legitimate narrative that he might be killed were he to return to his home, he is discredited by his failure to obtain a phone number, an act that seems unfathomable to the judge. The judge and lawyer representing the Home Office employ narrative logics focused primarily on orienting details to discredit the position of the applicant as a victim. By offering his own hypothetical narrative from narrative logics familiar to him, the judge contradicts and rejects the applicant's story.

Like many failed asylum cases, this case could be attributed to cultural ethnocentrism in political asylum hearings. Although cultural misunderstanding plays a role in producing suspicion, here we have attempted to demonstrate how the interrogation process produces hypothetical narrative logics through control of the orienting details. These narrative logics are used either to confirm the applicant's claim to be a victim or to reject that position and instead assign a different one—for example, economic migrant or persecutor. How Rusesabagina is seen—whether as an opportunist or as a participant in genocide—depends on narrative logics, as does the story of Letty Cottin Pogrebin's Uncle Isaac, the designated survivor.

Many asylum cases are based on culturally specific narrative logics—for example, the logics of bribery, of managing family responsibilities, and of discretion regarding stigmatized sexual minorities. How an asylum seeker is positioned as a credible narrator depends on the credibility of these narrative logics. Although on the surface political asylum hearings often focus on discrepancies in background, or orienting, details, often the motivation for finding these discrepancies is related to suspicion of the narrative logic of the applicant's claim. By challenging an applicant's narrative logic, the asylum hearing officer produces a suspicious subject.

Assessments of the credibility of asylum applicants occur within ideological, politically motivated discourses. Here we have described the moral geographies that differentiate between, for example, opportunism and situational ethics. Each of these operates according to narrative logics. Pogrebin's cousin Isaac, the designated survivor, is a case of situational ethics; if we accept Pogrebin's account, we understand the necessity of what he did, however horrendous. In contrast, according to Kayihura and Zukus, Rusesabagina, the hotel manager featured in the film *Hotel Rwanda,* was an opportunist, and he should not be seen not as a hero. Narrative logics can easily falter and fall under the lens of suspicion. Finding fault with details, although primary to the interrogation process in a hearing, occurs within the larger context of these moral geographies that position a narrator as victim, perpetrator, or opportunist and that are crucial for considering a person as deserving of asylum.

NOTES

1. For example, Peter Tinti and Tuesday Reitano discuss a continuum for the category of smuggler, from trafficker to ad hoc alliances of small businesses providing transport (2016, 32).

2. "John Demjanjuk's Nazi War Criminal Trial in Germany," Simon Wiesenthal Center, http://www.wiesenthal.com/site/pp.asp?c=lsKWLbPJLnF&b=5648009, accessed August 21, 2018. We discuss the role of nongovernmental organizations in pursuing war criminals in Bohmer and Shuman 2007b.

3. Rwandan ambassador to the Netherlands Immaculee Uwanyiligira claims that Rusesabagina is a genocide denier and that "there is a far more sinister connection that warrants exposing. Rusesabagina is also accused of sponsoring militia, military, and paramilitary forces that committed the genocide in Rwanda. These days, they operate in eastern Democratic Republic of the Congo under their new name Democratic Forces for the Liberation of Rwanda (FDLR (Houttui 2012).

4. See Kate Parker Horigan's discussion of the competing narratives produced by the changing status of Hurricane Katrina victims as they lost their homes, sought protection, and were characterized as villains or victims (2018).

5. As Mark Freeman (2002) points out, one of the things at stake in counternarratives about public politicized events is the possibility of a collective narrative. He describes counternarratives as "culturally-rooted aspects of one's history that have not yet become part of one's story" (202). See also Roht-Arriaza and Mariezcurrena 2006.

6. Marisa Cianciarulo argues that the identification of inconsistencies is an ineffective means of assessing asylum claims. She writes, "The focus on minor inconsistencies would be an ineffective means" of perfecting the asylum system. "A terrorist bent on gaining access to lawful immigration status will likely not make mistakes on his or her asylum proceedings but rather will be well-rehearsed and thoroughly coached" (2006, 131).

7. As defined by William Labov and Joshua Waletsky (1967), orientation "orients the listener in respect to person, place, time, and behavioral situation" (32).

8. For example, the officer considering the case of a North African applicant in the film *A Well-Founded Fear* accepts her assertion that she was raped by a soldier and the assertion that such attacks are common but does not consider her to be sufficiently afraid of being personally targeted. As we have discussed elsewhere, publicity can have an effect on the determination of applicants' vulnerability; they may be regarded as more likely to be harmed were they to return (Bohmer and Shuman, 2007b).

9. See Jaber F. Gubrium and James A. Holstein's (1998) discussion of the production of scripts as part of narrative exchange.

10. Our discussion of tellability builds on work by Neal Norrick (2005), Anna De Fina and Alexandra Georgakopoulou (2011), and Shuman (2006).

11. We have been especially interested in political asylum cases that depend on regarding a non-Western cultural practice as anathema. In other work, we have discussed how the narrative logics of fear and bribery are central to many political asylum narratives (Bohmer and Shuman, 2007a).

REFERENCES

BBC News. 2011. "Hotel Rwanda's Paul Rusesabagina Lantos Award Condemned." November 17, 2011. http://www.bbc.co.uk/news/world-africa-15771902.

Blommaert, Jan. 2001. "Investigating Narrative Inequality: African Asylum Seekers' Stories in Belgium." *Discourse and Society* 12 (4): 413–49.

Blundo, Joe. 2014. "Rwanda Survivor's Book Challenges Hollywood." *Columbus Dispatch*, June 5, 2014.

Bohmer, Carol, and Amy Shuman. 2007a. "Producing Epistemologies of Ignorance in the Political Asylum Application Process" *Identities: Global Studies in Culture and Power* 14 (5): 603–29.

———. 2007b. *Rejecting Refugees: Political Asylum in the 21st Century*. New York: Routledge.

———. 2010. "Contradictory Discourses of Protection and Control in Transnational Asylum Law." *Journal of Legal Anthropology* 1 (2): 211–29.

Cianciarulo, Marisa Silenzi. 2006. "Terrorism and Asylum Seekers: Why the Real ID Act Is a False Promise." *Harvard Journal on Legislation* 43 (1).

De Fina, Anna, and Alexandra Georgakopoulou. 2011. *Analyzing Narrative: Discourse and Sociolinguistic Perspectives*. Cambridge: Cambridge University Press.

De Fina, Anna, Deborah Schiffrin, and Michael Bamberg, eds. 2006. *Discourse and Identity*. Vol. 23. Cambridge: Cambridge University Press.

Ebert, Roger. 2004. "Hotel Rwanda." December 21, 2004. http://www.rogerebert.com/reviews/hotel rwanda-2004.

Freeman, Mark. 2002. "Charting the Narrative Unconscious: Cultural Memory and the Challenge of Autobiography" *Narrative Inquiry* 12 (1): 193–211.

George, Terry, dir. 2004. *Hotel Rwanda*.

———. 2015. "How a Film Could Get You 25 Years in Jail!" *Huffington Post*, April 11, 2014. https://www.huffingtonpost.com/terry-george/how-a-film-could-get-you-_b_5135407.html.

Gubrium, Jaber F., and James A. Holstein. 1998. "Narrative Practice and the Coherence of Personal Stories." *Sociological Quarterly* 39 (1): 163–87.

Haviland, John B. 2003. "Ideologies of Language: Some Reflections on Language and US Law." *American Anthropologist* 105 (4): 764–74.

Horigan, Kate Parker. 2018. *Consuming Katrina: Public Disaster and Personal Narrative*. Jackson: University of Mississippi Press.

Houttuin, Saskia. 2012. "Paul Rusesabagina: Hero or Villain?" Rwanda Central, January 31, 2012. http://www.rwandacentral.com/fullstory.aspx?frIDNews=487&Paul%20Rusesabagina:%20hero%20or%20villain?

Jackson, Michael. 2002. *The Politics of Storytelling: Violence, Transgression, and Intersubjectivity*. Copenhagen: Museum Tusculanum Press.

Jacquemet, Marco. 1996. *Credibility in Court: Communicative Practices in the Camorra Trials*. Vol. 14. Cambridge: Cambridge University Press.

———. 2009. "Transcribing Refugees: The Entextualization of Asylum Seekers' Hearings in a Transidiomatic Environment." *Text and Talk: An Interdisciplinary Journal of Language, Discourse and Communication Studies* 29 (5): 525–46.

———. 2011. "Crosstalk 2.0: Asylum and Communicative Breakdowns." *Text and Talk: An Interdisciplinary Journal of Language, Discourse and Communication Studies* 31 (4): 475–97.

———. 2013. "Transidioma and Asylum: Gumperz's Legacy in Intercultural Institutional Talk." *Journal of Linguistic Anthropology* 23 (3): 199–212.

———. 2015. "Asylum and Superdiversity: The Search for Denotational Accuracy during Asylum Hearings." *Language and Communication* 44:72–81.

Kayihura, Edouard, and Kerry Zukus. 2014. *Inside the Hotel Rwanda: The Surprising True Story . . . and Why It Matters Today*. Dallas, TX: BenBella Books.

Labov, William, and Joshua Waletzky. 1967. "Narrative Analysis: Oral Versions of Personal Experience." In *Essays on the Visual and Verbal Arts*, edited by June Helm, 12–44. Seattle: University of Washington Press.

Lawrance, Benjamin N., and Galya Ruffer, eds. 2014. *Adjudicating Refugee and Asylum Status: The Role of Witness, Expertise, and Testimony*. Cambridge: Cambridge University Press.

Malkki, Liisa H. 1995. "Refugees and Exile: From 'Refugee Studies' to the National Order of Things." *Annual Review of Anthropology* 24:495–523.

———. 2007. "Commentary: The Politics of Trauma and Asylum; Universals and Their Effects." *Ethos* 35 (3): 336–43.

McFadden, Robert D. 2012. "John Demjanjuk, 91, Dogged by Charges of Atrocities as Nazi Camp Guard, Dies." *New York Times*, March 17, 2012. http://www.nytimes.com/2012/03/18/world/europe/john-demjanjuk-nazi-guard-dies-at-91.html.

Modan, Gabriella Gahlia. 2008. *Turf Wars: Discourse, Diversity, and the Politics of Place*. Malden, MA: Blackwell.

Norrick, Neal R. (2005). "The Dark Side of Tellability." *Narrative Inquiry* 15 (2): 323–43.

Pogrebin, Letty Cottin. 1991. *Deborah, Golda, and Me: Being Female and Jewish in America*. New York: Crown.

Ranger, Terence. 2005. "The Narratives and Counter-narratives of Zimbabwean Asylum: Female Voices." *Third World Quarterly* 26 (3): 405–21.

Roht-Arriaza, Naomi, and Javier Mariezcurrena, eds. 2006. *Transitional Justice in the Twenty-First Century: Beyond Truth versus Justice*. Cambridge: Cambridge University Press.

Shuman, Amy. 2006. "Entitlement and Empathy in Personal Narrative." *Narrative Inquiry* 16 (1): 148–55.

Shuman, Amy, and Carol Bohmer. 2004. "Representing Trauma: Political Asylum Narrative." *Journal of American Folklore* 117 (466): 394–414.

———. 2010. "Narrating Atrocity: Uses of Evidence in the Political Asylum Process." DIIS working paper 2010:25. Danish Institute for International Studies, Copenhagen.

Thomas, Patricia. 2016. "Pilot the Dinghy or Die: Traffickers Forcing Migrants to Take the Helm." *Columbus Dispatch*, December 13, 2016.

Tinti, Peter, and Tuesday Reitano. 2016. *Migrant, Refugee, Smuggler, Savior*. London: Hurst.

Conclusion

AMY SHUMAN AND BRIDGET M. HAAS

In the introduction to this volume, we observed how media attention to the death by drowning of three-year-old Alan Kurdi quickly shifted to accounts of refugees turned away in one European country after another, followed by new policies of closed borders and deported asylum seekers. His story is a story of a refugee who died in transit. As we conclude this book, we observe that the discourse about asylum increasingly includes not only the persecution refugees experienced in their homelands but also the violence that they experienced at the hands of smugglers or in the harsh conditions of transit (Squire 2017). Notwithstanding the fact that the UN Convention Relating to the Status of Refugees states that asylum seekers cannot be penalized for illegal entry, the illegality of their border crossings often marks them as suspicious, blurring the asylum seeker with the smuggler and the person who is a victim of violence with the person who has, or might, perpetrate violence. Asylum seekers have always been multiply vulnerable; today their vulnerability translates not necessarily into an obligation to provide protection but instead into a warrant for suspicion.

Until recently, the suspicion driving assessments of credibility focused primarily on whether applicants were who they claimed to be, and applicants who could not satisfy credibility assessments were suspected of being economic migrants or opportunists of other sorts. Many still are accused of trying to game the system. Applicants have also been suspected of nefarious identities, especially of being threats to national security, as when President Franklin D. Roosevelt suspected Jewish refugees of being spies (Bohmer and Shuman 2018). Contradicting this suspicion, however, following World War II, some countries knowingly harbored Nazis. The discourses about discovered Nazis rarely characterize them as present dangers and instead portray them as living ordinary lives, blending into their new communities and even becoming model citizens. In contrast, suspicions of contemporary refugees and immigrants have widened, and many asylum seekers are suspected of being not only spies but also criminals, gang members, or traffickers. The discourse of people fleeing violence and seeking safety competes with the discourse of people who bring violence from elsewhere with them. To be sure, Lynn Stephen (2017) has asserted that particular populations of migrants are constructed as "preemptive suspects"—those that are perceived as always already dangerous. This marking of people as "preemptive suspects"—ironically, as Seth M. Holmes (2017) notes, in the name of "security"—serves to justify their exclusion and exploitation. The essays in this volume critically consider how migrants are marked and labeled both outside of and inside of political-legal arenas, as well as the relationships between these two fields.

To better understand the political asylum process and the contemporary public discourses of fear and suspicion, the contributors to this volume have turned to culturally specific understandings of the circumstances of political asylum hearings and asylum seekers. Our goal has been to engage in rigorous and thoughtful inquiry that might challenge some of the uninformed assumptions that often drive these suspicions.

The universal application of political asylum policy and law is relatively recent, dating to the 1951 creation of the UN refugee convention. Before then, individual regulations applied to particular situations. Article 14 of the UN's Universal Declaration of Human Rights, accepted in 1948, "recognizes the right of persons to seek asylum from persecution in other countries.[1] Initially, the 1951 refugee convention applied to European refugees from World War II; the 1967 protocol expanded the right to asylum to anyone fleeing persecution. Individuals have the right to seek asylum, but states do not have the obligation to provide it. However, states are obligated to consider applicants "without discrimination as to race, religion or country of origin" (UN General Assembly 1967). In addition to the policies that restrict states from penalizing individuals for illegal entry, according to the policy of nonrefoulement, states are also restricted from returning people to the country they are fleeing if they would be subject to persecution.[2] At the same time, according to article 3 of the convention, states can refuse to grant asylum to someone deemed to be a threat to national security.

The 1951 refugee convention's policies did not anticipate the great variety of violent situations that have created today's population of 65 million displaced people, including 22 million refugees and asylum seekers. Unlike refugees, asylum seekers make their way to a country of refuge as individuals. To gain asylum, individual asylum seekers need to be recognized as belonging to one of the categories that warrants asylum as stipulated by the convention. This crucial recognition, applied to people fleeing quite different circumstances, requires knowledge of cultural differences, the kind of knowledge described by the authors of these essays.

Each of the authors in this volume describes and draws insights from particular cultural or political situations that have significance or serve as obstacles to assessments of credibility in the political asylum process. Political asylum procedures and policies not only operate in but also foster the tension between universal principles and culturally specific situations. The policy is, necessarily, designed to apply equally to individuals from a variety of circumstances, but the question of whether individual cases conform to the policy's requirements inevitably depends on particular circumstances.

As ethnographers and cultural theorists, the authors of these essays are attuned to how people use cultural resources to negotiate their flight from atrocities and to attempt to find refuge elsewhere. Additionally, we recognize the ways that our voices are used often in the place of the voices of the asylum applicants. John Haviland describes how his voice of expertise did not necessarily contribute to justice but instead served "to lubricate and legitimize the wheels of bureaucracy itself, including its systematic and structural injustices." As scholars, we are often peripheral to political asylum policymaking and to the hearing processes that determine whether someone is given refuge or deported. Some of us have had firsthand experience with the political asylum process, whether serving as translators, assisting as advocates of other kinds, or documenting the experiences of refugees; all of us undertake our work with deep respect for the struggles of refugees.

The essays in this book attend to the cultural misunderstandings, faulty translations, and unchallenged assumptions that often serve as obstacles in the political asylum process. Neither cultural differences nor differences in forms of violence and persecution sufficiently account for the difficulties asylum seekers face. As several of the authors discuss, asylum seekers become suspect in a variety of ways, whether because they are assumed to be liars, whether they are feared to be terrorists, or whether they or the persecution they describe are not legible to the immigration officials. The assessment of credibility can falter in many ways and at many different points in the assessment process. The authors of these essays are not arguing that more knowledge, more accurate translations, greater attention to particular circumstances, or better evidence alone would be a remedy for overcoming those obstacles. Instead, we are interested in how suspicion fills in the lack of specificity or verification, and we discuss the institutional discourses and practices that are served by maintaining those obstacles.

In discussions that bring together technologies of truth and technologies of suspicion, these essays discuss how the political asylum process is often undermined by ongoing tensions between states' understandings of (or refusal to comply with) obligations and the question of who deserves asylum. Many scholars studying political asylum (including lawyers who describe the complexity of particular cases) have identified how success or failure hinged on assessments of credibility, and not surprisingly discussions of credibility have dominated political asylum discourse. These discussions and documentations are important and continue to shed light on fault lines in the system.

As both Benjamin N. Lawrance and John B. Haviland demonstrate, the vernacularization of knowledge and the attention to the particular cultural circumstances that could help explain a case do not necessarily lead to success for the applicant. To the contrary, such details can make the case seem even more incomprehensible and less credible when the cultural specifics do not conform to officials' expected categories.

Earlier work in political asylum research explored the centrality of assessments of credibility in political asylum hearings and, for example, discussed how minute and seemingly irrelevant discrepancies in an applicant's account led to refusals. Recognizing that the asylum officials were surely aware of the flaws in the system, scholars increasingly turned to an examination of how those practices might support shifts in policy and serve as rationales for rejecting the majority of asylum seekers. As several of the authors point out, the judgments of asylum officers are known to vary widely from one adjudicator to the next. Bridget M. Haas considers the relationship between credibility and deservingness and, based on her interviews with asylum officers, observes how applicants are positioned as deserving and entitled and how the officials position themselves either as saving lives or as distancing themselves from the geographically distant violence and persecution described by the applicants. She demonstrates how credibility is cocreated and notes, "It is in the breakdowns of knowledge and decision-making that we can better understand the (often invisible) power of technologies of truth—even if enacted and reproduced ambivalently—and the symbolic violence that these technologies effect."

Marco Jacquemet writes that "credibility is gained incrementally but is lost catastrophically." A single error can have huge consequences. The fault lines in the system are clear in the use of digital information sources. In his analysis of the uses of digital technologies, Jacquemet finds that digitization can offer speed in finding information, but at the same time, using digital sources accurately depends on understanding how they work, where they are limited, and where they are useful. The technologies themselves inevitably create distortions, whether in the form of faulty or imprecise translations or assumptions about proper names for people and places.

Jacquemet describes the case of a Yazidi applicant who produced an image on his cell phone to establish his credibility. In Jacquemet's terms, the case depended on two different systems of technology, both technologies available to the official in the form of "sedimented knowledge encoded into court records, prior cases, and archived materials" and the "storable, transmissible, and portable" knowledge stored on a cell phone. Contrasting the sedentary and the mobile, Jacquemet suggests the concept of the "trans-idiomatic environment of the asylum hearing, allowing people to reach a mutual understanding without relying on a common language or forcing a recalcitrant interpreter into cooperating."

Questions of proof take a different turn in the cases documented by Rachel Lewis. Applicants fleeing persecution as sexual minorities are required to demonstrate that they are openly gay according to the officials' stereotypical expectations of what gay behavior should look like. Lacking visibility, these applicants are not legible to the officials. Lewis pushed the point further, describing them as "unthinkable" and "unrepresentable." Sara McKinnon similarly discusses how Euro-American concepts of sexual identity used by immigration officials privilege Western concepts of public visibility. As Haas, Amy Shuman, and Carol Bohmer point out, these cases, like many others, lack evidence and rely instead on the applicant's narratives. Here, we want to observe that the demand for evidence is intricately connected to the legibility of applicants.

Connecting legibility and credibility can be helpful for understanding what might appear to be quite separate conversations about the credibility of a particular applicant and the larger suspicion of political asylum applicants generally as fraudulent, dangerous, or needy, or all three. Charles Watters describes the how the receiving country's possible compassion and the applicant's desire for a better life can constitute contradictory aspirations. McKinnon similarly points to how aspirations and anxieties become connected in political asylum discourses. Ilil Benjamin's study of volunteers working at an immigration nongovernmental organization in Tel Aviv provides a particularly clear example of discourses caught in the crossroads between compassion for desperate refugees and disillusionment. The fact that some of the refugees were economic migrants taking advantage of the system challenged the volunteers' trust more generally and thus their willingness to advocate on behalf of asylum seekers. Further describing mutual suspicion in the asylum process, Haas points out that not only the asylum seekers but also the adjudicators have become figures of mistrust. Like the cynical volunteers Benjamin observed, the adjudicators studied by Haas brought their own moral conceptions, both subtle and overt, to their assessments. Often, situational ethics and judgments about opportunism motivate the assessment process.

In the introduction to this volume, we proposed that current suspicions of asylum seekers are rooted in the complex relationships between the obligation to accept and assess asylum seekers and the question of who is deserving of asylum. Many of the essays tied these assessments to the question of how an applicant becomes legible. Often applicants who were able to establish that they had experienced persecution and violence in their homelands were nonetheless unable to qualify for asylum because they were not legible within recognizable categories. The categories that warrant asylum—political opinion, race, religion, nationality, or membership in a particular social group—are all potentially complex, but the category of social group is particularly subject to interpretation. Several of the authors of these essays discussed instabilities in the category of social group, whether because the group itself is newly recognized in asylum law (in the case of gender) or because the group requires the officials to look beyond their own recognizable categories of victim and participant in violence, a topic discussed by Shuman and Bohmer.

The political asylum hearing process is extensive and constantly changing, in part because new categories, such as gender violence, are determined to warrant asylum; some kinds of violence and persecution were not originally anticipated in the UN doctrine (especially, but not exclusively, gender-based violence, including persecution of sexual minorities, domestic violence, and rape).[3] McKinnon points out that immigration officials alter categories of gender by separating gender-based and sexuality-related persecution. Some applicants are more legible than others. Applicants' stories of persecution might be credible, but they still might be disqualified for asylum if they are not considered to belong to one of the recognized categories for political asylum. They are reinscribed as victims of criminal acts rather than victims of recognizable categories of persecution. The question of who deserves asylum is not only a question of credibility (as important as that is, especially when proof is impossible) but also, and perhaps more significantly, a question of whether the applicant is legible within the system. Some applicants were determined to be deserving but only when they were reassigned to a category considered more legitimate. McKinnon points out that immigration officials alter categories of gender by separating gender-based and sexuality-related persecution.

Questions of social group membership raise new credibility issues and prompt new forms of suspicion. Some categories seem to be completely unfamiliar to the immigration officials, who do not seem to recognize the possibility of the forced migration documented by Haviland or the supernatural claims discussed by Lawrance. Lawrance describes how the use of country of origin information (COI) can result in "bureaucratic erasure" based on narrow understandings of the cultural complexity of the situations asylum seekers flee and the means they use to escape. Without this greater complexity, assessments are likely to be inaccurate.

Lawrance discusses how COI is considered in deliberations about individuals who claim to be persecuted on account of witchcraft. The country of origin has long been a consideration in political asylum deliberation, and both lawyers and others who assist asylum seekers are aware that the success of an application can hinge on attitudes toward the country of origin. If the country of origin is regarded as an ally of the nation of refuge, the asylum seeker will likely face more scrutiny. These attitudes can have exponentially important consequences if particular populations are suspected as potentially dangerous (for example, in current anti-Muslim discourses). Lawrance described a case in which a young woman was married to and sent to live in London with an older man, a mystic, who died shortly after she arrived. She was accused by her community of causing his death by witchcraft, and she feared retribution if she were to return. However, the asylum adjudicators considered her to be a trafficked young woman rather than a woman fleeing retribution for allegedly using witchcraft. The adjudicators were familiar with trafficking but not with witchcraft.

In many of the examples described in these essays, we see how categories can easily be reassigned. In particular, the categories of trafficking, forced marriage, and other forms of coercion require complex understandings of who is protecting whom. In his chapter on Chiapan asylum seekers, Haviland asks whether removing children for their protection might be itself a form of trafficking and urge us to carefully consider who counts as a protected individual. As his story of "R" illustrates, the designation of protection is attached to particular narratives. As the victim of child abuse, R was deemed eligible for protection. Her more complicated narrative, including her story of fleeing because her parents did not approve of her relationship with her boyfriend, and the even more complicated relationships of people who exploited her would not necessarily be so successful in asylum hearings.

The very local circumstances that Haviland describes occur in the context of larger, geopolitical questions. In her chapter, Nadia El-Shaarawi argues "for an anthropological approach . . . that pays attention to the ways in which these larger geopolitical questions are made and remade in everyday encounters during the resettlement process." As the essays in this volume demonstrate, intersections and contradictions among local circumstances and global policies intensify in the political asylum process.

The political asylum process is not only complex and cumbersome—it also suffers from misleading, if not erroneous, discourses that confuse credibility about an applicant's case with other sorts of suspicion, such as whether the applicant is actually an economic migrant attempting to gain the system or is a terrorist. Misleading assumptions and associations create a false dichotomy between secure borders and protecting refugees and obscure the more difficult questions of what are the obligations of states toward people fleeing violence and who is deserving of protection. How is it that narratives of violence, persecution, and desperation are translated into narratives of opportunism?

As we send this book to press, the situation for the world's refugees has worsened. The discourses of obligation discussed by El-Shaarawi compete with discourses of fear and restriction, and even individuals whose vulnerability is directly attached to assisting Western military campaigns (translators, for example) are frequently denied the protection that political asylum was designed to afford. The seemingly quixotic suspicions, not tied to verifiable dangers, combined with the equally random-seeming methods of assessing asylum seekers lead some scholars and policymakers to ask whether the suspicions and methods serve as a quasi-rationale for limiting asylum. Are the limits motivated by the fear of immigrants more generally? We have tried to address some of the central fault lines in the political asylum process within the larger context of discourses about what is posed as a contradiction between protecting borders and protecting refugees. How is it that the politics of protection, as outlined in the 1951 convention, have become so intertwined with a politics of suspicion? The essays in this volume suggest that we can begin to untangle unwarranted suspicion by understanding that the technologies of truth and the technologies of suspicion are intricately connected. The technologies for assessing credibility are part of institutional frameworks and are never neutral. The legal categories of asylum are necessarily malleable, subject to interpretation, and open to application to unfortunately new forms of persecution. In a changing system, responsive to new situations, assessments of credibility will always be partial and always will be subject to questions of what makes an asylum seeker recognizable. Without that recognition, an asylum seeker becomes suspect. The slippage from protection to suspicion rests at least in part on recognition.

Driven by fear of violence and often desperate to escape, asylum seekers endure extraordinary difficulties to arrive in a country of possible refuge, only to face suspicion that they are not who they say they are, that their stories are untrue, that they are economic rather than political migrants, or that they are terrorists. To be granted asylum, asylum seekers must prove that they have a "well-founded fear" of returning to their home countries. However, fleeing fear, they sometimes find that they are themselves feared.

NOTES

1. Universal Declaration of Human Rights, www.un.org/en/universal-declaration-human-rights/.

2. United Nations Convention Relating to the Status of Refugees, article 33(1), 1954, United Nations Educational, Scientific, and Cultural Organization, http://www.unesco.org/new/en/social-and-human-sciences/themes/international-migration/glossary/refoulement/.

3. Sara McKinnon (2016) recounts the history of asylum refusals of individuals whose persecution on account of gender did not qualify (2) and provides a detailed account of how determinations about gender align with state interests (25).

REFERENCES

Bohmer, Carol, and Amy Shuman. 2018. *Political Asylum Deceptions: The Culture of Suspicion.* Cham, Switzerland: Palgrave Macmillan.

Holmes, Seth M. 2017. "Commentary: Marking 'Preemptive Suspects'; Migration, Bodies, and Exclusion." *Latin American Perspectives,* September 17, 2017. https://doi.org/10.1177/0094582X17699915.

Jubany, Olga. 2017. *Screening Asylum in a Culture of Disbelief: Truths, Denials, and Skeptical Borders.* Cham, Switzerland: Palgrave Macmillan.

McKinnon, Sara L. 2016. *Gendered Asylum: Race and Violence in US Law and Politics.* Urbana: University of Illinois Press.

Squire, Vicki. 2017. "Governing Migration through Death in Europe and the US: Identification, Burial and the Crisis of Modern Humanism." *European Journal of International Relations* 3 (3): 513–32.

Stephen, Lynn. 2017. "Creating Preemptive Suspects: National Security, Border Defense, and Immigration Policy, 1980–Present." *Latin American Perspectives,* March 20, 2017. https://doi.org/10.1177/0094582X17699907.

UN General Assembly. 1967. Protocol Relating to the Status of Refugees. January 31, 1967. United Nations, Treaty Series, vol. 606, p. 267. http://www.refworld.org/docid/3ae6b3ae4.html.

Contributors

Ilil Benjamin completed her PhD at Cornell University and is currently a full-time lecturer at Johns Hopkins University, where she teaches courses on refugees, human rights, public health, and medical humanitarianism. Her first book project, based on her dissertation, explores tensions between frontline aid workers' priorities and their NGOs' larger agendas in Israel and Palestine.

Carol Bohmer, a lawyer and sociologist, is a visiting scholar in the Government Department at Dartmouth College and a teaching fellow at King's College, London. She has worked in the area of law and society, examining the way legal and social institutions interact. She is the coauthor with Amy Shuman of *Rejecting Refugees: Political Asylum in the 21st Century* and *Political Asylum Deceptions: The Culture of Suspicion.*

Nadia El-Shaarawi, MPH, PhD, is an assistant professor of global studies at Colby College. Her research focuses on forced migration, mental health, temporality, and humanitarianism in the Middle East and North Africa. She has conducted fieldwork with urban Iraqi refugees in Cairo, where she explored the lived experiences of navigating the bureaucratic process of refugee resettlement. She has also worked with Iraqi and Syrian refugees in Jordan and is beginning a new collaborative project (with Maple Razsa) on the Balkan migration route and the politics of the "refugee crisis" in Europe. Prior to joining Colby, Nadia was the Global Migration Postdoctoral Fellow at the Kenan Institute for Ethics at Duke University. She received her PhD in anthropology and her MPH in international health from Case Western Reserve University and an MSc in medical anthropology from Oxford University.

Bridget M. Haas, PhD, is a National Research Service Award Fellow in the School of Medicine and an adjunct assistant professor of anthropology at Case Western Reserve University. Specializing in medical and psychological anthropology, her research interests include political asylum, refugee health and mental health, immigration policy and health outcomes, and child health and well-being. She is completing a book based on her fieldwork exploring the lived experiences of asylum claimants in the United States. Her current research project is focused on the psychotherapeutic treatment of refugees and asylum seekers who are survivors of torture.

John Beard Haviland, PhD (Harvard), is a distinguished professor of anthropology at University of California, San Diego, and a linguistic anthropologist of the social life of language. He works among Tzotzil (Mayan) speakers in highland Chiapas, Mexico, and in diaspora (including many in the United States, especially those who run afoul of the law, for whom he frequently acts as both Tzotzil interpreter and expert anthropological witness). His ethnographic research also extends to communities of speakers of Guugu Yimithirr and other nearby Paman languages in the Cape York Peninsula in northeastern Australia and recently to the deaf (and hearing) inventors of a first-generation sign language in Chiapas.

Marco Jacquemet is a professor of Communication Studies at the University of San Francisco. His current scholarship focuses on the communicative mutations produced by the circulation of migrants, languages, and media idioms in the Mediterranean area. He is writing a book based on this research, called "Transidioma: Language and Power in the 21st Century." His most significant English publications to date are *Ethereal Shadows: Communication and Power in Contemporary Italy* (coauthored with Franco Berardi) and *Credibility in Court: Communicative Practices in the Camorra's Criminal Trials*. He is also active in Italian and European mediactivist and refugee rights networks.

Benjamin N. Lawrance is a professor of African history at the University of Arizona, Tucson. He is the author or coeditor of ten books, notably *African Asylum at a Crossroads: Activism, Expert Testimony, and Refugee Rights* and *Adjudicating Refugee and Asylum Status: The Role of Witness, Expertise, and Testimony*. He has served as an expert in approximately four hundred asylum claims by West Africans in immigration courts and tribunals.

Rachel A. Lewis is an associate professor and the director of graduate studies in the Women and Gender Studies Program at George Mason University. Her research and teaching interests include transnational feminisms, queer theory, media and cultural studies, sexuality, race and immigration, human rights, transnational sexualities, and feminist and queer disability studies. She has published articles in *Feminist Formations, Sexualities,* the *International Feminist Journal of Politics, Social Justice,* the *Journal of Lesbian Studies, Women and Music: A Journal of Gender and Culture,* and *Music and Letters.*

Sara L. McKinnon is an associate professor of rhetoric, politics, and culture in the Department of Communication Arts at the University of Wisconsin–Madison. Her research and teaching is in the areas of intercultural rhetoric, globalization studies, and gender studies. She is the author of *Gendered Asylum: Race and Violence in U.S. Law and Politics,* which charts the incorporation of gender provisions in US refugee and asylum law within the context of broader national and global politics. Her current work examines rhetoric that frames Mexico as violent, in order to understand the geopolitical stakes and material consequences. Drawing on archival research and field work, this project examines how violence in Mexico is imagined, the material impacts of this discourse, and what this image of the country does for US political-economic interests.

Amy Shuman is a professor of folklore in the Department of English at Ohio State University, where she is also a fellow of the Mershon Center for International Security. Her research focuses on personal narratives told in everyday life and includes studies of refugees and artisan stone carvers in Pietrasanta, Italy. She is the coauthor with Carol Bohmer of *Rejecting Refugees: Political Asylum in the 21st Century* and *Political Asylum Deceptions: The Culture of Suspicion.*

Charles Watters is a professor of well-being and social care and director of the Centre for Innovation and Research in Wellbeing at the University of Sussex. His work centers on the reception and treatment of forced migrants around the globe and the impact of different modalities of care on refugee and migrant well-being. His current research interests include ethnographies of migrant place-making in reception centers and urban areas and examination of factors influencing the well-being of refugee children in schools. He has held a range of international advisory positions on migration, refugees and health and is the founding editor of the *International Journal of Migration, Health and Social Care*. His publications include *Refugee Children: Towards the Next Horizon*.

Index